Blind Injustice

Blind Injustice

*A Former Prosecutor Exposes the Psychology
and Politics of Wrongful Convictions*

MARK GODSEY

University of California Press

University of California Press, one of the most distinguished university presses in the United States, enriches lives around the world by advancing scholarship in the humanities, social sciences, and natural sciences. Its activities are supported by the UC Press Foundation and by philanthropic contributions from individuals and institutions. For more information, visit www.ucpress.edu.

University of California Press
Oakland, California

Library of Congress Cataloging-in-Publication Data

Names: Godsey, Mark, author.
Title: Blind injustice : a former prosecutor exposes the psychology and
    politics of wrongful convictions / Mark Godsey.
Description: Oakland, California : University of California Press, [2017] |
    Includes bibliographical references and index. |
Identifiers: LCCN 2017013390 (print) | LCCN 2017016659 (ebook) |
    ISBN 9780520962958 () | ISBN 9780520287952 (cloth : alk. paper)
Subjects: LCSH: Judicial error—United States. | Prejudices—United
    States—Psychological aspects. | Criminal justice, Administration of—
    Political aspects—United States. | Evidence, Criminal—United States. |
    Discrimination in criminal justice administration—United States. |
    False imprisonment—United States.
Classification: LCC KF9756 (ebook) | LCC KF9756 .G63 2017 (print) |
    DDC 345.73/0122—dc23
LC record available at https://lccn.loc.gov/2017013390

Manufactured in the United States of America

24 23 22 21 20 19 18 17
10 9 8 7 6 5 4 3 2 1

Contents

Acknowledgments

This book is dedicated to my parents for their example of open-mindedness and openheartedness. To Berea College in Kentucky, where my parents attended school, for setting my family on a path of education, intellectual curiosity, and questioning. To the staff, students, clients, exonerees, Boards of Advocates, and supporters of the Ohio Innocence Project, particularly the Rosenthal Family, as fellow warriors. And, finally, to my wife, Michele Berry Godsey, for being my partner in sharing psychological intrigue and in fighting injustice.

I would like to thank the following people who assisted me greatly in the research and/or polishing of this book: Liza Dietrich, Tom Wells, Taylor Freed, Beckie Taylor, Laura Hills, Martin Yant, Phil Locke, Mindy Schechter, Jim Maxson, Kathy Brinkman, Richard Leo, Brandon Garrett, Nancy Petro, Jim Petro, Lou Bilionis, Barry Scheck, Rob Warden, Anne DeLyons, Karla Hall, John Cranley, Michele Berry, Caleb Baum, Rachelle Barr, and Megan Wamsley.

About This Book

This book is intended for anyone with an interest in criminal justice, psychology, the forensic sciences, civil rights, or politics.

It is also designed to serve as the primary or a supplementary textbook for undergraduate and law school courses on wrongful convictions. Instructors wishing to assign this book may contact the author, Mark Godsey, who will share a database containing supplementary videos, clinical studies, and selected case documents to help enrich a curriculum for each chapter. Professor Godsey teaches this book in conjunction with the Netflix docu-series *Making a Murderer* or the Academy Award–winning docu-series *OJ: Made in America*. Instructors wishing to follow one of these models are welcome to contact him for more details.

For readers interested in learning more, please join the Facebook group Blind Injustice.

1. Eye Opener

My client Ricky Jackson was sentenced, as he says it, to "death by electrocution." He narrowly escaped the chair in the 1970s before spending nearly forty years in prison for a murder he didn't commit—a national record that no one sets out to break. On a chilly Cleveland morning in November 2014, I walked with him as he left prison at age fifty-seven and entered a world that barely resembled the one he knew in 1975 as a kid who had just turned eighteen—Ricky's age when the state of Ohio first sought to kill him.

And I sat in court with Raymond Towler, who spent twenty-nine years in prison for a rape he didn't commit. Raymond is a peaceful and philosophical man, and an incredible artist and musician. A renaissance man. I was there when the judge banged her gavel and said to Raymond, after he had suffered through decades in prison, "You are free to go." After that, the judge left her bench, embraced Raymond, and, with tears in her eyes, recited the Irish blessing:

May the road rise up to meet you.
May the wind be always at your back.
May the sun shine warm upon your face;
the rains fall soft upon your fields,
and until we meet again,
may God hold you in the palm of His hand.

So far in my career as an innocence lawyer my Ohio Innocence Project represented and helped free twenty-five people like Ricky and Raymond who together were sent to prison for a combined 470 years for crimes they didn't commit. Some of them, like my client Nancy Smith, were ripped away from the arms of their children, and were able to hold them again in freedom only after they had become adults. Others, like Ricky Jackson, returned to a world that contained no remaining family members or friends with whom they had any sort of intimate connections.

. . .

I got to know my late friend Lois Rosenthal because she was naturally drawn to the problem of wrongful convictions. Lois was not a lawyer. Rather, she was a philanthropist and social justice activist of the best kind. She and her husband, Dick, have transformed my hometown of Cincinnati with their generosity and philanthropic spirit. For this reason, the Contemporary Arts Center, as well and many other things in town, bear their name. Lois was instrumental in establishing and building the Ohio Innocence Project, the organization that I cofounded in 2003 and still run today. The primary mission of the Ohio Innocence Project is to free innocent people from prison, like Ricky, Raymond, and Nancy.

Through the years, whenever I described a new case to Lois—in other words, when I told her about a prisoner whose case we had recently investigated and for whom we had discovered new evidence proving innocence— she would ask, "How could this happen?" Over and over again through the years she has asked me: "How could this person have possibly been convicted in the first place?"

And a few months later, when I would inevitably tell her that despite the strong evidence of innocence we had amassed the prosecutors were fighting back hard and were refusing to admit a mistake, she would ask: "Why? Why do they do that? Why can't they admit their mistakes? How can they let an innocent person stay in prison? How can this be?" Lois could never understand why the system fights back the way it does. The way it twists the law and facts to keep these injustices from seeing the light of day. And the way it resists reform. The way it makes heart-wrenching mistakes and then stubbornly refuses to change and improve.

Lois is not alone. Anyone who has been introduced to the problem of wrongful convictions in this country has asked these same questions. Indeed, I frequently speak on the topic of wrongful convictions, and the first questions I'm always asked as soon as I finish a speech are: "Why does this happen?" "Why do the prosecutors make it so hard to obtain justice for these poor people?" "Why isn't the system changing to reduce these problems?"

I receive these questions over and over again. I wrote this book to try to answer them. I decided to write it because my unusual career has given me a unique perspective that has allowed me to answer these questions in a way that most others can't. As an innocence lawyer and activist, I have routinely witnessed the unjust behavior of police, prosecutors, judges, and defense attorneys, and how this behavior has caused untold pain to thousands of innocent people suffering at the hands of the system. In other words, I have witnessed the things that puzzled Lois and others.

Before becoming an innocence activist, however, I served for many years as a hard-nosed prosecutor. As a result of this unique juxtaposition, I now look back on my years as prosecutor and see that I engaged in this same type of conduct and had the same mindset that I now know causes tragic injustices. As did others around me. So this book is a kind of confessional and memoir, which, because of my personal journey, provides a behind-the-scenes look at the psychological and political factors that cause wrongful convictions in a way that no book previously has. It is also the story of one person's evolution, a story of my enlightenment and discovery.

In this book I explain how flaws in the human psyche, and political pressures, cause actors in the criminal justice—police officers, prosecutors, judges, and defense lawyers—to behave in bizarre and incredibly unjust ways without being aware that they are doing so. I talk about how, individually and as a society, we are by and large blind to these problems. We are in denial. Indeed, ours is a system of blind injustice.

And finally, I explain the steps we must take to improve—to become aware of the problems, and to open our hearts and minds—in order to create a more just and accurate system.

．　．　．

Earlier in my career, I served for many years as a federal prosecutor in New York City, where I prosecuted high-level felonies that frequently made the local news and sometimes even the national news. Organized crime cases. Hijacking cases. Terrorism cases. Major fraud cases. And cases involving corrupt high-level politicians. I won local law enforcement awards for "aggressively fighting crime," and a national award from U.S. Attorney General Janet Reno for "superior performance" that only a small number of prosecutors nationwide obtain. I was a prosecutor's prosecutor.

In 2001, I went back to my hometown of Cincinnati to serve as a criminal law professor at the Chase Law School, part of Northern Kentucky University near Cincinnati. Chase Law School had an organization called the Kentucky Innocence Project. It was part of a national network of organizations, typically based at law schools, which use law students to try to free the wrongfully convicted from prison. The professor who supervised the Kentucky Innocence Project was on sabbatical my first year of teaching, so I, as the new criminal law professor on the block, was asked to fill in and help supervise the students that year. But as a former prosecutor, I was skeptical. I didn't believe that innocent people were sent to prison in this country. I didn't really want to do it. But as a new professor, wanting to please my new bosses, I couldn't really say no. So I grudgingly agreed.

At my first meeting with the law students in the Kentucky Innocence Project, two students reported on their meeting with an inmate named Herman May, who was in prison for rape. They had just returned from visiting him in prison. With great emotion and passion, they talked about how they "looked into his eyes" and could see his sincerity, could feel his pain, and came to "know" he was innocent. I sat there and listened to their description and internally rolled my eyes. "How naïve," I thought. "What a bunch of gullible, bleeding-heart law students."

I asked the students about the evidence that convicted May in the first place. It turned out that May had become a suspect because he was caught pawning a guitar that had been stolen from a car in the same neighborhood and on the same night of the rape. Acting on a hunch derived from this coincidence, the police put May's picture in a photo spread and showed it to the rape victim. The victim identified May, and then testified at trial that May was the man who had raped her.

Semen from the perpetrator had been collected by a hospital from the victim's body at the time of the rape. The victim had testified at trial that she was not sexually active then, and therefore the semen belonged to the rapist. But DNA testing of the semen was not possible at the time of May's trial. So May was convicted and sent to prison.

Based on the certainty of the victim's eyewitness testimony, I believed May was guilty. In fact, I *knew* it. The students were hopeless romantics, I thought, if they actually believed that this guy might be innocent given how confident the victim was in her identification.

But the Kentucky Innocence Project moved the court for DNA testing of the semen using new scientific techniques. The DNA test results came back and confirmed that the DNA profile in the semen from the rape did not match the DNA profile of Herman May. May was released from prison after serving thirteen years for a crime it appeared he had not committed.

This was, needless to say, an eye-opening experience for me, the prosecutor's prosecutor. I was shocked. Suddenly the stories told by the students as to how May, as a teenager, had been taken in tears from his high school social studies class by the police and whisked to the police station, only to have pubic hairs plucked from his groin for forensic analysis, had new meaning. And it made me feel a little sick that I had scoffed at those stories just months before, thinking he had deserved it. I was confused as to how this could have happened.

Shortly thereafter, I attended the national Innocence Network conference. There, I met many men and women from around the country who had served ten, fifteen, or even twenty-five years in prison for crimes they did not commit. I attended lectures from scholars and lawyers about new knowledge that had come to light about weaknesses in our criminal justice system. This was the first time that I truly experienced the innocence movement. It caused me to slowly, but surely, start to see things in a new light. I began to understand that there was more going on than I had previously seen, and that there were problems in the system that I, as a prosecutor, should have seen, but about which I had simply been in denial.

The next year I got a job at the University of Cincinnati College of Law. At the time, Ohio was the one of the largest states in the country that did not have an innocence organization. With John Cranley (at the time of this writing, the mayor of Cincinnati), and others, I founded the Ohio Innocence Project at my new law school in 2003. By that time, I was a believer.

Since that time, my project has investigated thousands of cases of Ohio inmates claiming innocence. While our investigations have confirmed the guilt of many, as mentioned earlier we have freed twenty-five men and women on grounds of innocence.

Nationally, more than two thousand people have been identified as victims of wrongful conviction since 1989. The number continues to grow weekly. The details of these cases are maintained on the National Registry of Exonerations website, run by a collaboration of several prominent universities and law schools.[1] But I now know that this number is just the tip of the iceberg, because DNA and other new evidence is available in only a small percentage of cases. Many more inmates, with no evidence to work with, simply have no way of proving their innocence.

But the mere fact that innocent people in our system are occasionally wrongfully convicted is not what prompted me to write this book. Indeed, the revelation that innocent people in this country too often go to prison, while once earth-shattering, is by now old news.

Rather, I was impelled by my personal experience. From my perch as a prosecutor turned innocence advocate, I have witnessed bizarre human behavior that has left me both fascinated and shaken. I have seen how witnesses get it wrong but adamantly believe they are right. How witnesses have their stories twisted and rearranged by the police and prosecutors, without even realizing they have been manipulated and without the police and prosecutors realizing they have altered witnesses' statements to fit their theory of the case. How prosecutors, police, judges, and defense attorneys develop tunnel vision and make irrational case-decisions because they refuse—no matter the evidence—to question their initial instincts. How politics and internal pressures have caused people in the system to act unjustly and unfairly, all the while in denial about their true motivations. How they have become stubborn and arrogant about their ability to divine the truth, while they are in denial about their human limitations. And I have seen how these human flaws have resulted in tragic, gut-wrenching injustices.

In the end, the most lasting and important result of the innocence movement will not be the innocents who have been freed. Rather, I believe that it will be the new understandings in psychology that it has spawned, and the way that new understanding will reform the criminal justice system. The innocence movement led social scientists to study human perception, memory, and error with renewed vigor, resulting in a better understanding of the human mind. Psychologists began asking, "How could ten witnesses have taken the stand and said they were all positive that this man was the perpetrator, while DNA testing proves that it wasn't him?" "How could a regular person, with above-average intelligence, have confessed to murder, and even become convinced that he did it, when we now know from DNA testing that someone else did it?" "How could a supposedly neutral CSI forensic scientist take the stand and say that the defendant's fingerprint matches the fingerprint on the bloody knife, when we now know that isn't true?"

The answers are startling. And they not only help explain the many wrongful convictions but they call into question many of the basic premises of our criminal justice system, and even how we come to perceive "the truth" in our daily lives.

I have been fortunate to be deeply involved in these developments both from an academic perspective—researching and teaching the clinical developments in psychology—and as an innocence lawyer/former prosecutor, which has given me a front-row seat to how these psychological principles play out in the real world. This book is therefore designed to illustrate these principles from both an academic and a real-world perspective. Each chapter explores a distinct psychological human weakness inherent in the criminal justice system, such as confirmation bias, memory malleability, eyewitness misperception, tunnel vision, credibility-determining errors, administrative evil, bureaucratic denial, dehumanization, and the system's internal political pressures. I discuss what we have learned about these issues from academic and clinical studies in psychology, but also describe cases from my own career as a prosecutor and innocence lawyer and show where these principles distorted the truth or resulted in grave injustices. Because they are also relevant outside of the criminal justice system, I attempt to show

how these psychological problems can cause us to lose sight of the truth in our everyday lives as well, both at work and at home.

As I'll explain, the psychological flaws behind wrongful convictions are a triple-whammy. They not only contribute to the wrongful convictions in the first instance, but they make us unable to see or comprehend the errors as they are happening. In other words, they blind us to their impact. Then the same psychological problems cause us to deny the mistakes after-the-fact when a wrongful conviction is claimed twenty, thirty, or even forty years later. In other words, the psychological issues at work create the problem, blind us to the problem as it's unfolding, and then insulate the problem from introspection and discovery after-the-fact. As a result, we as a society are in collective denial about our biases, misperceptions, and memory problems. Prosecutors, judges, police officers, jurors, witnesses, defense attorneys, media reporters—*everyone*—have bought into the myths of the system and confidently go about their business unaware of the thin ice they are walking on. Though new breakthroughs in science and psychology are quickly eroding the myths of the past, players in the system by and large ignore them, resist the "new," and confidently assert their opinions in ignorance of their flimsy foundations.

But let me first offer a few caveats. Number one, I am not a psychologist. Rather, I am a lawyer. However, my unique seat as a prosecutor turned innocence advocate has enabled me to perceive strange human behavior "in the field" in a way that psychology professors might only dream about. I became so fascinated by the personal psychology that I started to see after joining the innocence movement that I began researching psychological doctrines to better understand the unsettling human behavior I was seeing every day in the courtroom, and to better comprehend how I had behaved as a prosecutor. So although this book is partially a book about psychology written by a lawyer, I believe that it will shed light on the relevance of important psychological doctrines in real-world settings.

A second caveat is that I will not discuss systemic racism in this book. Racism is undoubtedly a major psychological phenomenon that taints outcomes in the criminal justice system. But although extremely important, that problem has been explored elsewhere and is so complicated and pervasive that it could easily dominate the book. The purpose of this book is to bring to light other issues that aren't as widely discussed and debated.

Third, I am at times quite critical of actors in the criminal justice system, particularly police officers, prosecutors, judges, and defense attorneys. But when I am being critical, it is not because I believe that any of these professional positions are generally filled with bad people. Quite the contrary.

I have a deep respect for law enforcement and consider myself a supporter of it. I also have a deep respect for defense attorneys, who perform a thankless job of vital importance, and for judges as well. Rather, I believe that the unjust actions of the professionals described in this book occur because they are *human*. All of us would act in similar ways were we in their shoes, without the proper guidance and training. Indeed, I have engaged in these unjust activities myself, as a prosecutor, as I detail in this book. I believe that it is only through a process of recognizing and understanding our human limitations—our psychological flaws and the structural, political flaws of our system—that we can gain the requisite humility that will allow us to make the criminal justice system a true system of *justice*.

Fourth, I frequently discuss things I did as a prosecutor, and things that "we" did in my prosecutor's office, meaning myself and my fellow prosecutors. In doing so, I refer to what I believe was the custom and practice in my office, based on what I was taught and what I observed. However, for most of the practices I discuss, there was no formal training; rather, new prosecutors picked up the customs and practices from their supervisors and senior prosecutors on the go. Therefore, when I say "we did X in my prosecutor's office," I am referring to what I believe was the general custom and practice, but I cannot be certain that this was the practice of every single prosecutor in my office.

Finally, this is not a doomsday book. At the end, I will offer some solutions that could help mitigate the problems in our system. While there will always be human error in any system run by humans, there are steps we can take to make our criminal justice system more accurate. And we have a duty to explore, learn, and take those steps. As with many problems in life, awareness and acknowledgment of our human weaknesses is half the battle. But I also address procedures that can be implemented in the criminal justice system to minimize the distortions of truth that humans inherently bring to each and every inquiry.

2. Blind Denial

It didn't take long after I left the prosecutor's office and began litigating innocence cases for me to see firsthand the levels of extreme psychological denial to which prosecutors and police often succumb to avoid admitting that they convicted an innocent person. One of my first innocence cases, which eventually resulted in my first exoneration, was that of Clarence Elkins, who was in prison for raping and murdering his mother-in-law and assaulting and raping his niece in Barberton, Ohio, in June 1998.

Elkins's mother-in-law, Judy Johnson, had been attacked by an intruder in her living room in the middle of the night. The scene left behind was from a horror movie. The perpetrator raped and violently beat her, leaving a bloodbath over the floors and walls surrounding her body. He then went into a bedroom and beat and raped Elkins's six-year-old niece and Johnson's granddaughter, Brooke Sutton, leaving her for dead as well. But Brooke fortunately survived. After she regained consciousness the next morning, she told police that the attacker "looked like" her Uncle Clarence, but this soon became "it *was* my Uncle Clarence." Even though Brooke had only seen the attacker in the dark for a few seconds—and while under great stress—before he knocked her unconscious, the police immediately arrested Clarence and charged him with rape and murder before performing any other investigation. Although Elkins had a clean record and an alibi—witnesses placed him more than thirty minutes away from Johnson's house at the time of the murder—based on the questionable testimony of a child, the state of Ohio sought the death penalty against Elkins. The jury rejected the death penalty but convicted Clarence, and he was sent away to prison for life.

Clarence screamed his innocence when he was arrested, during his trial, and for years thereafter from his prison cell.

9

In 2005, my team at the newly formed Ohio Innocence Project heard those screams and took over the case to have DNA testing performed on the crime scene evidence. As a result of advances in DNA testing since the time of Elkins's trial, the lab was able to find male DNA on the swabs taken by the coroner from Johnson's vaginal cavity after her murder. This DNA did not belong to Elkins. Since Johnson was not sexually active at the time of her murder, any male DNA inside her vaginal cavity had to have come from the man who raped and murdered her. Moreover, the same unknown man's skin cells were found on Brooke Sutton's panties, which the perpetrator removed after knocking her unconscious so he could proceed to rape her. Only the actual killer could have deposited his DNA inside Johnson's vaginal cavity and on Brooke's panties on the night of the attack. And since that DNA didn't match Elkins, it logically meant that he was 100 percent innocent of the crimes.

I assumed when our DNA test results came back that the prosecutors would drop the charges against Elkins and set him free, and then begin looking for the true killer. After all, it was clear that Elkins was innocent and that therefore a cold-blooded killer was still loose on the streets. I was new to postconviction innocence work, and I was naïve. So I was very surprised when the prosecutors pushed back and insisted that Elkins was still guilty. And they didn't just push back, they fought with anger and venom and with ridiculous arguments that simply didn't make any sense.

The prosecutors responded to our DNA evidence by arguing that Elkins, despite the brutality of the attack, somehow must not have left any of his DNA anywhere at the crime scene. The male DNA we found during our testing, they said, must have been put there by some sort of innocent contamination that occurred before or after the crime. They suggested—hold on to your hat here—that perhaps a male juror during Elkins's original trial had opened up the evidence bags when no one was looking and, for example, rubbed his hands over Brooke's filthy, bloody panties, putting his DNA all over them in the process.

But the prosecutors didn't have any evidence that this incredibly farfetched scenario had actually taken place. They didn't have, for example, an affidavit from a male juror—or any other man—saying he had opened the evidence bags and placed his DNA all over the evidence. Indeed, the prosecutors were just making this up. And their theory was flatly contradicted not only by common sense but by the actual evidence in the case. The envelope containing Johnson's vaginal swabs had remained sealed throughout Elkins's trial. The "chain of custody" documents showed that the envelope had been properly sealed and preserved from the time the vaginal swabs were first collected at the coroner's office right after the murder occurred until the time that the swabs were DNA tested years later. The seal had never been improperly broken. And there was no way possible that a male juror or anyone else could have placed his DNA on the vaginal swabs *through* the properly sealed envelope.

To counter this inconvenient fact, the prosecutors threw out other bizarre arguments, suggesting for example that the male DNA found in Johnson's vaginal cavity could have come from Johnson shaking hands with some unknown man earlier in the day that she was murdered, thereby getting male DNA on her hands, and then Johnson masturbating or otherwise touching the inside of her vagina with her own hands, causing this man's DNA to rub off inside her vagina in the process. Wow! And the prosecutors couldn't explain how, if this were true, the man who shook Johnson's hand somehow got his DNA on Brooke's panties.

At our 2005 hearing to free Clarence, the prosecutors presented these silly arguments in court with passion and conviction. In fact, despite the clear evidence of innocence that our DNA testing had uncovered, the lead prosecutor continued to refer to Elkins as "the rapist Clarence Elkins." At one point when making his arguments to the court, for example, he stopped, pointed at Elkins sitting next to me in his orange jumpsuit and shackles, and dramatically called him this. After all the indignity that Elkins had suffered from being wrongfully convicted and imprisoned for so many years, I was amazed that he could sit there so coolly while this prosecutor continued to refer to him that way after DNA testing had already demonstrated his innocence. But he somehow endured it with grace.

When I spoke in court and explained the DNA test findings to the judge, the lead prosecutor and his second-chair prosecutor would roll their eyes and let out one exasperated sigh after another. During each break in the courtroom proceedings, the lead prosecutor and I would have cameras and microphones stuck in our faces as soon as we walked out into the hallway. He would always insist that Elkins was absolutely guilty, and that this DNA stuff was all smoke and mirrors.

The certainty in his voice, and his level of confidence in his position, blew my mind. To me, it was like the prosecutor standing up in court and arguing with great emotion and passion that the moon is made of cheese. I began asking myself questions that I would end up asking myself many times in future innocence cases when seeing similar reactions from prosecutors: Does this prosecutor realize his arguments don't make sense and he's just putting on an act for political reasons, or does he really believe what he's saying? Is he lying? Is he evil, trying to keep an innocent man in prison? Or is he just not very smart and truly doesn't understand the DNA test results? Which is it, stupidity or evil?

But years later, after hearing other prosecutors take similar positions in other cases, I eventually knew my answer. The prosecutor *did* believe what he was saying. He wasn't putting on an act. And he wasn't evil. Because Elkins's innocence conflicted with everything he had internalized for years about the system to which he had dedicated his life, he was in a form of psychological denial that prevented him from evaluating the evidence objectively. He literally could not mentally or emotionally accept the truth.

In Elkins's case, it turned out that the judge was in denial too. Despite the weakness of the prosecution's argument and the clarity of our DNA evidence, she denied our motion to free Elkins, meaning that he would have to spend the rest of his life in prison.

So in desperation, the investigation continued. Elkins's then-wife Melinda, and private investigator Martin Yant, who had been trying to find the true killer, soon identified a strong suspect—an individual named Earl Mann. Mann had a history of violence, and had been living two doors down from Judy Johnson at the time of the crimes. He even looked quite a bit like Elkins. We learned that in 2005 Earl Mann was serving time for other crimes in the same prison as Elkins. Out of thirty prisons in Ohio, Elkins and Mann ended up not only in the same prison but in the same cellblock.

In an ironic twist of fate, Elkins was able to collect one of Mann's cigarette butts in prison and mail it to our DNA lab. The lab confirmed that Earl Mann's DNA matched the unknown man's DNA from Johnson's vaginal cavity and Brooke's panties. But even after subsequent testing of Earl Mann's blood confirmed the same result, the prosecutors still didn't want to believe that Clarence was innocent. It took an eventual confession from Mann, and the heroic intervention of Ohio Attorney General Jim Petro on Elkins's behalf, for the prosecutors to finally capitulate and agree to exonerate Elkins.[1] In December 2005, Clarence Elkins walked out of prison a free man. Not long after, Earl Mann pleaded guilty, and is now serving life in prison for the rape and murder of Judy Johnson and the assault and rape of Brooke Sutton.

. . .

In my work as an innocence lawyer, I have seen good people—prosecutors and police officers—callously commit what I would call "acts of evil." In using the phrase "good people," I recognize that the line between good and evil is thin and that no person is all good or all bad. We are complicated creatures, and I do not intend to engage in a philosophical debate about the coexistence of good and evil in the human condition. Rather, I use this phrase in the everyday sense to refer individuals who do not suffer from some sort of personality disorder, like sociopathy, but rather, are typical everyday people who, for the most part, try to do the right thing and try not to unnecessarily cause catastrophic pain to others through their actions.

In that sense, I have seen prosecutors and police—who I think are generally "good people," commit egregious acts of evil. In case after case where we have developed strong evidence that our client is an innocent person suffering in prison, police and prosecutors have denied our claims in knee-jerk fashion without even looking closely at the evidence, and have made intellectually dishonest arguments in court to keep the innocents suffering in prison. And sometimes judges have gone along with them.

Indeed, of all the psychological phenomena I have observed over the past twenty-five years from my seat as a prosecutor turned innocence advocate, the most fascinating one for me has been the fervent denial that I have witnessed far too often from those deeply invested and imbedded in the system. Many of these people will admit in the *abstract* that innocent people are *sometimes* convicted and sent to prison for crimes they didn't commit. They have all read the newspapers and seen stories on exonerations of prisoners; in 2015 and 2016, these exonerations occurred in this country at a rate of about three per week. But when a specific case is presented to them that their office was involved with many years earlier, they invariably say that *this* case is not one of those where an innocent person was convicted, no matter the evidence.

It reminds me of public surveys about the U.S. Congress. When asked whether Congress is doing its job, the public gives it very low marks, often as low as a 10 percent approval rating. But when the public is asked whether *their* congressperson is doing a good job, the public hands out high marks, often exponentially higher than those for Congress as a whole.[2] But if each specific congressperson is doing a great job according to his or her constituents, how can Congress as a whole be viewed so poorly? Because the public thinks that it's always "other people's congresspersons" who are stinking the place up. In like fashion, law enforcement officials who will admit that wrongful convictions sometimes occur firmly resist the notion that any of the defendants *they* convicted are innocent.

As Professor Daniel Medwed has stated in his book *Prosecution Complex*, prosecutors succumb to denial "to avoid 'facing the unfaceable'"—that the inmate might be innocent. He added, "Denial may lead prosecutors to behave in a churlish fashion, even after an official declaration of innocence, by refusing to apologize or engaging in petty behavior that strains the bounds of logic."[3] One could say the same about police. In some instances, denial manifests itself in prosecutors forcing exonerees through vengeance retrials, even though no evidence of guilt remains.[4] The foreperson of the jury in the vengeance retrial of exoneree Derrick Deacon said after his jury acquitted him, "There was no case. There was never a shred of evidence against Derrick Deacon. Why did they try him a second time if he's been in jail for 24 years?"[5]

A phrase has been adopted in the innocence movement to describe the theories that police and prosecutors will sometimes adopt to avoid facing reality: the *unindicted co-ejaculator,* which is a play on the phrase *the unindicted co-conspirator,* a legal term common in American courtrooms. In its simplest form, this notion arises when a man has been convicted years earlier of raping a woman and the woman's testimony is that she was not sexually active before the rape and that only one man committed the rape. Then, when DNA test results come back years later showing that the DNA of the convicted man does *not* match the semen collected after the rape, prosecutors change their story and say that there must have been *two* rapists. They maintain that the defendant committed the rape but that he must have done it with someone else, and that this unknown man—the "unindicted co-ejaculator" (though prosecutors don't use that term)—was the one who left his semen behind. The defendant raped her too, he just didn't ejaculate.

In other cases, police and prosecutors may dig in their heels and insist over and over—without any evidence—that the DNA test results obtained from the prosecutor's own state lab *must* be wrong; that an error must have occurred somewhere in the testing process.[6] But if prosecutors were using DNA test results from their own lab to try to *convict* someone, they would treat such a suggestion from the defense as ludicrous.

I can't count the number of times in innocence cases I have sat in the courtroom and listened to prosecutors espouse theories like this, when I have wanted to stand up and say to the judge and everyone in the audience, "Wait a minute. Are these people serious? Is this some kind of a joke? Is there a hidden camera around here somewhere? Am I on TV? Am I on Mars? Am I losing my mind? Because if I'm hearing this right, either they're crazy or I'm crazy." Of course, I never say this, but the temptation sometimes arises again when I see the judge nodding along with the prosecutor's bizarre arguments. This extreme, mind-blowing level of denial that I have seen in cases like this left me scratching my head so much that I decided to dive into the psychology behind it, which ultimately led me to write this book. I was so bewildered by what I was seeing that I had no choice but to turn to psychology for answers.

· · ·

In my career as an innocence lawyer, I have had case after case where my client has suffered in prison long after the evidence proved them innocent. We develop a strong case for innocence and present it in court, but the client remains in prison because the prosecutors fight back with frivolous theories like the "unindicted co-ejaculator" theory or the "masturbating grandmother" theory in the Elkins case. And while my office has eventually freed many of these clients, most of them suffered in prison for many additional years after the evidence of innocence first surfaced because of this type of reaction from law enforcement and courts. And I have cases now where my clients have been proven innocent by DNA testing but still remain in prison after years of litigation. The collective state of denial in these cases has stretched beyond the prosecutors and trial judges, through the appellate courts and beyond. Although we have a better chance of an objective hearing the farther away we get from the prosecutor's home field, finding an open-minded judge down the road is a crapshoot. There's no guarantee that an innocent person will ever find justice, even with strong evidence of innocence on his side. Such is the level of denial that we too often see in our system.

I have visited these innocent clients in prison and been shaken by their anguish and agony over missing their children, or not being present when their mothers and fathers passed away. My client Nancy Smith, who we eventually freed many years later with strong evidence of innocence, was like a bear caught in a leg trap whenever I visited her in prison, in a constant state of agitated pain—mentally tortured, really. Nancy had been a bus driver for a daycare center in Elyria, Ohio. After intense media coverage of an alleged daycare molestation case in another state in the early 1990s, copycat claims of child molestation began popping up at daycare centers all across the country. A common thread in these cases was that many of these daycare centers, as in Nancy's case, were funded by Head Start, a federal program that offered deep pockets for the alleged victims' families, or otherwise offered opportunities for rich civil settlements. As in Nancy's case, many of the families that made allegations in these cases later received multimillion-dollar settlements. These cases are now known collectively as the "Daycare Hysteria Cases," and it is widely believed that many of the individuals charged in these cases are innocent, and many have been exonerated.[7] Indeed, the Daycare Hysteria Cases were a modern-day witch hunt, like the Salem witch trials. But I digress.

In Smith's case, the parents of the children, who later received millions in settlements, alleged that on a particular day, Smith did not deliver their three- and four-year-old children to daycare after picking them up in the morning, but instead took them to a strange house where Nancy and her "boyfriend" molested the children before taking them home at the end of the day. The children changed their stories repeatedly before trial, and their stories involved wild accusations such as Nancy and her boyfriend making them drink urine and sticking them with needles. Child-abuse experts who have studied cases such as this will tell you that stories of this nature are a red flag. When children have not actually been abused, and are too young to understand sex or what real sexual molestation typically looks like, they will often give bizarre and incredible answers to questions like, "What bad things did they do to you?"

Years after Nancy was convicted and sentenced to prison, evidence surfaced that all of the children were marked present at school on the day the alleged abuse happened. In addition, Nancy had an adult bus aide on her bus that day, who later verified that the wild tales didn't happen—the kids had been dropped off at school and taken home at the end of the day. Moreover, between dropping the children off in the morning and taking them home at the end of the day, Nancy always went to a second job. Work records showed that she was present at her second job on the day in question. A video of the children being interviewed by police also surfaced, which demonstrated that the children had been coached by their parents to incriminate Nancy and her alleged accomplice. Although it's hard to believe, Nancy's attorney at trial did no investigation and didn't bother to call the bus aide as a witness or investigate to find any of the documents that would have proven her innocence. Nancy spent nearly fifteen years in hell as a result of the allegations, while the accusing families got rich. After the evidence of innocence surfaced, Nancy was released in 2009, and the farce of her case was later depicted on an hour-long episode of *Dateline NBC*.[8]

But long before she was freed, back when the odds of her exoneration seemed a remote dream, I visited her in prison. To this day I have never witnessed a person in deeper emotional pain than Nancy Smith was that day. She was in utter agony over not being present to raise her four children. After she was wrongfully convicted, her younger children had been passed around from relative to relative, as Nancy had been a single parent. Her children had not had sufficient stability over the years, and one child had developed serious psychological problems and addiction issues as a result.

And there was nothing she could do to help them. She was so confused as to why this was happening to her that she couldn't sit still when she spoke. Her whole body shook and she cried so hard that I could barely understand what she was saying to me. She was in a state of nonstop, extreme mental torture.

On my drive home from the prison that day, I thought about the horrible injustice she faced—having to remain in prison and away from her children even though the evidence of her innocence was now strong. The reality of her mental torture was so overwhelming that it made me feel physically ill. The pressure I felt to free her—which at the time early in the investigation seemed like a longshot—made me pull my car over to the side of the road because I thought I was going to vomit.

I have had many sleepless nights over other cases. And that's just what I have experienced as a lawyer. I cannot imagine the pain and anguish that the innocents themselves and their families have suffered.

The mother of Dean Gillispie, a man we eventually proved innocent and freed in 2011, told me shortly after we took over her son's case in 2003, "This is the first time since Dean was kidnapped by the state of Ohio that our family has been able to enjoy Christmas. Just knowing that someone is listening, and that someone else is finally taking up the fight with us, made it feel a little like Christmas." But by 2003, she and her family had already experienced twelve Christmases without her son. And they would have to go through eight more Christmases before we finally brought Dean home as a free man. In fact, Dean had to spend an additional three years in prison after we had collected the evidence demonstrating his innocence simply because of the resistance from the prosecutors and the trial judge, who were as appallingly close-minded as the prosecutor in the Elkins case.

When I look at these cases, I see police officers, prosecutors, and judges who took unreasonable and intellectually dishonest positions that stripped innocent people of their freedom and caused tremendous human suffering for entire families. These acts could be considered acts of evil. But, as I will explain below, I believe that these actors in our criminal justice system are normal, good people. Indeed, if they *were* evil, then one would have to conclude that a high percentage of police officers and prosecutors in our system are evil, because so many of them react in this way to postconviction innocence claims. But they're not evil. They're just normal, regular people. They are the kind of people who would help an old man cross the road, or who would shovel the snow from a sick neighbor's driveway. They're the type of people who get invited to speak to high school civics classes, and talk to the students about our great system of justice. Everyone thinks they're wonderful, and the kids in the class want to grow up to be like them. Then they go back to their offices and commit acts of heartbreaking, callous injustice in cases like these because they are operating under a bureaucratic fog of denial.

Three psychological factors combine to cause good people to create this kind of "evil" outcome in our criminal justice system: cognitive dissonance, administrative evil, and dehumanization.

COGNITIVE DISSONANCE

Cognitive dissonance is a psychological phenomenon that can cause us to push aside or deny information that conflicts with our most deeply held beliefs.[9] The theory holds that humans cannot maintain two conflicting beliefs for long because it causes great internal discomfort or dissonance. To resolve the feelings of dissonance, we must take action to alleviate the conflict, which often means that we hold fast to the belief that is most important to our psyche, while subconsciously moving ourselves into a state of denial about the competing belief.[10] And in many cases, we don't just deny the information that conflicts with the belief that we have chosen to maintain, but, in order to make ourselves feel better about our initial feelings of discomfort, we strongly lash out against the competing belief, convincing ourselves that it is dead wrong and must be soundly defeated. We rationalize that our most important belief is absolutely correct, and then overcompensate for that rationalization by lashing out against the competing belief to soothe the internal discomfort that appeared when our deep belief was first challenged.

Many who supported the Nazi party in Germany during World War II eventually came to realize that their political party was committing mass genocide against the Jews and other targeted groups. For most, I'm sure, that realization caused initial feelings of dissonance. They loved the political party that was giving them a deep sense of self-worth by lifting Germany up as a world power, but they also knew that genocide was immoral. At that point, faced with beliefs that were in tension with one another, they had a choice. They could leave the Nazi party and not participate in its activities. But this could mean making great personal or professional sacrifices, which many were not willing to make. Or they could keep participating in the party but put their heads in the sand and convince themselves that the genocide wasn't actually happening, but rather was nothing more than wild rumors propagated by the enemy. Or, to make themselves feel better about what their beloved country was doing, they could go "all in" and aggressively adopt the ideology of the party, convincing themselves that killing Jews was the morally right thing to do in the circumstances and defensively lashing out against anyone who suggested otherwise.

While some Germans left the party, and some even chose to heroically save Jews, many chose to either deny what was happening or overcompensate by aggressively adopting the party's position regarding the "Final Solution." The closer they were in the hierarchy to the concentration camps, the harder it was for them to deny what was taking place, so the more likely they were to go "all in" in order to internally justify their actions and avoid dissonance.

Humans engage in cognitive dissonance about more mundane matters as well. If we smoke, we know that it is bad for our health. We can't continue to smoke while simultaneously stressing out about the health consequences—that's an intolerable situation that our subconscious will not allow us to maintain for long. So we must do something to resolve the dissonance. One option is that we can quit smoking, which of course some do. Others continue to smoke but rationalize away the dissonance. They may adopt the mantra that they will quit soon and thus won't suffer of any of the health effects associated with long-time tobacco use. They perpetuate this mantra that they will "quit soon" year after year, decade after decade, even though to any objective observer it eventually becomes clear that they will never quit. Or they convince themselves that if they quit smoking they will gain weight, which brings with it health risks like diabetes that they decide are greater than the risks associated with smoking. "Diabetes runs in my family," they will say, "and smoking is the only thing that keeps me thin. I unfortunately have to pick my poison. I don't have a choice."

Or they might convince themselves that they enjoy smoking so much that it outweighs the health risks. "Why would I want to live ten years longer if I'm not enjoying myself in the meantime," they tell themselves. "Smoking calms me down, and makes my life enjoyable. I can't concentrate at work when I'm not smoking. I'm a better person when I smoke. I'd rather have a pleasant shorter life than a longer life filled with constant stress and worry about health issues. I need to just cut myself a break and chill out."

Many decades ago, the father of the cognitive dissonance theory, psychologist Leon Festinger, infiltrated a cult whose members had been convinced by their leader that the world was going to end that year on December 21 at midnight. Members of the cult who followed their leader to a specified location at the end of time would be picked up by a spaceship and saved, they believed. Many of them sold their homes and gave away all of their possessions, believing they would not need them in outer space.

Festinger wanted to know how the group would react when the prophecy didn't come to pass. At midnight, nothing happened. No spaceship appeared, and the world didn't end. By two o'clock in the morning, the group was becoming very tense. At a quarter to five, however, the leader suddenly received a new prophecy and announced that God had decided to spare the world because of the faith and adherence of this little cult. Their impressive showing of faith, the leader claimed, had changed God's mind. As Festinger predicted, members of the cult were enthralled and now believed in their leader more than ever before. With exhilaration, they called the press to report the miracle, and began proselytizing with renewed vigor about the miracle they had been fortunate enough to witness.[11]

· · ·

As I've said, I believe that the vast majority of police and prosecutors are good people. They go into law enforcement to help others. To make the world a better place. To stop crime and provide a voice for the victims of crime, and to fight for justice. They internalize their fight for good, and it becomes an essential part of their self-identity and psyche. They naturally buy into the notion that their colleagues around them express: "We are the good guys, who put our lives on the line for the safety of others." And it's true. Law enforcement personnel have dedicated their lives to the public good. Many prosecutors, for example, are lawyers who could earn much more money in private practice but choose to make less in order to serve the public good.

When these individuals first entered the criminal justice system many years earlier, it appeared to be an impressive machine that had been honed and tweaked over the many decades of its existence to near-perfection by the intellect, wisdom, and hard work of the generations before them, tracing back to our nation's founding fathers. They had been fortunate to become a part of it, to be shown its ways, and to eventually carry the torch for the next generation. And through their careers, they each invested their lives in the system, believing deeply and proudly that they were contributing to something that was both noble and greater than the sum of its parts—bigger than any one person. And from that belief they formed part of their identity and sense of noble self-worth.

So, as developments both in the innocence movement and the field of psychology have called into question some of the basic assumptions at the core of the system, these individuals have often reacted with defensiveness, if not great hostility. When someone has suggested in a particular case that an innocent person may have been wrongfully convicted, they've denied it, often coming up with outlandish theories as to why the defendant is guilty—despite, as we have seen, DNA test results clearly demonstrating innocence. Or when someone has suggested that system-wide reforms are necessary—like those to make eyewitness identification or forensics more reliable—they often scoff and continue carrying out their work the way it's always been done, refusing to hear or even consider the proposed reforms.

Of course, when someone comes along and says, "Your office convicted an innocent man and sent him to prison for thirty years, while the true perpetrator stayed out on the street and raped and killed three women because of your mistake," it is naturally difficult to accept. It could cause intolerable dissonance. It conflicts with everything those in the system believe about themselves and the system to which they have dedicated their lives and have attached their sense of self-worth.

So when they hear this, they have a choice. They can objectively examine the claim to determine if it is true. But that is very difficult for most humans to do. Instead, many instinctively have a knee-jerk reaction. They refuse to examine the new evidence critically and come up with outlandish theories in order to maintain their deep-seated beliefs about the system's fairness. And they react with anger toward those who are challenging their beliefs and their identity. When told that the criminal justice system is systemically flawed and needs to be overhauled and reformed in many respects, they react with similar defensiveness and indignation.

Professor Daniel Medwed, who served as an innocence lawyer earlier in his career, spoke to my class and described the shock he felt when he first witnessed this psychological phenomenon at work. In his first case as an attorney for an innocence organization in New York, his team developed overwhelming evidence that their client was innocent. He told his students, "This evidence is very strong. The prosecutors are all reasonable people and just want to reach the right answer. We won't need to file a motion in court to free our client, we'll just go meet with the prosecutors and show them our evidence, and I'm sure they'll agree with us and set him free." But he was wrong. And naïve. And he lacked an understanding of human psychology, just as I did when I first entered this line of work. The reaction from the prosecutors, and the way they spun the new evidence in ridiculous ways to avoid conceding innocence, shocked Medwed. The prosecutors' reactions fascinated Medwed so much that he went on to focus his later scholarly career as a law professor on the psychology behind such reactions, writing several articles on the subject and eventually publishing *The Prosecution Complex*.

· · ·

We have a law in Ohio, as in all other states, that requires police and prosecutors to turn over biological crime-scene evidence for DNA testing in postconviction cases if certain legal requirements are met. In probably more than a hundred Ohio Innocence Project cases, my office has sought DNA testing through this statute on behalf of an inmate claiming innocence. In my early years doing this work, I would call up the prosecutor's office in question and say, "This inmate wrote us and says he's innocent. We looked up the case and it seems there should be DNA we could test to find out if he's telling the truth. Will you consent to release the DNA so we can get it tested? We'll pay for the testing. If you consent, we won't have to waste time litigating the issue in court."

The answer was almost always "No." I then would stress, "We're not saying he's innocent yet. I'm just saying there is DNA we could test that will give us the answer, and it doesn't cost you anything, so why can't we just test it?" Still the answer would almost always be "No." One prosecutor said to me during such a call, "The name of your program—Ohio Innocence Project—bothers me. How did you come up with that name? It's insulting. I get it—you're representing these people and you want to get them off. But none of these people are actually innocent, of course."

So now, years later, unless we are dealing with one of a few counties in Ohio that I have learned will sometimes consent to the testing, we don't even bother calling and asking. We just file a motion in court saying that our client is entitled to DNA testing under Ohio's DNA law, knowing it's going to be opposed aggressively by the prosecution.

When I talk about this during speeches, members of the public always ask, "Why won't the prosecutors consent to the DNA testing?" The only answer I can provide is that they're in such denial, and are so confident that any person their office has ever convicted is guilty, that they see it as a silly waste of time. But this defensive attitude not only is unjust, it wastes tons of taxpayer money. Indeed, when we're forced to fight for testing in court, it often takes years of litigation, tying up precious court time and resources in the process.

In one case, after getting a request for DNA testing from an inmate, I contacted the local prosecutors and asked them for consent to test the DNA in his case. I told them we would pay for the testing. Although there was plenty of biological material that could easily determine whether the inmate's claims of innocence were true, the prosecutors refused to consent. So we had to litigate the matter in court. After extensive litigation the trial court denied our motion, despite the fact that it was pretty clear the inmate was entitled to testing under Ohio's DNA law. A year or two later, once we got the case away from the prosecutor's home court, an appellate court found that the trial court judge had "abused his discretion" in denying testing under Ohio's

DNA law. So the case was remanded back down to the trial court with an order to submit the biological material to a lab for DNA testing.

The DNA testing went forward, and it confirmed the inmate's guilt. This is not an uncommon occurrence for those of us in the innocence movement. We, of course, cannot know when first seeking testing whether an inmate is innocent or not. We simply want to find out by testing the DNA. I tell my students that a DNA test result confirming guilt is the best answer one could hope for. I tell them, "If you're sitting around hoping that an innocent person is in prison, while the real perpetrator is out committing more crimes, you're sick." So when we got the test results back confirming this inmate's guilt, I was nonplussed. I was happy that we got a definitive answer. I did in that case what we always do with such test results—I moved to dismiss the DNA motion and end our representation of the inmate.

Typically, when we file such a motion after a client is confirmed guilty, the prosecution files a written motion agreeing, and the trial court enters an order ending the matter without the prosecutors or the defense attorneys having to come to court. It's all done in writing through the mail or, more recently, through electronic filings. But in this case, once we filed our motion to dismiss, the prosecutors filed a motion saying they wanted to have a hearing in court to discuss the matter further. I was confused by this request. It seemed like a waste of time. Everyone was in agreement that the DNA testing confirmed the inmate's guilt and the matter should be quickly resolved, so why did we need to waste time coming to court to discuss whether the motion should be dismissed? Nevertheless, out of courtesy, I did not oppose this curious request.

The night before the hearing in court, a reporter I had gotten to know fairly well called me and said something to the effect of, "The elected prosecutor himself is coming to court tomorrow, instead of just his assistant prosecutors, and he's having this hearing because he wants to blast the Ohio Innocence Project for wasting taxpayer money and taking up their time and the court's time for a guilty rapist. He's alerted the media so that we'll all be there tomorrow to get the story. I'm just giving you a heads-up."

After I got off the phone, I contacted the prosecutor's office and reminded them of my earlier offer to pay for the DNA testing without having to litigate, pointing out that we could have confirmed the inmate's guilt years earlier with no cost to taxpayers. But since they had refused to consent to the free testing back then, a lot of time and money had been wasted. In other words, the waste of taxpayer money was the prosecution's fault.

The next morning before the court hearing, the reporter called me back and said, "They've called off the media. The elected prosecutor is no longer coming. He's just sending one of his minions." The hearing lasted about sixty seconds and was a nonevent. It too was a waste of time. But not only had the prosecution's resistance to DNA testing wasted taxpayer money by requiring several years of litigation before the testing finally went forward, the prosecutors were so hostile to the DNA testing motion that they were chomping at the bit to publicly embarrass the Ohio Innocence Project for allegedly wasting taxpayer money on behalf of a guilty inmate. They pulled back from doing so only because they had been reminded that the waste of taxpayer money was no one's fault but their own.

Any lawyer in the innocence movement could provide example upon example where prosecutors fought back against innocence claims with a closed-minded attitude and denials that anyone their office had convicted could possibly be innocent. I've already provided numerous examples in this book. Here's another one. It occurred when I was still new to this line of work and still somewhat naïve.

The Ohio Innocence Project had a client, Rico Gaines, who had been convicted of murder based primarily on questionable eyewitness testimony. Years later, after Rico had spent many years in prison, the prosecution's star witness recanted, explaining that his testimony at trial had been wrong.

I now know that's typically not enough to win an innocence case. When the prosecution's witnesses recant years later, it doesn't move the needle for the courts. The courts simply assume that the "guilty murderer" or his family members pressured the witnesses to recant.

But in this case we had more than that. A man who lived on the street where the murder occurred contacted us and said he had seen the shooting. He was near the street at the end of his driveway when he saw and heard a dispute between several people on the street in front of him, and ducked down behind his car and peeked around to watch as the shots were fired. He saw the murder happen right in front of him. He not only knew that our client had not been involved, but he could identify the shooters as shady characters from his neighborhood who had a reputation for crime and violence.

He explained that he had been afraid to come forward at the time of the original trial because he had teenage children in the house and didn't want to put them at risk by testifying against such unsavory characters. But now his kids were grown and gone, and he had learned from the newspapers that the true culprits were imprisoned for other crimes. So he no longer feared for the safety of himself or his children. This new witness was not a friend of our client, and had no apparent motive to lie.

In addition, ballistics reports showed that the murder could not have happened the way the prosecution alleged at trial through their snitch witnesses. The reports corroborated what this new witness was saying about how the murder went down.

We contacted the prosecutors and informed them of this new evidence. We told them that we would give them access to the new witness, and they could even polygraph him if they wanted. They declined. They didn't want to meet or polygraph our witness. So we had the witness polygraphed ourselves, and he passed. Although I know polygraphs are not particularly reliable, we sometimes use them for our witnesses anyway because a positive result can on occasion help sway prosecutors. But because we couldn't get anywhere with the prosecutors, we filed a motion in court to exonerate Rico based on this new evidence.

After our motion was filed, the prosecutors contacted us and said they'd changed their minds. They would like to meet the new witness and see for themselves if he was telling the truth, they now said. Excited that the case was maybe going somewhere and that the prosecutors seemed willing to examine it with an open mind, we called up the witness and made arrangements for him to go to the prosecutor's office for an interview. When he arrived, however, they didn't interview him. Instead, they placed him under arrest for a series of unpaid, delinquent traffic tickets. They booked him and put him through the entire arrest process. This witness had to call his church and ask his pastor to pull money together from other church members to pay all of his outstanding tickets so that he could be released. Once his account was paid, the prosecutors sent him on his way.

The message was clear—the prosecutors were not, in fact, going to approach the case with an open mind, but would use any means available to them to intimidate the witness from testifying at our upcoming exoneration hearing.

We eventually were able to free Rico from a life sentence after he had spent nine years in prison. But the prosecution, as in so many other innocence cases, denied the prisoner's innocence at every turn without once making a good-faith effort to be objective or to seek the truth.

Although there are, of course, exceptions, this sort of behavior from prosecutors in postconviction innocence cases is considered the norm. When I tell these stories during speeches, the public becomes confused. They repeatedly ask me, "Why would the prosecutors do this? Don't they want the just result?" "Don't they want the truth?" They look at me like they don't believe me. So I was glad when the public could finally see a clear example of this sort of recalcitrance in the Netflix docu-series *Making a Murderer*. In 1995, when Steven Avery was in court fighting to overturn his wrongful conviction for the rape and assault of Penny Beernsten, a prosecutor from a neighboring county called the sheriff's department in charge of Avery's case and informed them that a man they had just arrested, Gregory Allen, had confessed to committing the rape. But the officer who took this call not only failed to disclose it to the court or Avery's lawyers, he didn't even write it down. He told a few supervisors about it and they all then blew it off.

Years later, after Avery was finally exonerated through DNA testing that proved Allen was the actual perpetrator, the Wisconsin Attorney General's Office commenced an investigation, at which time the sheriff's department finally documented this phone call from years before.

Why did they fail to take action when the call first came in? Because of a form of psychological denial. There was no doubt in their minds that Avery was guilty of attacking Penny Beernsten, so the phone call was irrelevant to them. Or, more precisely, they suffered from cognitive dissonance and it conflicted with their belief in Avery's guilt, so they shoved it aside. Human beings have a very hard time changing their minds once the die is cast. One psychological study shows that gamblers at a race track who have already placed their bet on the pending race (and thus can't go back) are far more confident that they have made the right choice than gamblers who have picked their horse but are still waiting in line to place their bets.[12] There's something about putting your money down that causes your mind to harden. Once prosecutors and police have obtained a conviction, they have put their money down. They have placed their bet, and there is no going back.

· · ·

I suffered from this problem to some degree myself as a prosecutor. Here's just one example. For two or three years when I was a prosecutor I spent a lot of time with a particular cooperating "snitch." He was someone we had arrested who then "flipped" and became an informant for us to work time off his sentence. (Informants plead guilty to the crime they were arrested for committing, and then agree to delay their sentencing for sometimes up to several years until their period of cooperation ends. And then they get leniency at sentencing depending on how helpful they were to law enforcement during their period of cooperation.) I met frequently with this informant as I prepared him for his potential testimony in various trials. I found him to be quite intelligent and funny. And he seemed quite honest. We developed a good working relationship. I liked him. On one occasion, for a reason I can't remember, I made a passing reference to his confession—how he had confessed in the back of the squad car when first arrested a few years earlier. When I mentioned his confession, he snickered.

I said, "What? Why did you laugh?" He said, "I did the crime, but I didn't confess in the squad car like Detective ——— said. He just made that up. I couldn't believe it when my lawyer showed me his report about my confession. It doesn't matter, I was gonna plead guilty anyway. I'm not gonna fight something I did."

To say that a detective fabricated a confession is a serious allegation that must be examined closely. But at the time, I just brushed off his comment as nonsense and didn't give it a second thought. It seemed ridiculous to me. So I just changed the subject. But when I look back at it now, I know that this informant had no motive to lie. He had admitted to the crime and pled guilty years before, and had become an informant right away. Why would he make up a story about a fabricated confession two or three years later? It could start an investigation that might force him to make accusations against one of the detectives he was now working with, and who would have a lot of influence over the length of prison sentence he would eventually receive when his cooperation period ended. So he had a strong incentive *not* to lie about that. And it's not like the informant had an agenda to bring up the confession with me because he wanted to start a beef. The topic came up by happenstance and in passing, and I was the one who brought it up. The informant was nonchalant about the whole thing, and he allowed me to quickly change the subject.

And when I think back, I remember that before we first arrested this informant I had put a lot of pressure on that detective to get a confession. I told him that the case would be tough and that since he always seemed to be able to get people to confess I really hoped he could "work his magic" and get a confession from this guy as well.

And because I swept the informant's allegation under the rug, I didn't determine if there were any pending cases involving disputed confessions obtained by this detective. I'm sure any defense attorney handling such a case would have liked to know that evidence existed that the detective who had just ostensibly obtained a disputed confession from her clients may have, on at least one prior occasion, fabricated a confession. It didn't even occur to me make such an inquiry. The first time it occurred to me was when I recalled this incident while I was writing this chapter. Just like the officer in *Making a Murder* who took the call that Gregory Allen had confessed to the rape for which Steven Avery was serving time, I thought it was ridiculous misinformation that didn't deserve a second thought.

Although to this day I don't know whether the informant was telling the truth about the allegedly fabricated confession, I do know that I blew off his allegation because of cognitive dissonance. I swept it under a mental rug because it didn't coincide with my beliefs about the system. And I believe that if I had brought it up to my supervisors and asked what should be done, they likely would have blown it off as well. No internal investigation would have commenced. Indeed, I might have been *chastised* for being gullible enough to take an informant's word over a police officer's word. We believe a snitch when he gives us information that helps us send someone to prison for life, but when he challenges our basic beliefs about the system, his allegations are promptly denied as nonsense without a closer look.

. . .

As an innocence lawyer, I am constantly frustrated by how police departments in Ohio stonewall my office's request for police files. When we start working on a case, the first thing we do is send the police department in question a public records request, under Ohio's public records law, to get the original police file so we can evaluate how the investigation was conducted and what evidence was collected. When my office first started doing this work, from 2003 until about 2009, we routinely received the police files in response. But after a few highly publicized exonerations, many police departments stopped turning their files over to us. Sometimes they just ignored our letters. Or when they responded, they didn't send the file but instead sent a letter claiming that the investigation was still ongoing, which relates to one of the exceptions under the public records law. They claimed the investigation was ongoing even in cases where our client had been convicted decades previously. So there was no way, in reality, the investigation was actually still open. This all happened in a manner that made it seem orchestrated, as many departments across Ohio started behaving this way at exactly the same time. It's like they all agreed at a statewide meeting of some sort that they might be able to stop the Ohio Innocence Project from getting so many exonerations if they agreed to stop turning over their files to us. One of the clinical professors working in my office, Donald Caster, eventually had to sue the Columbus Police Department under the public records law to try to create some new precedent that would end this chicanery. We won that lawsuit in 2016.

I now think back to when I was a prosecutor and received my first public-records request in one of my old cases. I was told by supervisors that I had to call some federal office in Washington DC to learn what I was supposed to do. I made the call. The person on the other end said something to the effect of, "If you can assert that the investigation isn't closed, then just say that and don't turn over the file. For example, if there is any suggestion in the file that your defendant may have committed the crime with someone else, and there wasn't enough evidence to arrest that person, or you didn't pursue that other person at the time, then you can honestly say the investigation is still open. It is possible that someday someone will walk into your office and give you enough evidence to arrest that other person." Even though I wasn't working on the case anymore, and hadn't thought about the case for years, I thought of an unlikely scenario that allowed me to assert that the case wasn't completely closed, as I was instructed, and then never thought about the case again. It didn't bother me one bit. I was glad I had such an easy avenue to stop the "bullshit."

. . .

Cognitive dissonance has fueled an aggressive backlash against proposed changes in the forensic sciences in recent years. As the innocence movement, psychological research, and new breakthroughs in science have exposed fallacies in many areas of forensics (as I will discuss in depth later), those who make their livings in these fields have lashed out at those offering new ideas as if they were heretics in the fourteenth century challenging the Church's sacred truths.

Take the field of shaken baby syndrome (SBS). For the past two decades, hundreds if not thousands of people in this country have been convicted based on a medical theory that we now know is invalid and can lead to wrongful convictions. This medical theory stated that if a dead or severely injured infant is reported to the hospital with three specific symptoms— bleeding in the retinas of the eyes, bleeding under the dural matter of the brain (subdural hematoma), and brain swelling—then the baby had to have been shaken by a caretaker. Only intense shaking, the theory went, could cause those three symptoms to be present at the same time. So if a parent or a babysitter called 911 when an infant lost consciousness, and it was later determined that those three symptoms were present, whoever was caring for the infant at the time would be charged and likely convicted of murder (or assault if the baby lived) for allegedly shaking the baby.

We now understand, however, that various conditions and illnesses can cause these three symptoms. "Short falls"—such as falling off a couch or diaper-changing table—can cause these symptoms as well in some circumstances. Accordingly, many individuals charged with murder under this theory have been acquitted in recent years, if they have had the funds to pay for medical experts to dispute the prosecution's experts espousing the shaken baby syndrome theory. And several people who were previously convicted under this theory have since been exonerated after spending years in prison, if they were lucky enough to have an independent-thinking judge examine the medical literature with an open mind.[13] But many convicted under this theory remain in prison. And many of them may be entirely innocent.

These new developments have caused quite a reaction among some pediatricians who made their living testifying for the prosecution in these cases. They have lashed out with venom at the doctors and neurosurgeons who have suggested that the original shaken baby syndrome theory could be wrong. Rather than responding on the merits of the issues, they have at times made the doctors questioning the status quo feel threatened. One doctor who challenged the status quo was even charged with perjury in a case after he testified for the defense, but he was ultimately acquitted. In the UK, Dr. Waney Squier, one of the world's leading neuropathologists, who was once a believer in SBS, was disciplined in 2016 for declaring under oath her belief that SBS is an improper diagnosis in many cases.[14] In response, a group of more than twenty leading pathologists and other leaders in this field from around the world published the following editorial:

> We are concerned that Dr. Waney Squier, perhaps Britain's foremost scientist in the field of pediatric neuropathology, who has been a consultant at the John Radcliffe hospital for 32 years, was struck off the medical register by a General Medical Council panel on Monday, based on her testimony in so-called shaken baby syndrome (SBS) cases. She was accused of various things, including showing too little respect for the views of her peers.
>
> Every generation has its quasi-religious orthodoxies, and if there is one certainty in history it is that many beliefs that were firmly held yesterday will become the object of knowing ridicule tomorrow. Whether this will be the fate of SBS, time will tell. However, the case of Dr. Squier follows another troubling pattern where the authorities inflict harsh punishment on those who fail to toe the establishment line.
>
> It is a sad day for science when a 21st-century inquisition denies one doctor the freedom to question "mainstream" beliefs. It is a particularly sad day for the parent or carer who ends up on the wrong end of another doctor's "diagnosis" that an infant was shaken, when the child may have died from entirely different, natural causes.[15]

The merits of this debate and the reactions of prosecutors and the medical establishment are captured perfectly in the documentary film *The Syndrome*. Anyone interested in this issue should watch this fascinating documentary to see cognitive dissonance on full display and the paltry level of discourse of the medical establishment when responding to claims that they may have had it wrong all these years. For example, in the film, a doctor invested in this field plays his guitar and leads the audience at a shaken baby syndrome conference in a karaoke-style sing-along of the following satirical lyrics, to the tune of "If I Only Had a Brain" from the *Wizard of Oz:*

I will say there is no basis, for the claims in shaking cases,
My opinion's in demand.
Though my theories are outrageous, I'll work hard to earn my wages
If I only get ten grand.
I could be an honest person, say abuse, of this I'm certain
Like Oz across the land.
But my wallet says it's needin' so I'll say it's all rebleedin'
If I only get ten grand.
Oh, I will tell you why the State's proof is not there,
Make my claims for causes that are very rare,
No proof for them, why should I care?
I don't care what other docs say, I will claim they're short falls always,
Professing on the stand.
Bleeding bad within the brain, or say I'll not abuse again
If I only get ten grand.
Other things cause bleeds in eyes, confessions are all lies,
I'm like a one-man band.
Anecdotes do not make science, research has no reliance
If I only get ten grand.
Oh, I will tell you why the State's proof is not there,
Make my claims for causes that are very rare,
No proof for them why should I care?
I'm attacked by many critics, but defense guys like to get us
Cause I support their plan.
They'll decry me as a chorus, I don't care my skin's not porous
Cause I always get ten grand. I want to get ten grand.
I really need ten grand.

When defenders of the original SBS theory have responded on the merits, it usually involves a claim that the theory must be true because some of the individuals arrested for shaking an infant later confessed to doing so. The confessions, they say, prove the theory right. This highlights the problem with the medical profession incorporating fields outside of their area of expertise into their medical diagnosis. It is apparent that these doctors do not fully understand the phenomenon of false confessions, to be discussed later in this book. That's not surprising, because most of the public does not understand the phenomenon of false confessions, including many judges, unless they have studied the psychological literature and have seen it play out in the courtroom. They also do not understand that a parent who just lost a child—perhaps the worst horror that could happen in one's lifetime—are extremely vulnerable to false confessions. This is particularly true when they are told by the police that a confession is the only way that they might be able to receive leniency and someday reunite with their other children, or when they are told that, unless they confess, their spouse is going to take the fall for shaking the child.

Thus, with SBS, an incorrect medical theory may lead to a false confession. The false confession is then used to validate the incorrect medical theory in a circular feedback loop.

The forensic establishment has pushed back with similar close-minded vitriol to criticism of bite mark evidence. The only two independent agencies that have thoroughly examined this type of forensic evidence have issued reports that are quite damning. In a 2009 report, the prestigious National Academy of Sciences demonstrated the deeply ingrained problems with bite mark evidence, and the Texas Forensic Science Commission in 2016 ruled that there should be a moratorium on the use of this evidence in the state of Texas.[16] In response, the American Board of Forensic Odontology (ABFO) has fought back, and its supporters "have waged, aggressive, sometimes highly personal campaigns to undermine the credibility of people who have raised concerns," the *Washington Post* observed.[17] Supporters of the status quo have, among other things, filed troublesome ethics complaints against odontologists who have dared to question the establishment.[18]

In 2015, the ABFO conducted a study intended to demonstrate the reliability of bite mark evidence and to silence its critics. However, the study failed miserably. The thirty-nine forensic odontologists who participated gave at times wildly divergent views on the hundred cases included, showing the subjective and arbitrary nature of this "science." Professor Paul Gianelli, a member of the National Academy of Sciences, called the results "disturbing" but "not surprising," adding, "There have been a number of cases over the years in which one bite mark analyst testified that a mark was a human mark, while another testified it was something entirely different, for example a bug bite, or an indention from a belt buckle."

But the most curious outcome of the ABFO's study has been its efforts to suppress its own results. Concerned sources within the ABFO told the *Washington Post* that the organization's leadership was "shocked" and "reeling from" the results of its own study, and tried to cancel the panel at an upcoming conference at which the results were supposed to be announced. The panel ultimately went forward, but the presenters from the ABFO downplayed the significance of the study, criticizing the organization's own methodology in the study as flawed. And even after the study exposed deep fallacies in bite mark science, the ABFO encouraged its members to continue testifying about this "science" in courtrooms.

The ABFO ultimately decided not to publish or release its study. Paul Gianelli said in response, "If this were truly a science-based organization, I would not only expect them to be extremely troubled by the results of this study, I would expect them to want to publish the results. And sooner rather than later, so they could be considered in any pending criminal cases in which bite mark evidence is a factor."[19] Prosecutors who continue to support bite mark evidence have sometimes reacted with similar defensiveness, if not outright dishonesty.[20]

This type of reaction toward those who challenge the status quo has been evident outside the forensic sciences as well. In 2012, a Louisville detective informed the Kentucky Innocence Project (KIP) that a man he had interrogated had confessed to a murder for which one of the KIP's clients was in prison. But the detective's superiors were not pleased that he had disclosed this information to what they believed was a defense-oriented organization. The detective alleged that he was demoted as a result, and internal police department emails obtained by the media demonstrated that the police department was angry with him, saying he should have treated it as a "confidential matter" and should not have "stuck his nose" into the case. The detective ultimately won a $450,000 whistleblower settlement against the city of Louisville for the retaliatory actions that he suffered as a result of his actions.[21]

In 2009, a Kansas City inmate named Robert Nelson sought DNA testing to prove his innocence, but was denied by the court. He refiled his motion in 2011 asking the court to reconsider, but his motion was rejected again, this time because he had not used the proper form such motions require under the Kansas DNA statute. Nelson's sister then reached out to the court and asked to be provided with a motion from another inmate's case so that Nelson could have a proper template to follow. When she called, she reached court clerk Sharon Snyder, who provided her with a sample motion from another inmate's case that had been successful. The motion Snyder provided to Nelson's sister was a public document, not confidential. Nelson then filed his motion for a third time, this time following the correct procedure, and he was successful. The DNA testing went forward and proved him innocent, and he was exonerated after spending three decades in prison for a rape he didn't commit. But after the court learned that Snyder had shared a publicly available document with Nelson's sister, she was fired. Snyder was only nine months away from being eligible for retirement at the time.[22] On national television, Nelson later called Snyder his "Angel," and Snyder said that, despite being fired, she was not sorry for helping Nelson out and would "do it again."

ADMINISTRATIVE EVIL

Good people will typically act with goodness when acting alone. When acting alone, our internal moral compass is our only guide and the only thing to which we are beholden. But problems of cognitive dissonance and denial are magnified exponentially when good people are part of a large bureaucracy, like the criminal justice system, that marches in lockstep according to predetermined policies and procedures. In a large bureaucracy, individuals are just cogs in the wheel doing what they're "supposed to do." No single person can be seen as the cause of any single injustice. Rather, responsibility is defused. The "system" is responsible, not the individuals.

Because the actors in a bureaucracy are beholden to its policies and procedures—the "party line"—they are conditioned not to check or even consider their internal moral compasses as they would when acting alone. And because everyone around them is following the same policies and procedures, they have a stilted sense that, if they are following them and doing what they are told to do, they are doing what is right. In other words, in large bureaucracies the practices and procedures of the group become the guiding lights and replace the internal moral compasses of individuals.

This phenomenon has been called "administrative evil." It is the process that allowed "good" German people to participate in the Holocaust as cogs in a large wheel. As one professor of organization studies has said:

> The prevailing cultural context in the modern age, with its emphasis on technical rationality, has enabled a new and dangerous form of evil. The Holocaust was the signal event marking the emergence of administrative evil, but the tendency toward administrative evil, as manifested in acts of dehumanization and genocide, is deeply woven into the identity of professions in public life. The common characteristic of administrative evil is that ordinary people, within their normal professional and administrative roles, can engage in acts of evil without being aware that they are doing anything wrong. Under conditions of moral inversion, people may even view their evil activity as good.[23]

Numerous psychological experiments performed in the 1960s and 1970s demonstrated that ordinary people will commit callous acts of cruelty, when following rules and regulations as part of a group or in a bureaucratic setting, that they wouldn't commit when acting alone. In one famous study, Professor Stanley Milgram set out to demonstrate that Americans would not engage in cruel acts of evil when following instructions from an authority figure, as did the German people during World War II. Subjects in the experiment, conducted in a laboratory at prestigious Yale University, were told that they were participating in a memory experiment and would be acting as "teachers" under the supervision and instruction of a white-lab-coated "scientist." The teachers were told that their goal was to help other subjects—"learners"—to improve their memories.

With the "scientist" watching and providing instructions, the subjects were told to read a series of word pairs to the learners, who were confederates of Milgram, for the learners to parrot back from memory. When a learner recited the pairs correctly, the teachers were to simply acknowledge the correct answer. But if a learner made a mistake, the teachers were to administer an electric shock by flipping a switch on an elaborate console in front of them. Each time a learner made a mistake, the intensity of the shock would increase. Failing to provide an answer also counted as an incorrect answer that would result in a shock. There were thirty different shock levels on the console, starting at 15 volts and going up in 15-volt increments to 450 volts. Each level of shock had a different name on the console, with the highest levels saying "very strong shock," "intense shock," "extreme intensity shock," "danger: severe shock," and finally, ominously, "XXX."

The teachers could not see the learners, as they were in an adjacent room, but they could hear the learners, as the door between the two rooms was left open. Before the experiment started, the teachers were taken into the adjacent room and strapped to the electrodes on the learners' chair and given a shock at the 45-volt setting so they could get a sense of what the shock would feel like at one of the lowest levels. Although the 45-volt shock was not a dangerous level, it was enough to get someone's attention.

Unbeknownst to the teachers, the learners were actors, and the shocks they received never went above 45 volts, even when a teacher turned the switch to higher levels. The learners were told to grunt audibly at 75 volts, to complain that they were in pain starting at 120 volts, and to start begging for release at 150 volts. At 270 volts, they were told to start screaming as if in intense pain. Between 300 and 330 volts, the learners were told to no longer respond to the questions, but to simply scream in agony when the shocks came. At 330 volts, they were told to be unresponsive to both the questions and the shocks, as if they were unconscious or dead.

Milgram anticipated that the teachers would resist increasing voltage levels, so he instructed the scientist to engage in predetermined "prods." The first two times a teacher expressed hesitation, the scientist was instructed to simply say, "Please continue." After that, the scientist was instructed to say, in order, "The experiment requires that you continue," "It is absolutely essential that you continue," and "You have no other choice, you must go on." If the teacher continued to balk after receiving this final instruction, the experiment was terminated.

Before going forward with the experiment, Milgram asked a number of people, including psychiatrists, graduate students, undergraduates, and middle-class residents of New Haven, Connecticut, what they thought the outcome of the experiment would be. Every single person in the survey predicted that all teachers except a few sociopaths—more than 99 percent—would break off the experiment early on and would refuse to give anything beyond the lowest level of shocks to the learners. This comported with Milgram's own predictions.

The results of the experiment surprised everyone. More than 60 percent of teachers went all the way to 450 volts, well past the point where the learners had seemingly lost consciousness and might be considered dead. Milgram then repeated the experiment but modified it such that several teachers participated together in administering shocks as a group. In that scenario, 100 percent of the teachers administered shocks up to the maximum 450 volts.

Milgram had assumed, like those he had surveyed before the experiment, that American subjects would not allow the voltage to increase beyond minor levels. His plan was to perform the experiment on American subjects and then perform the same experiment in Germany. He hypothesized that, unlike Americans, Germans would follow the instructions to dangerous high-voltage levels, thus proving that something about German culture conditioned Germans to follow authority and bureaucratic instructions as they did during the Holocaust. But because the Americans fared so poorly, he didn't bother repeating the experiment in Germany.

Milgram's results mirror those of the famous "Stanford prison experiment," which was conducted in the basement of the Stanford psychology department. In this experiment, Professor Philip Zimbardo screened male student subjects for "normal" personality characteristics, finding eighteen subjects that did not exhibit particularly aggressive or passive dispositions. The eighteen young men were paid to participate for two weeks in what he called a "prison experiment," but Zimbardo assured them that they would be well cared for and not abused. He divided the men into two groups—nine prisoners and nine guards—and created an environment and infrastructure where the guards had to lead the prisoners through two weeks of typical prison life, enforcing rules and keeping the prisoners in line as would guards in a typical prison.

Although the experiment was slated to last for two weeks, Zimbardo was forced to cut it off after six days because the guards steadily and collectively slid down a path of sadistic discipline and abuse. Each day, the guards became more aggressive and abusive while the prisoners became more sullen and passive. By the sixth day, Zimbardo had been forced to release five of the prisoners because of depression and extreme anxiety. By that time, the guards had forced the prisoners to do such degrading things as defecate into buckets that were never emptied, to repeatedly chant filthy songs, and to clean toilets with their bare hands.

The Milgram and Stanford experiments could not be performed today because of the ethical guidelines enforced by human subject review boards that have proliferated in the past few decades. But they demonstrate the morality-stripping effects of bureaucratic hierarchy, obedience to authority figures, and group pressures. I doubt that many individuals in our society, if they had access to a device that administered shocks as in the Milgram experiment, would use such a device on their friends, family or neighbors. The idea would be abhorrent to them. They would never do it when acting alone, when their only guideline would be their internal sense of morality.

But when normal people are placed in a bureaucratic setting where doling out pain is part of the accepted structure, and are told to inflict pain, most do so without blinking. Why? Because in a bureaucratic hierarchy with authority figures above them and preset guidelines and procedures for individuals to follow, they think of their actions not as their own but as the actions of the institution to which they belong, and to which they have assigned great prestige. They defer to those in authority and to the institution. Each cog in the wheel has been conditioned to follow procedures and rules that have been set by the institution, and thus they do not follow their internal moral compass in the way they would if acting alone. The "power of the individual's conscience is very weak relative to that of legitimized authority in modern organizations." The "guiding value in most organizations is compliance with legitimized authority. Or, put another way, doing the right thing is almost always what is deemed good for the organization."[24] As one expert on organizational studies has said:

> Because administrative evil is typically "masked," no one has to accept an overt invitation to commit an evil act, because such invitations are almost never made. Rather, it may come in the form of an expert or technical role, couched in appropriate language, or it may even come packaged as a good and worthy project (moral inversion). Evil then occurs along another continuum: from acts that are committed in relative ignorance to those that are knowing and deliberate acts of evil (masked and unmasked). Individuals and groups can engage in evil acts without recognizing the consequences of their behavior, or when convinced their actions are justified or serve the greater good. Administrative evil falls within this range of the continuum, where people engage in or contribute to acts of evil without recognizing that

they are doing anything wrong. Typically, ordinary individuals are simply acting appropriately in their organizational roles—in essence, just doing what those around them would agree they should be doing—and at the same time, participating in what a critical and reasonable observer, usually well after the fact, would call evil.[25]

· · ·

I am a Woody Allen fan. Each of his movies has a plot, of course, which often includes a moral lesson. But Woody's characters frequently make passing comments, unrelated to the main plot, that infuse his films with other ideas important to Woody's moral universe. In the film *Hannah and Her Sisters,* one of Woody's characters explains to another character that he has been watching television all night, and adds, "You missed a very dull TV show on Auschwitz. More gruesome film clips, and more puzzled intellectuals declaring their mystification over the systematic murder of millions. The reason they can never answer the question 'How could it possibly happen?' is that it's the wrong question. Given what people are, the question is 'Why doesn't it happen more often?'"

I relate deeply to that comment, although I would modify it. I would change the last sentence to say, "The real question is: 'Why are we so blind to the fact that we commit injustices against each other every day because of the same bureaucratic mindset that we saw in Nazi Germany?'" Indeed, our society's primary "take away" lesson from the Holocaust is that we can't let it happen again. That, of course, is a paramount goal. But the problem is that we view how the Germans behaved during the Holocaust as an aberrational moment in history. It is that aberrational moment—and only that moment—that must be avoided in the future, we say. In reality, though, the bureaucratic mindset that allowed the Holocaust to happen exists all around us at all times, causing injustices that, while not on par with the Holocaust, are profoundly unjust nonetheless within their micro-context. By seeing the Holocaust only as a great aberration and failing to see how that mindset operates in smaller ways on a daily basis throughout our bureaucratic institutions, we are not learning as much as we could from that horrific period in history.

When prosecutors and judges cause great human suffering by blindly refusing to consider evidence of innocence, objectively speaking they commit acts of evil. But I am convinced that none of them see it that way. And, again, I don't think that they are bad people. Instead, I believe they are normal people just going about their business as they have been instructed to do—trying to shoot down the claims of the "bad guys" that come before them—without ever reflecting on their own morality or looking at the issue outside of the bureaucratic framework that they have been conditioned to follow. And they do this because they are human. They do what I believe nearly all of us would do in similar situations.

DEHUMANIZATION

The problems of cognitive dissonance and administrative evil proliferate in the criminal justice system in part because actors in the system systemically dehumanize criminal defendants. Dehumanization "is a psychological process whereby opponents view each other as less than human and thus not deserving of moral consideration."[26] Dehumanization is all around us, and is visible whenever and wherever humans systematically punish other humans through a bureaucratic apparatus. In times of war, for example, each side in the conflict dehumanizes the other. During World War II, Nazis dehumanized Jews; and Americans dehumanized "Japs," spreading dehumanizing propaganda and placing those of Japanese descent in internment camps. In colonial times, slave owners dehumanized Africans.[27] Racism in any form involves dehumanization.

In like fashion, police officers and prosecutors (and, to some extent, judges) are part of a bureaucratic structure whereby they are in some sense at war and are required to routinely inflict great pain and punishment on other human beings, including when they "deserve it" in some moral sense. And their psyches allow them to do so more easily by seeing those they punish as akin to "enemies." This alleviates dissonance. Criminal defendants become stereotyped as "evil," "guilty," "all the same," and not worthy of individual attention.[28]

Furthermore, the criminal justice system moves along at a great pace, with millions of cases coming and going at all times. Judges, police officers, prosecutors, and defense attorneys handle thousands of cases over their careers, with the human beings at their mercy veritably whizzing by. Before long, these system actors come to see criminal defendants as commodities—each an anonymous, faceless file with an assigned number, sitting in a file cabinet in their offices. To those files they apply the practices, customs, and bureaucratic rules and regulations that they have been taught, without really considering the files as human beings, or sufficiently considering whether the rules and regulations need to be adjusted on a case-by-case basis to reach the most humane results. It's an assembly-line mentality, each actor just a cog in the wheel applying bureaucratic rules in cookie-cutter fashion without thinking deeply about the impact of those rules and regulations.

I received my offer to work at the federal prosecutor's office in New York City when I was working at a large New York City law firm. A memo was circulated around the firm announcing my departure and why I was leaving. Because the U.S. Attorney's Office is a very prestigious place for a young attorney to work, I received hearty congratulations from the lawyers of the firm, including many who had spent time as prosecutors in that office prior to joining the firm.

One lawyer who had previously worked in that prosecutor's office didn't seem very happy for me, though. When others congratulated me in the hallway, she had an unsettled look on her face and then walked away without saying anything. I assumed maybe she didn't know what the group had been talking about. So I went to her office and said, "Hey, did you see I'm going to the U.S. Attorney's Office? I know you used to work there." She said, "Yes," without enthusiasm. I said, "Didn't you like it?" She said that she did at the time, but after she got some distance, she didn't like what the experience did to her. I asked what she meant. She said, "It made me a harsh, judgmental person. I dehumanized people. It took me a long time after I left to shake off that mentality. Maybe it's okay for some people, but in retrospect I realized it didn't really fit me."

Because I was excited about my new job, I shrugged off her comments. I then launched into the job with great enthusiasm, and did it well. I served for several years, handling high-level felonies of various sorts. Many received national media attention. I won awards. But now, years later, and having served on the defense side in the meantime, I know what she was talking about. And a part of me knew it even while I was a prosecutor.

Indeed, we clearly dehumanized defendants in my prosecutor's office. They were categorized as "the other." We each had so many cases that we often mixed up the names of our defendants. I went to court on more than one occasion and used the wrong name—I spoke about another defendant's case instead of the one that was before the judge at that time—before realizing my mistake. That was not an uncommon occurrence in my office. Defense lawyers did the same thing. The defendants were just case files to us. They were just interchangeable parts in the bureaucratic game we played. It didn't matter what their names were, nor did anything else specific to them as human beings. All that mattered were the facts of their cases and the standard set of rules we were supposed to apply to them.

In my office, we used the phrase "bad guy" to signal that our defendants were "others" upon whom we were to inflict punishment and apply our bureaucratic customs and practices, without individualization. I recall one instance early in my prosecutorial career when I presented a plea deal to my supervisor in a particular case. My supervisor wanted to make sure I wasn't being too soft, so he asked me what my defendant had done to get himself in trouble. I told him. He responded, "He's a *bad guy*—you can't give him that deal." Whenever the phrase "bad guy" was used—which was invariably in every case—it meant, "Don't be such a softy and do what you're supposed to do—hammer him." We were the good guys. They were the bad guys. Bad guys weren't worthy of nuanced thoughts outside of the preset rules and regulations that we were supposed to apply to them in assembly-line fashion. It was very black and white.

When this dehumanizing mentality goes to extremes, it perpetuates things like the "two-ton contest," in which prosecutors in Chicago competed to see who could be the first to indict "four thousand pounds of flesh." The contest resulted in prosecutors going after the heaviest defendants they could find.[29] While no one that I know of in my prosecutor's office engaged in anything like a "two-ton contest," I can relate to the mentality, because I lived it. Criminal defendants are nothing more than "things," "commodities," and "bad guys," and the whole process is a bureaucratic game.

· · ·

In one of my cases as a prosecutor, a group of teenagers hijacked a postal truck and stole thousands of dollars from it. The truck's daily route went from post office to post office around New York City at the end of each day to pick up the cash and money orders that the post offices had collected throughout that day. By the end of each day, it typically contained tens of thousands of dollars. The teens hijacked the truck with semiautomatic assault weapons, forced the driver to drive behind an abandoned building, fired a gun into the air, and then stuck the hot, smoking barrel into the driver's mouth, making him cough and choke. At gunpoint, they told him to unlock the safe. They then absconded with the money.

I was assigned the case after the initial arrests and bail hearings, so I didn't know what any of the defendants looked like when I took over the case. To me, the case was just a file. The defendants were just numbers. Shortly after I took over the case, lawyers for two of the teens reached out to me and said their clients would like to plead guilty and testify against the others in exchange for leniency. However, the attorney for another defendant, who I'll call Ward, made clear that his client was not going to plead and planned to go to trial. So I met with the two teenage defendants who wanted to cut a deal, had them plead guilty, and signed them up as cooperators to testify against Ward.

The process of preparing these teens to testify against Ward was very tedious and time-consuming. They were in custody, so each time I worked with them on their testimony they had to be brought to my office by U.S. marshals and then returned to jail when I was done. They had grown up in the projects, deprived and without much parental involvement or emphasis on education. So, when practicing their testimony and asking a question like, "What happened next," I would often get an incomprehensible answer. Such was the state of their education and inability to express themselves clearly.

In order to make them good witnesses, I had to spend an inordinate amount of time working with them. I had to teach them how to tell a story in a clear, linear fashion. I had to teach them, for example, that if they used five different "he's" in a single sentence, the jury would get confused. Indeed, if left to their own devices, they might answer the question "What happened next?" like this: "First, they said let's go at four, and then he called me and said let's wait longer, and then she came over and looked at my beeper for a minute and then agreed with him, and then he agreed too, and then we all decided to go get some food first, and then he finally said okay I'm ready." They needed to slow down and use proper names, I told them, rather than "he," "they," and "we," so that jurors could follow the story. Also, they used so much street slang that it was hard to understand them. So I had to teach them how to talk in a way that jurors could comprehend. But they were so accustomed to their way of speaking that it was like pulling teeth to get these lessons to sink in.

So over the months leading up to Ward's trial, I had to spend day after day with these two teenagers preparing their testimony. Through that time, I grew very fond of them. Despite their limited education, they were very smart. And aspects of their personalities were very kind and charming. I quickly came to believe that they were essentially "good" people, who had just grown up under extremely difficult circumstances, with little positive guidance and few good role models, and had made some bad choices as a result.

I became protective of them, even paternalistic. I wanted them to succeed in life after the case was over. So I tried to give them the life lessons that they had never received at home. I discussed philosophical issues with them, and tried to get them to focus on what they were going to do with themselves after the case was over. And they were so young that they touched my heart as naïvely innocent. For example, one of the teenagers would get exhausted after a few hours of trial preparation, so I would sometimes let him watch his favorite show—the cartoon *Spider-Man*—in the conference room during our afternoon breaks. He had to watch the show with a U.S. marshal in the room.

I decided pretty early on that I was going to fight for them at their sentencings, and get them as little prison time as possible, so that they could move past this experience and do all the positive things in their lives that I had talked to them about doing.

That was very different than how I viewed their co-defendant Ward. As I prepared for his trial, I became more and more convinced that he was the ringleader of the hijacking, and that he was a depraved individual who was spiraling out of control at the time of the crime. I was sure that if we didn't get a conviction, it was just a matter of time before he actually killed someone. I hated him for that. When preparing for trial, he was my enemy and the one that I needed to take down for the betterment of society. I pictured him as a very tough, mean, evil person. I had placed the "enemy image" on him—the image that we placed on all such people who we were targeting for punishment.

Shortly before the trial started, the judge called us in to resolve the final pretrial motions. Ward was brought to court for this proceeding in a prison jumpsuit with handcuffs and shackles. This was the first time I had seen him. And I couldn't take my eyes off him. I believe he was eighteen at the time, but he could have passed for fourteen. He was a kid. He was physically small. He had a baby face. He looked scared to death but he tried to hide it. At this hearing, he sat at the defendant's table next to his lawyer and pretended to understand what was going on, nodding emphatically when the judge or his attorney said various things, and then hurriedly scribbling down notes on a notepad like he was writing down something important and playing a key role in his defense. Yet his demeanor was quite innocent, naïve, and scared, just like my cooperating witness's when he told me that *Spider-Man* was coming on and nervously asked if he could watch it.

And what really killed me was that no one was there for him. That was very unusual, as most defendants have family and friends who show up at all the court proceedings for moral support. Ward, on the other hand, though just a kid, didn't have a single person—not even a parent—there in the courtroom to support him. From that fact alone, I knew what kind of life he had had. I knew he had lived the same kind of deprived life as had my two cooperating witnesses for whom I had hope and had tried to take on a fatherly role.

The sharp contrast between how I had pictured Ward and how he actually appeared in all his humanity made me feel disoriented and very uncomfortable. Although I had never allowed myself to feel this way toward a criminal defendant, for some reason I felt very sad for him. After the hearing was over, I went back to my office and closed the door. I was shaken. I felt like I had been kicked in the gut. I choked back tears for a good ten minutes, pacing in my office and ignoring my ringing phone. I couldn't stop thinking about how he was exactly like my two cooperating witnesses who I had grown so fond of, and how no one had been present in courtroom to support him. He, like my cooperating witnesses, no doubt had good qualities. Indeed, my witnesses were best friends with this kid and had grown up with him. They had all raised each other in the projects because no one else was there to raise them.

But I knew intellectually that Ward deserved to be punished for his crime. And I had a job to do. My job was to punish him—to try to send him to prison for the thirty years that the crime called for. So I tried to shake off my reaction to him at the hearing and move forward. But I couldn't completely shake it. The trial started, and it wasn't fun for me like most trials were when my competitive juices flowed. I was internally conflicted and continued to feel empathy for him because no one was there to support him. Each morning, I almost prayed that someone would be there in the courtroom for him, but no one ever materialized.

So when one of my witnesses didn't provide the helpful testimony that I anticipated she would, I looked for an excuse to cut a deal and walk away from the case. Even though I probably still could have gotten convictions on all counts, I told my supervisor of the problem that had arisen and sought permission to offer Ward ten years in prison instead of the thirty years he was looking at if he were convicted on all counts. In talking with my supervisor, I probably oversold the depth of the problem in my case to ensure that my deal would be approved. My supervisor approved the deal, and Ward took it. He went away to prison for ten years.

I then fought to get the smallest sentences possible for my two cooperating witnesses. I don't remember their sentences, but they were minimal, perhaps two years in prison. A few years later, I saw one of them in the hallway of the courthouse after he was released from prison. He had come back to the courthouse to check in with his parole officer. He told me that he had turned his life around, had received his high school degree in prison, and was now in college on a baseball scholarship. It made me feel good. It was a success story. But I wondered whether, if Ward had made the decision to cooperate in exchange for leniency, he too would now be in college on his way to a successful life.

I knew that I had made a fatal mistake as a prosecutor. I had grown fond of my cooperating witnesses—I had humanized them—and through that process I had humanized Ward. And once that happened, I couldn't perform my job as I was supposed to. Rather, I cut a perhaps unnecessary deal that gave Ward tremendous leniency. In passing the criminal laws that Ward had violated, Congress—and the people who elected their representatives—had decided that thirty years in prison was the appropriate sentence for Ward's crime. But I didn't want to inflict that level of punishment on him. Because I had humanized him, I put my own personal feelings over the bureaucratic rules, in effect allowing my feelings to trump the very laws I was supposed to follow.

I don't know for sure, but I don't think that any prosecutors in my office ever had to choke back tears in their office over the humanity of a criminal defendant. If so, it wasn't talked about. Ever. No one talked about defendants in a humanizing manner. And I didn't talk about my feelings toward Ward with anyone but my wife.

· · ·

I never allowed what happened in the Ward case to happen again. And so, after working to get myself back into the prosecutorial mindset, I reacted with shock and indignation when a judge complained to my supervisor that I had jubilantly celebrated after inflicting punishment on a defendant in another case. In that case, it was almost Christmas. The jury had come back with its guilty verdict at about 5:30 in the afternoon, just after our office Christmas party had started in the law library of our office. Several federal judges were in attendance at the party. With a fellow prosecutor who had tried the case with me, and a band of FBI agents who had worked on the case with us, I came bounding into the Christmas party yelling, "We won! Conviction on all counts, baby!" as everyone at the party lined up to give us high fives, with glasses of Christmas punch in their other hands.

It didn't occur to me that our celebration was inappropriate—that's what we always did when we won a case. Indeed, in another case, after the jury returned a guilty verdict early one evening, the NYPD detective on the case drove my fellow prosecutor and me across town to have a celebratory dinner. His sirens were blaring and his lights flashing, making rush-hour traffic stop as we cut through red lights and crowded Manhattan intersections as if we were rushing to a crime scene. My fellow prosecutor and I laughed our heads off in the back seat of the squad car, giddy from the victory.

But while most of the judges in our building, I think, would not have given a second thought to our Christmas party celebration, one of them was deeply offended. He wrote a note to my supervisor complaining about my conduct and saying something to the effect of, "A criminal conviction is not something to celebrate. It's necessary, but criminal defendants are people too, and it is a gut-wrenching experience for their families. Reacting with jubilation is not appropriate for such a somber event. No one wins in the criminal justice system." When this note came in, my supervisor read it aloud to a bunch of us standing around, and we thought it was crazy. "What a jerk," we said. "Who does he think he is?" "What a clueless a-hole," we laughed. Of course, I was not told to refrain from such celebrations in the future. It was an accepted part of our culture.

• • •

A few years ago, the Ohio Supreme Court overturned on appeal the exoneration of one of our clients, Nancy Smith. She is the woman I described earlier in this chapter who had been wrongfully convicted of child sexual molestation and was in such agony while she was in prison because she was separated from her four children. After she was exonerated and released, she had been able to reestablish relationships with her now-grown children, and was spending her time joyously babysitting all her grandchildren while their parents worked during the day.

The Ohio Supreme Court did not take issue with the merits of Smith's exoneration; rather, the court overturned it on a technical ground, saying that the trial court that exonerated her did not have the jurisdiction to do so in the manner in which it had been done. This meant that Smith would have to go back to prison immediately. We had grounds to potentially correct the error, and could continue to litigate to have her exoneration reexecuted in a proper manner, but such litigation could take a year or two, or even longer, and Smith would have to go back to prison until she was reexonerated in a manner that passed legal muster. And there was no guarantee that she would be exonerated again—there is always a risk of unexpected obstacles along the way, or new judges with different views taking over the case. Going back to prison, even if she might be reexonerated later, was an intolerable and unimaginable nightmare to Smith.

After the Ohio Supreme Court ruled, the prosecutors were apparently worried that Smith would be fully exonerated again at some point. So they offered her a deal. Each of the various counts of child molestation she had been convicted of carried a few years in prison. The prosecutors offered to exonerate her of some of the charges, but leave intact the charges that justified the number of years she had already spent in prison before her first exoneration. So under this deal, she would have already served all the time required for the convictions that would remain intact. The rest of the charges would be dismissed. To take this deal that would ensure she would never go back to prison, Smith had to agree to give up all appeals of the charges that would remain intact, and agree never to sue any public officials or departments over her wrongful conviction.

This was a torturous choice for Smith. She could continue to fight for complete vindication, but she would have to go back to prison in the meantime, and immediately. Since she simply could not imagine going back to prison, she had no choice but to take the deal.

The courtroom was packed with Smith's family on the day the court proceeding was held to finalize the deal. Everyone was in absolute agony, not sure if she was making the right decision. Indeed, either choice was intolerable—it was truly a choice between two evils.

The reason I'm telling this story, however, is because of the way the judge conducted himself that day. The judge who had exonerated Smith a couple years earlier had recused himself from the proceeding, so a visiting judge from a nearby county took his place for the day. Apparently completely oblivious to the human suffering in the room, the judge walked out into the courtroom and immediately cracked a joke. Pretending like he didn't know the courtroom would be full of cameras, he ran his fingers through his hair and laughed aloud, saying cutely, "If I had known there were going to be all of these cameras here today, I would have gotten myself a haircut." When his joke was met with silence, he quickly scanned the courtroom as if he were surprised that he had not received a round of hearty, approving laughter from the peanut gallery. He then continued through the thirty-minute proceeding in a similar way, nonchalant and, in my opinion, hamming it up for the cameras in a joking, light-hearted fashion.

Although there is technically nothing "wrong" with this judge acting in the manner that he did that day, I tell this story to illustrate what I saw as a complete incongruity between the actual human suffering in the courtroom and the oblivious, dehumanizing manner in which the judge apparently saw the whole affair. It was like watching a doctor crack jokes while telling a patient and his family that he has six weeks to live.

And I know how the judge saw it. He saw the proceeding as I did when I was a prosecutor. It was just another day at the office, where he had to deal with another anonymous, faceless defendant—just another file on his docket to which he was to apply his bureaucratic rules without awareness of the humanity around him.

. . .

In my innocence work, I have tried on occasion to break through the institutionalized dehumanization to help prosecutors see my clients and their families as suffering human beings. But it has never worked. I tried this unsuccessfully in Dean Gillispie's case, for example. A little background on Dean's case is necessary here.

Dean had been arrested and convicted in 1991, when he was twenty-five, for raping three women. The serial rapist in the case had a distinct modus operandi. He abducted the women in broad daylight in public parking lots, flashing a badge and posing as a police officer and claiming the women had stolen something in a nearby store, and then forced them at gunpoint to drive their cars to an isolated area—behind a building or into the woods. Once there, he dropped his pants and forced them to perform oral sex on him. He said very specific things to his victims during the rapes, like, "I work as a contract killer for the CIA," "I'm from Corpus Christi, Texas, and Columbus, Ohio," and, "I do this because I was molested by my grandfather when I was twelve." The victims described him as having a dark tan, wearing a medallion on a chain around his neck, a smoker, blonde or light brown hair with a reddish tint, and acne along his jaw line, among other characteristics. The victims worked with the police to create a composite sketch, which was plastered on posters all over the Dayton area.

Two years passed with the crimes unsolved before Dean was arrested. At the time he was arrested, Dean had a lot of friends, no criminal record, and a good job with a bright future. He was from a hard-working middle-class family in Dayton, with no criminal history. It's fair to say that Dean was popular and loved by many. But Dean had made enemies with management personnel at his factory job over union disputes. Serious enemies. And after one dispute when tempers flared high, one of his supervisors took Dean's factory employee photograph and went to the police department investigating the unsolved rapes and said, "This guy Dean looks like the rapist on the wanted posters." The wanted poster had been on the wall at the factory for two years prior to this, but the supervisor did not try to implicate Dean until after things really heated up between them.

According to what the jury heard at trial, the rookie detective in charge of the case at the time put Dean's photograph in a line-up with photographs of five other men, and all three victims identified Dean as the rapist. Then they identified him at trial. There was no other evidence against Dean but the identifications of the three victims. No forensics. Nothing. At trial, Dean had an alibi—witnesses testified that he had been in Kentucky camping with friends on a weekend when two of the rapes had occurred, and one of them even had the trip recorded in a diary. But the prosecutor told the jury Dean's friends were covering for him. Despite the fact that Dean has fair skin and burns rather than tans, had gray hair since high school, couldn't wear a chain or medallion around his neck due to thick chest and neck hair, didn't smoke, didn't have acne along his chin line at any time, and his other physical characteristics contradicted the victims' original descriptions of the rapist in many other ways, the jury convicted him. Indeed, as I'll discuss later, despite the unreliability of human memory and eyewitness identification testimony (which the criminal justice system has not fully recognized yet), when three rape victims take the stand, cry, and assert with great emotion that they are "positive" the defendant is the man who raped them, it is nearly impossible for a defendant to overcome it in the courtroom. Dean was sent to prison for twenty-two to fifty-six years.

After Dean served twenty years in prison, my office cleared him in two different courts on two different grounds. First, our investigation revealed that the jury had been misled about how the case against Dean started. We tracked down the original detectives on the case—the detectives who had the case when it was cold, before the rookie detective who arrested Dean took over the case. These experienced detectives told us that Dean's work enemy—his supervisor—had tried to implicate Dean earlier when they were still in charge of the case. But the two detectives investigated Dean and very easily eliminated him as a suspect. In addition to Dean not matching the physical description given by the victims, one of the victims had called in a few days after writing her initial police report and said she forgotten to include the fact that she saw the waist and inseam size of the perpetrator's pants on a tag along the outside belt line when he dropped his pants and made her get down on her knees to perform oral sex on him. When this call came in, the detectives wrote a new, shorter report about the pants size of the perpetrator and put it in the file. As soon as Dean's work enemy brought Dean's name forward as a potential suspect, they looked up Dean's height and weight in the Department of Motor Vehicles records, and could see that there was no way Dean could ever fit into pants of that size. They also were experienced enough to recognize when a person was trying to implicate someone from a vendetta, and it was clear to them that Dean's supervisor was implicating Dean out of spite, so palpable was his hatred. So they wrote up a report eliminating Dean as a suspect and placed it in the case file.

Both detectives then left the department—one moving to Florida and the other to Arizona—and the rookie detective took over the cold case. By coincidence, the rookie detective just happened to be friends with Dean's work enemy, and their families had known each other for years. Dean's work enemy then brought Dean's photograph back over to the police department for another bite at the apple with a more sympathetic ear. The earlier reports written by the previous detectives eliminating Dean as a suspect then disappeared from the file, as did all information in the file exonerating Dean—such as the report with the perpetrator's pants size—and the rookie detective went forward as if Dean was a new suspect. He got the victims to identify

Dean in the photo line-up. At trial, the jury never learned what had really happened, and didn't have all the facts. Neither did Dean's defense attorney. Based on testimony from the two original detectives in the case, a federal judge threw out Dean's conviction in 2011 and he was freed.

Our investigation also revealed who likely committed the rapes. An anonymous tip came in implicating another suspect. A thorough investigation by my office demonstrated that the named suspect had a history of flashing a badge and posing as a police officer to commit crimes, including abducting women. He also was known to tell people that he was a contract killer for the CIA, was from Texas and Columbus, and that he had been molested by a male family member when he was twelve—just like the rapist. According to witnesses who knew him well, he tanned deeply in the summer (the rapes occurred in August), smoked, had light brownish hair with a reddish tint, and wore chains and medallions in the late 1980s when the rapes occurred. By examining his arrest record and talking to former girlfriends who had called 911 on him at one time or another in the past, we learned his sexual preference is for oral sex exclusively. When his partners requested intercourse, he was unable to perform.

For our hearing in state court, we created a chart to illustrate the similarities between this suspect and the rapist. On the right is half of the perpetrator's face from the victims' composite sketch made in 1988. On the left is half of this suspect's face from a photo taken in 1990. We merged the two half-faces together for comparison purposes (see fig. 1).

After we presented this evidence in state court, Dean's conviction was thrown out a second time, this time on the ground that the jury likely would have acquitted Dean had it been made aware of the powerful new evidence implicating this alternative suspect.

Now back to the point about my attempts to get prosecutors to see my clients as human beings rather than numbers in a file. After the evidence of Dean's innocence first surfaced and while Dean was still in prison, I asked for a meeting with the prosecutors to convince them not to oppose Dean's upcoming parole request. I wasn't asking them to exonerate Dean yet, but merely not to oppose his parole so that he could be released from prison while we litigated his potential exoneration. After I spent about an hour presenting my evidence of innocence, which included the police misconduct in the case, the elected county prosecutor said in a huff, "What I am supposed to do about this? I thought you just wanted us to not oppose his parole? Why are you telling me all this stuff about alleged innocence and police misconduct that has nothing to do with parole?" I wanted to respond, "For one, you could investigate the police misconduct." As the case pro-

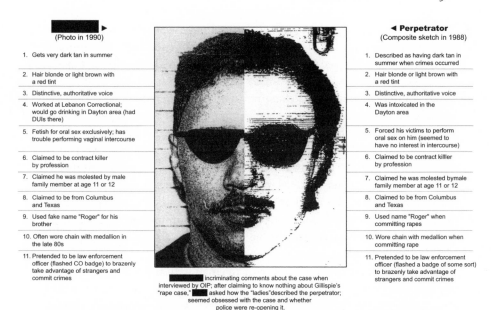

	▶				◀ **Perpetrator**
(Photo in 1990)					(Composite sketch in 1988)

1. Gets very dark tan in summer	1. Described as having dark tan in summer when crimes occurred
2. Hair blonde or light brown with a red tint	2. Hair blonde or light brown with a red tint
3. Distinctive, authoritative voice	3. Distinctive, authoritative voice
4. Worked at Lebanon Correctional; would go drinking in Dayton area (had DUIs there)	4. Was intoxicated in the Dayton area
5. Fetish for oral sex exclusively; has trouble performing vaginal intercourse	5. Forced his victims to perform oral sex on him (seemed to have no interest in intercourse)
6. Claimed to be contract killer by profession	6. Claimed to be contract killler by profession
7. Claimed he was molested by male family member at age 11 or 12	7. Claimed he was molested by male family member at age 11 or 12
8. Claimed to be from Columbus and Texas	8. Claimed to be from Columbus and Texas
9. Used fake name "Roger" for his brother	9. Used name "Roger" when committing rapes
10. Often wore chain with medallion in the late 80s	10. Wore chain with medallion when committing rape
11. Pretended to be law enforcement officer (flashed CO badge) to brazenly take advantage of strangers and commit crimes	11. Pretended to be law enforcement officer (flashed a badge of some sort) to brazenly take advantage of strangers and commit crimes

███ incriminating comments about the case when interviewed by OIP; after claiming to know nothing about Gillispie's "rape case," ███ asked how the "ladies"described the perpetrator; seemed obsessed with the case and whether police were re-opening it.

FIGURE 1. Comparison of victims' composite sketch of perpetrator and image of alternative suspect in the Dean Gillispie case. From Dean Gillispie court files.

ceeded in the years that followed, this prosecutor's office not only opposed Dean's exoneration, but it did nothing about the police misconduct, even after the federal judge threw out Dean's convictions on that basis.

In any event, at the end of that hour meeting, the assistant prosecutor who had tried Dean's case to the jury years earlier told me that I was too late—that he had already sent a letter to the parole board opposing Dean's release on parole. He showed me the letter. It was very short. In one part it said something to the effect of, "It is true that Dean Gillispie has passed polygraphs, but this is only because he is such a depraved sociopath that he can trick a polygraph."

This sentence really jumped out at me because I knew that the prosecutor didn't really know Dean but had only seen him in court. He had never talked to Dean. I knew that he was only capable of seeing Dean as an "enemy," as I initially saw Ward and all similar defendants I was trying to send to prison. Anyone who actually knows Dean, however, knows that he is one of the smartest, warmest, and most unselfish people they have ever met. Which is why he is loved by so many. Dean had become my friend by that time through my many prison visits, and I had grown to love and respect his family and empathize with their suffering. I knew at the time that the prosecutor's stilted view of him not only was dead wrong but was that of an institutionalized bureaucrat who couldn't see past the dehumanizing stereotype he used for all people he inflicted with great punishment.

As we stepped out into the hallway after the meeting, I said to this prosecutor, "I'm going to give you an offer that I bet no defense lawyer has ever given you. Before you make such a statement about another person, don't you think you should get to know him first? So I'm gonna let you go visit him in prison, without my presence, and spend as much time as you'd like asking him questions and getting to know him. Sit with him for hours and look into his soul. After that, tell me if you still think he's a sociopath. Since we're dealing with the freedom of another human being, please consider making an effort to have some sort of basis for your opinion." The prosecutor seemed a bit surprised or rattled by this offer, and quietly responded that he would think about it.

A few days later, I followed up with an email with the same offer but got no response. After more time passed, I explained my offer to one of the original detectives on the case, Steven Fritz, who was sympathetic to Dean's case because had informed us of the police misconduct. Fritz had worked for years with the prosecutor in question, knew him well, and thought he was a good person. Fritz said he would talk to the prosecutor and try to get him to visit Dean in prison. Later, Fritz told me that after he emailed the prosecutor and asked him why he hadn't responded to my invitation. The prosecutor had emailed back saying something to the effect of, "Never talk to me about this subject again."

Looking back on it, the prosecutor's response doesn't surprise me. Again, prosecutors are conditioned to dehumanize, and meeting with Dean would have gone so far against the bureaucratic norms that my offer must have seemed bizarre. But his response reflects the unbending ethos of our criminal justice system.

. . .

Fighting injustice as an innocence lawyer is at times a frustrating and depressing job. The public sees only the Kodak moments on the news when we celebrate joyously with a newly freed inmate after a big win. When that happens, people call us "heroes" on our Facebook pages. But the reality is that constantly fighting a system that refuses to admit mistakes, dehumanizes our clients, and fights to keep innocents in prison is exceptionally draining and demoralizing. Particularly when working on a case where the evidence of innocence is strong but the prosecutors oppose the exoneration motion and the courts go along with them. My office has many clients now who we believe are innocent, and we have the evidence to prove it, but our clients remain behind bars. In some of these cases the evidence of innocence is overwhelming, including DNA test results.

A few years ago, a class of our Ohio Innocence Project law students made OIP T-shirts for their group. On the back they put a picture of a person wearing boxing gloves fighting a giant glacier. That's because the students realized pretty quickly that we fight a system that, like a glacier, is hard to move. I've had attorneys leave my office because of burnout and the psychological stress of fighting such a wall of resistance. Those who stay for the long haul must constantly pick each other up and give each other pep talks to remain focused and continue the battle.

One day after we found out that we lost a case for which we had amassed very strong evidence of innocence, the entire office was deflated. The students who had worked so hard on the case were in shock and crying. I sent the students and Jennifer Bergeron, the OIP attorney on the case, the following email, which I include to demonstrate how we deal with such demoralization:

Jennifer, Emily and Sean,

I know that you were very upset about the loss today. You guys did everything you could. There aren't many feelings worse than experiencing raw injustice so up-close and personal. It is hard to take. After I would visit Nancy Smith in prison, with her emotions so raw from missing her children, I would try to keep from throwing up the whole drive home. The injustice and pain was sickening, and I had lost time and time again and seemingly couldn't do anything to fix her situation.

I am so sorry how it turned out. As you know, the fight isn't over, and Al will continue to have the best fighting for him. It comes down to the luck of the draw—which judge you have, which makes it that much more upsetting.

I learned through time from doing this for so long that even when we lose for someone like Al, the mere fact that someone stood up for him has unbelievable value to his life and to humanity as a whole. Imagine the difference if you were Al and no one ever listened, or no one ever believed in you, and you had to spend the rest of your life in prison without anyone ever acknowledging that an injustice had been done to you, or without anyone ever saying you are worth fighting for.

But Al, in contrast, has had a group of smart, educated and caring people who were complete strangers come to him and not only believe in him, but work tirelessly for years for him. And the fact that it was such an uphill battle—and everyone knew it was a long shot from the beginning—made the fact that you joined him in the fight that much more meaningful. As Ricky Jackson said to us in jail the night before he was released, just having good, talented people say, "You matter to me, and I'm going to do everything I can for you" in some way rekindled his faith in humanity. It meant the world to him, even if it didn't result in his freedom. I know that others feel the same way, and although I don't know Al, I do know that he is a thoughtful person and no doubt feels that way too. Reaching out and fighting for another human being who no one else will fight for has incredible value in and of itself.

Years ago after we started working on Dean Gillispie's case, his mother said to me one January, "This Christmas was the first year since Dean got locked up that I enjoyed Christmas. Just knowing someone else believes in us and is willing to take up the fight in some way changed things for me." If we had never won Dean's case, I would always know that we had provided a human service to Dean and his family just by showing them that someone was willing to acknowledge what happened and stand with them.

My favorite line from *To Kill A Mockingbird* is when Atticus is talking to his kids and says something like, "I don't want you to get the idea that real courage is a big man with a gun. Courage is when you're licked before you start, but you start anyway, and you see it through to the end because it's the right thing to do."

If it was easy to win these, anyone could and would do this type of work. The real value, and the real courage, is doing something because it's right even if it has a high chance of ending in gut-wrenching injustice. Few will do that job, which is why it is so much more important to humanity in the long run. A lot of people tried to save Jews in WWII but failed—the Jews they were hiding were discovered and killed and so were the good people who tried to hide them. But even though they failed at what they were doing, and the Jews they were trying to save were executed, if people like that didn't exist our species would suck. People like that make us all better. They're heroes, even though they didn't accomplish their goal and ended in an epic fail.

This isn't WWII, but it's a little piece of injustice that matters just as much to this person. Thanks for fighting for Al, and filling that important void that no one else would fill.

—Mark

CONCLUSION

I close this chapter with excerpts of a letter written by former prosecutor Marty Stroud. When Stroud was a young man, he prosecuted Glenn Ford for murder and sent him to death row. Ford spent thirty years on death row in Louisiana before being fully exonerated in 2014. Immediately after he was exonerated and released, Ford took ill with cancer, and he died not long after in 2015. During his short period of freedom before his death, the state of Louisiana fought Ford's claim for compensation, ultimately prevailing and keeping Ford from receiving a dime. While Ford was still alive, the editorial board of the *Shreveport Times* published an editorial urging Louisiana to compensate him. In response, Stroud sent the following letter to the newspaper:

> This is the first, and probably will be the last, time that I have publicly voiced an opinion on any of your editorials. Quite frankly, I believe many of your editorials avoid the hard questions on a current issue in order not to be too controversial. I congratulate you here, though, because you have taken a clear stand on what needs to be done in the name of justice.
>
> Glenn Ford should be completely compensated to every extent possible because of the flaws of a system that effectively destroyed his life. The audacity of the state's effort to deny Mr. Ford any compensation for the horrors he suffered in the name of Louisiana justice is appalling.
>
> I know of what I speak.
>
> I was at the trial of Glenn Ford from beginning to end. I witnessed the imposition of the death sentence upon him. I believed that justice was done. I had done my job. I was one of the prosecutors and I was proud of what I had done.
>
> Members of the victim's family profusely thanked the prosecutors and investigators for our efforts. They had received some closure, or so everyone thought. However, due to the hard work and dedication of lawyers working with the Capital Post-Conviction Project of Louisiana, along with the efforts of the Caddo Parish district attorney's and sheriff's offices, the truth was uncovered.
>
> Glenn Ford was an innocent man. He was released from the hellhole he had endured for the last three decades.
>
> There was no technicality here. Crafty lawyering did not secure the release of a criminal. Mr. Ford spent 30 years of his life in a small, dingy cell. His surroundings were dire. Lighting was poor, heating and cooling were almost non-existent, food bordered on the uneatable.
>
> Nobody wanted to be accused of "coddling" a death row inmate.
>
> But Mr. Ford never gave up. He continued the fight for his innocence. And it finally paid off.
>
> And yet, despite this grave injustice, the state does not accept any responsibility for the damage suffered by one of its citizens. The bureaucratic response appears to be that nobody did anything intentionally wrong, thus the state has no responsibility. This is nonsensical. Explain that position to Mr. Ford and his family. Facts are stubborn things, they do not go away.
>
> At the time this case was tried there was evidence that would have cleared Glenn Ford. The easy and convenient argument is that the

prosecutors did not know of such evidence, thus they were absolved of any responsibility for the wrongful conviction.

I can take no comfort in such an argument. As a prosecutor and officer of the court, I had the duty to prosecute fairly. While I could properly strike hard blows, ethically I could not strike foul ones.

Part of my duty was to disclose promptly any exculpatory evidence relating to trial and penalty issues of which I was made aware. My fault was that I was too passive. I did not consider the rumors about the involvement of parties other than Mr. Ford to be credible, especially since the three others who were indicted for the crime were ultimately released for lack of sufficient evidence to proceed to the trial.

Had I been more inquisitive, perhaps the evidence would have come to light years ago. But I wasn't, and my inaction contributed to the miscarriage of justice in this matter. Based on what we had, I was confident that the right man was being prosecuted and I was not going to commit resources to investigate what I considered to be bogus claims that we had the wrong man.

My mindset was wrong and blinded me to my purpose of seeking justice, rather than obtaining a conviction of a person who I believed to be guilty. I did not hide evidence, I simply did not seriously consider that sufficient information may have been out there that could have led to a different conclusion. And that omission is on me.

Furthermore, my silence at trial undoubtedly contributed to the wrong-headed result.

I did not question the unfairness of Mr. Ford having appointed counsel who had never tried a criminal jury case much less a capital one. It never concerned me that the defense had insufficient funds to hire experts or that defense counsel shut down their firms for substantial periods of time to prepare for trial. These attorneys tried their very best, but they were in the wrong arena. They were excellent attorneys with experience in civil matters. But this did not prepare them for trying to save the life of Mr. Ford.

The jury was all white, Mr. Ford was African-American. Potential African-American jurors were struck with little thought about potential discrimination because at that time a claim of racial discrimination in the selection of jurors could not be successful unless it could be shown that the office had engaged in a pattern of such conduct in other cases. And I knew this was a very burdensome requirement that had never been met in the jurisprudence of which I was aware.

I also participated in placing before the jury dubious testimony from a forensic pathologist that the shooter had to be left handed, even though there was no eyewitness to the murder. And yes, Glenn Ford was left handed.

All too late, I learned that the testimony was pure junk science at its evil worst.

In 1984, I was 33 years old. I was arrogant, judgmental, narcissistic and very full of myself. I was not as interested in justice as I was in winning. To borrow a phrase from Al Pacino in the movie "And Justice for All," "Winning became everything."

After the death verdict in the Ford trial, I went out with others and celebrated with a few rounds of drinks. That's sick. I had been entrusted with the duty to seek the death of a fellow human being, a very solemn task that certainly did not warrant any "celebration."

In my rebuttal argument during the penalty phase of the trial, I mocked Mr. Ford, stating that this man wanted to stay alive so he could be given the opportunity to prove his innocence. I continued by saying this should be an affront to each of you jurors, for he showed no remorse, only contempt for your verdict.

How totally wrong was I.

I speak only for me and no one else.

I apologize to Glenn Ford for all the misery I have caused him and his family.

I apologize to the family of Mr. Rozeman [the victim] for giving them the false hope of some closure.

I apologize to the members of the jury for not having all of the story that should have been disclosed to them.

I apologize to the court in not having been more diligent in my duty to ensure that proper disclosures of any exculpatory evidence had been provided to the defense.

Glenn Ford deserves every penny owed to him under the compensation statute. . . .

I now realize, all too painfully, that as a young 33-year-old prosecutor, I was not capable of making a decision that could have led to the killing of another human being. No one should be given the ability to impose a sentence of death in any criminal proceeding. We are simply incapable of devising a system that can fairly and impartially impose a sentence of death because we are all fallible human beings.

I end with the hope that providence will have more mercy for me than I showed Glenn Ford. But, I am also sobered by the realization that I certainly am not deserving of it.[30]

This poignant letter captures the tunnel vision, cognitive dissonance, administrative evil, and dehumanization that affected Ford's trial and postexoneration compensation battle. Stroud was able to recognize these psychological factors, and see the system's resistance from a different angle, in part perhaps because of his character, but also because he had spent many years away from the prosecutor's office before Ford was exonerated. Stroud has spoken to my class via Skype, telling my students that most of his former colleagues in his prosecutor's office—particularly those that never left law enforcement—did not share the views that he expressed in this letter. I can understand the prosecutor mentality. I certainly saw things in a different light as time passed after I left my prosecutor's office—things that I could not have seen while I was still there. As one police officer has said, reflecting back on his actions he now regrets, and the mentality he had as a police officer, "Getting away from the job really freed up my mind."[31] Upton Sinclair once observed, "It is hard to get a man to understand something when his salary depends on him not understanding it."[32]

We resist justice and fairness in some instances because we are human. Humans act differently, and less justly, when they are part of a large system that diffuses responsibility and creates certain bureaucratic mindsets. Such behavior is inevitable to some degree, and sometimes even necessary, particularly for those whose job it is to routinely inflict punishment on other human beings. There is no doubt that we must protect our hearts from the pain that we must sometimes inflict.

But we must learn that there are times when we must step out of these roles, and out of such mindsets, for true justice to prevail. May Marty Stroud's words and example begin to show us the way.

3. Blind Ambition

I practiced as a prosecutor in the federal system. In the federal courts, judges are appointed for life by the president of the United States. They never have to run for reelection or solicit campaign donations. They don't have to worry about getting the endorsement of the local police union or the prosecutor's office for their next campaign. While individual federal judges I appeared before sometimes had reputations for being somewhat "pro-defense" or "pro-prosecution," you never got the sense that the judges behaved in certain ways because of external political pressure. Rather, they tended to act according to their own compasses—their own idiosyncratic beliefs about right and wrong, fairness and morality.

When I left the federal prosecutor's office and founded the Ohio Innocence Project in my home state, and started appearing routinely in front of elected state judges, I experienced culture shock. In some cases I had a hard time telling the difference between the prosecutor and the judge. I was told before I started by attorneys working for innocence organizations in other states, "You likely won't get a fair shake in many cases until you get the case away from the local judge who is politically entrenched with the local prosecutor, even if they're not in the same political party. You'll probably lose in the prosecutor's home court, even if the evidence of innocence is strong. But you *might* eventually get justice later the farther you get away from the local judge and the local prosecutor, like at some higher appellate court or, most probably, in federal court once you take the case to federal habeas review." After years of experience and seeing this phenomenon at work firsthand over and over again, I now unfortunately have to pass this advice on to others. And while I have admittedly encountered some elected judges who appear immune to such political pressures, and have the courage to remain truly independent no matter the cost, many if not most seem determined to side with the prosecution whenever they can, even if it means bending the law or the facts a bit to do so.

In one of my first innocence cases that went to court, the case of Chris Bennett, which I litigated with the OIP cofounder John Cranley, the elected judge was visibly hostile from the get-go both to us and to any evidence of innocence we presented. Bennett had been convicted of driving a van drunk and causing an accident that killed his friend, who was the only other person in the van with Bennett. The van crashed on a country road, and when the police arrived Bennett was sitting in the driver's seat with a head injury and in a semiconscious state. His friend's body was draped over the engine console that protruded between the two front bucket seats, and his legs stretched onto the passenger side floor. Based on no investigation whatsoever and nothing more than the position of the two occupants when they arrived (and the fact that Bennett's blood test showed he was highly intoxicated), the police arrested Bennett and charged him with aggravated vehicular homicide. In the hospital, Bennett was diagnosed with amnesia from the head injury; he couldn't remember anything about the crash, including who was driving. Unable to defend himself, he pled guilty and was sent off to prison.

Bennett wrote to us from prison and said his memory had started returning to him in snippets. He remembered being in the passenger seat and bracing himself for the crash. Because he remembered crashing into the windshield, Bennett said if we could find the totaled van, his blood and DNA would be imbedded in the cracks of the smashed windshield on the passenger side of the van, proving he was not the driver. Even though many months had passed from the time of the crash and our receipt of Bennett's letter, one of my law students, Mary Macpherson, was able to find the van sitting in a junkyard scheduled to be demolished the following week. We went to the junkyard, found the van, and were astonished to see that the spiderweb cracks in the windshield were still caked in dried blood, with large amounts of what appeared to be human hair imbedded in the cracks as well. Subsequent DNA testing of the hair and blood confirmed Bennett's story. His DNA was all over the passenger side of the van, including his blood and clumps of hair at the point of impact on the windshield directly in front of the passenger seat, while none of his DNA was found on the driver's side.

But our students went further and conducted the investigation that the police or defense attorney never did. They knocked on doors along the country road where the crash occurred. In the house nearest to the location of the crash, they found a man who said he heard the crash and found the van before anyone else arrived, including the police. When he arrived, Bennett was sitting in the *passenger* seat unconscious with his arm hanging out the passenger side window, and Bennett's friend appeared dead on the floor between the two seats in the same position where the police later found him. After a moment, Bennett regained semiconsciousness, tried to stand up, and then stumbled over his friend's body into the driver's seat where the police later found him. Even though he was attending to Bennett's injuries when the police arrived, neither the police or the defense attorney ever bothered to ask him what he saw as the first responder. This new witness gave us a sworn affidavit.

We took this new evidence to court to try to free Chis Bennett. But the judge seemed to greatly resent what we were trying to do. For the first two days of the hearing, he gave me the cold shoulder but was friendly and warm with the prosecutors. When John and I presented our evidence he often just sat on his bench and appeared to read briefs from other cases. He even took phone calls from the bench as we presented evidence, bending down so you could just see only the top of his head. But you could see that he was holding a phone up to his ear and whispering into it. Not just for a few minutes here or there, but for long stretches of time.

Although we presented strong evidence of Chris Bennett's innocence at that three-day hearing, including the DNA test results, the judge ultimately issued a decision denying our motion to exonerate Bennett. His decision didn't even mention the DNA test results—he just ignored any evidence that was inconvenient for the result he apparently wanted. Fortunately, the advice I had been given by other innocence attorneys around the country ultimately proved true in that case, as we eventually won Bennett's case in a higher court once we got away from the politics of the prosecutor's home field and reached more objective judges.

What struck me about the judge in the Chris Bennett case was not just his cold behavior toward us or the way he flatly refused to fairly consider the evidence. What struck me the most was how he treated the prosecutors. Even though when the case started we had filed a motion to exonerate Bennett that included hundreds of pages of evidence demonstrating Bennett's innocence, the judge granted the prosecutors' repeated requests for delays in filing their response. In fact, after we filed our motion, the prosecutors sought and received six straight motions for delay before finally responding to our motion to exonerate Bennett. This delayed the case for month after month while Bennett sat in prison waiting for his day in court.

At one point during this string of delay motions, I asked for a status conference to explain to the judge that we had an innocent man sitting in prison who deserved to have his case heard in a timely fashion. When I made this argument to the judge in a teleconference, he said, "Are you suggesting that *my* prosecutors are trying to unfairly delay the case?" He emphasized the word "my" and drew it out. And that was how he spoke of the prosecutors throughout the remainder of the case. Whenever I made any suggestion that the prosecutors were delaying or engaging in other activity that wasn't entirely justified, he called them "*mmyyyyyy* prose-cutors," and would say, "Are you suggesting *mmyyyyyy* prosecutors would do that?" I wanted to say, "Judge, they're not *your* prosecutors. You don't own them, and they don't own you. You represent the judicial branch. They represent the executive branch. The two branches are supposed to be separate and independent. You aren't on the prosecutor's team."

When we got Bennett's conviction overturned after getting the case away from the prosecutor's home court, an appellate court found that the judge had abused his discretion and ignored relevant evidence in denying Bennett's motion. But Bennett sat in prison for an extra year or two as a result of this judge's actions. As one of my first cases in a court with elected judges, I couldn't believe the way the judge had acted. I had never seen anything like it.

In Dean Gillispie's case, discussed in depth in the last chapter, when we filed our motion to exonerate and free Dean from prison, the judge in the case was rumored to be considering a future run for mayor of Dayton, Ohio, the city where the case was being decided. Dean had been convicted many years earlier, but had always maintained his innocence, and our investigation turned up strong evidence of it. My co-counsel was Jim Petro, who had just left his position as attorney general (AG) of Ohio and was now in private practice while kicking around the idea of running for governor of Ohio. Petro was one of the few politicians I had encountered at that time who was open to the idea that the system sometimes convicts innocent people, and I had worked closely with him when he was AG of Ohio. Indeed, AG Petro had helped to free one of my clients, Clarence Elkins, when the local prose-cutors and the judge in Akron, Ohio, had refused to exonerate Elkins even after DNA testing proved him innocent. Petro used his bully pulpit as the AG of Ohio to pressure the local prosecutors into doing the right thing, ultimately resulting in Elkins's exoneration and release. Immediately upon leaving office and entering private practice, Petro called me and said he wanted to volunteer as co-counsel on some Ohio Innocence Project cases. I asked him to help out with Dean Gillispie's case, and he agreed.

Petro had a history with the judge in Gillispie's case. Prior to serving as AG, Petro had been the auditor of Ohio, and the judge, prior to taking the bench, had served as the county auditor in Dayton, which required him to work closely with Petro. Because the judge and Petro were both politically active, the two had occasion to speak now and then. Petro told me that during these conversations the judge always expressed fascination and surprise that he would represent Gillispie, who had been convicted of multiple rapes, while preparing to run for governor. After one such conversation, Petro said to me, "We of course didn't talk about the Gillispie case directly, but he commented how brave he thinks I am, and how surprised he is that I'm considering a run for governor and that I would, at the same time, represent someone in prison who had been convicted of such horrendous crimes."

When Petro reported such conversations to me, he didn't necessarily take it as a good or bad sign. I, however, feared that it was a bad sign, that the judge was politically attuned to the fact that it would be very difficult to take the side of a convicted rapist while running for governor of Ohio—or running for mayor of Dayton, for that matter. I knew that Petro was a rare bird and didn't care about such things. Petro only wanted to do what his conscience told him was right. But I believed that Petro was a maverick in a small minority of politicians.

And my fears turned out to be true. Before leaving the bench to run for mayor, the judge did everything in his power, in my opinion, to defeat our attempts to exonerate and free Dean, ignoring the evidence and spinning it any way he needed to reach the result he wanted. We ultimately got the judge's decision reversed twice on two different grounds—once on appeal in state court and once again in federal court. The reviewing courts found that the judge had unreasonably applied the law and abused his discretion as a judge. As a result, Dean was eventually exonerated and freed after spending twenty years in prison for rapes he didn't commit. But the obstacles that this judge put in his way had cost Dean more than three additional years of his freedom.

Although the judge in Dean's case seemed biased against our attempts to free Dean from day one, one particular incident stands out. Here a little more case background is needed.

As I said before, Dean's case involved police misconduct. He was freed when a federal judge found that important evidence for the defense—including a report that the rapist wore pants of a size that Dean could not have fit into—had been lost or destroyed by the police and never turned over to the defense prior to Dean's trial. One of our other claims of police misconduct involved Dean's alibi. On a weekend when two of the rapes had occurred, Dean had been camping out of state with a large group of friends. Although his friends testified at his trial to this fact, and one of them even had a diary showing that Dean had been with them out of state that weekend, Dean's defense team had never been able to find any receipts at the campground to back this up. We had reason to suspect, however, that when the investigation first began so many years earlier, the detective in charge of the investigation, or someone else in his department, had beaten Dean's defense team to the campground and had taken the receipts before Dean's team ever got a chance to collect and review them. At trial, though, the detective testified that no one from his police department ever went to the campground and took the receipts.

After it became known in the press that the Ohio Innocence Project was looking into Dean's case, we were told through the grapevine that a law enforcement official from Dayton had information that could be helpful to us, and was willing to meet with us. Upon meeting him, he told us that the detective in Dean's case had admitted to him after Dean's trial that he or someone from his department actually *had* gone to the campground and taken the receipts. But this police officer was reluctant to sign an affidavit, expressing his fear of personal and professional repercussions for crossing the blue line and testifying against another officer. He had come forward, he said, simply because he wanted us to know the truth. "Keep digging," he told us, "you're on the right track."

After this meeting, I had several more conversations with this police officer in which he expressed these same fears, and continued to say he wouldn't sign an affidavit for fear of crossing the blue line. As I continued to push, he started claiming that his memory of the conversation with the detective had suddenly faded (even though he had just recently told us that his memory on this point was very strong, with 100 percent certainty). So I got one of my students who had been present at the original meeting to write an affidavit about what this officer had told us, attaching the notes he had taken during the meeting. I also wrote up my own affidavit about what the officer had said. When I filed the affidavits in court, the prosecution filed a response with an affidavit from this police officer in which he claimed that the student's notes of the meeting were inaccurate. He also said that our affidavits contained fabrications. The officer further claimed that I had tried to get him to sign a defense affidavit that contained falsehoods. In other words, he was now suggesting, in essence, that he had never said those things to us about the police getting the campground receipts.

What the prosecution didn't know when they had this police officer draft his affidavit, however, was that I had previously recorded two of my final conversations with the police officer on the sly. I knew from experience that, once we publicly exposed what he had told us, he would be under great pressure from law enforcement to deny it and call us liars. So, anticipating this, I wore a wire in one meeting with him and had a recording device set up for a subsequent phone conversation. And my recordings showed that the officer was misleading in his carefully worded affidavit filed by the prosecution. For example, in his affidavit the officer claimed that he didn't want to sign the defense affidavit because, in essence, it was not true or accurate. But in the last conversation I had with the officer, which was recorded, he said he wanted to be subpoenaed to testify for Dean rather than sign an affidavit, because that way it would make it look like he was being *forced* to cooperate with the defense, which would give him political "cover." He said he wanted to "do the right thing," despite "county politics," and would "let the chips fall where they may." That was, of course, before the prosecution got to him.

So I filed a response with the judge that included discs containing the recorded conversations. The law enforcement officer was, in my opinion, caught red-handed in a misleading cover-up. But the judge in Dean's case, who was about to run for mayor, did nothing about it. He did not even grant us a hearing. He denied our motions, meaning that Dean would have to finish out his prison sentence for a possible thirty-six more years.

But what is most interesting is what happened next. Immediately after he denied all our motions and the case went to higher courts, the judge asked for a phone conference with the prosecution and the defense. When I learned of the scheduled phone conference, I was confused. The case was over before this judge. He was done with it. He had denied our claims and we were now moving on to higher courts. Why did the judge want to talk to the parties in the case now? This was most unusual. The only thing I could think of was that the judge was concerned about the police officer's troublesome affidavit and wanted to know what the prosecution was going to do about it. But I knew better than that. Given the hostility that the judge had shown toward our efforts to exonerate Dean, I doubted that could be the reason.

The phone conference consisted of the judge, myself, Jim Petro, and the prosecutors. When it started, the judge said something to the effect of, "I asked for this call because I have evidence of a federal crime sitting on my desk. Professor Godsey secretly recorded a police officer without his consent, which is a federal crime. So I am alerting the parties that I am sending this evidence—the recordings—from my case file to the federal prosecutor's office in Dayton for investigation and possible prosecution of Professor Godsey." An awkward silence then ensued, until Jim Petro said, "Judge, that's not a federal crime. And it's entirely legal in Ohio." The judge then asked the prosecutor, "Is that true?" The prosecutor said it was not a federal crime, or any kind of crime at all, as far as he knew. The judge then hemmed and hawed, muttering a bit inaudibly to himself, and then said something to the effect of, "Oh, well I think it might be, I guess I'll have to look into it some more . . . Bye." And he hung up the phone.

I never heard anything again from this judge about my alleged federal crime.

It bears underscoring: This judge, the same judge who was overturned on appeal for abusing his discretion and unreasonably applying the law when denying Dean's claims and thereby forcing Dean to languish in prison for three additional years, had sitting on his desk evidence that a police officer had made problematic statements under oath in a sworn affidavit filed in his court. The affidavit could, in my opinion, possibly even have resulted in a perjury prosecution against the police officer. But the judge was so aligned with law enforcement, and had so lost his independence and neutrality, in my opinion, that his concern was not the misconduct of this police officer, but whether he could cause a bogus federal prosecution to be brought against the defense attorney who had the audacity to secretly record a police officer and catch him in misconduct. To this day, nothing has ever happened to the officer who filed the troublesome affidavit. The judge went on to lose his race for mayor.

. . .

The public believes that the American criminal justice system is structured to favor the accused. Defendants are privileged with numerous constitutional rights, such as the right to remain silent, the right to a speedy trial, the right to an attorney even if they can't afford one, and the right to call witnesses in their defense and to cross-examine the prosecution's witnesses. They are presumed innocent until proven guilty, and the prosecution has the burden of proving the defendant's guilt beyond a reasonable doubt. The defense doesn't have to prove anything.

I have heard many judges and prosecutors over the years paint a picture of police and prosecutors as calm, rational actors, under no pressure to solve any particular case, who just want to fairly and objectively develop a case against the perpetrator so that they can obtain justice for the victims, but who are unfairly hampered in that effort because the odds that are so steeply stacked against them.

The reality, however, is anything but this. Police and prosecutors are under great pressure to solve heinous crimes and hold someone accountable for them. In doing so, they must show determination and aggression to identify suspects and steely resolve to convict them. The fact that most prosecutors in this country are elected, and the public wants prosecutors who are "tough on crime," creates a pressure to solve, arrest, and convict. As a result, the calm, "just the facts, ma'am" detective or prosecutor often depicted on television is too often a myth. Their jobs are competitive, they are judged on their success rates, and they are under pressure to obtain convictions in order to move up.

Elected judges experience political pressure as well. The vast majority of defendants in this country charged with serious crimes like murder or rape have their cases adjudicated by judges who will someday have to face reelection. Although it is difficult to measure how elections affect judges, and few judges will admit—to others or even to themselves—that the election process causes some judges to tilt in favor of appearing "tough on crime," many lawyers who practice before elected judges, particularly defense attorneys, perceive that it often does. And statistics back this up. Particularly in jurisdictions where both the prosecutors and the judges are elected, the two branches of government, executive and judicial, often appear to march together with a self-congratulatory focus on obtaining convictions while appearing "tough on crime" in a competitive, showy fashion, with each official trying to one-up the other. Politics makes it a game, it seems, and it's a game they must play well to succeed.

Defendants and defense attorneys, on the other hand, operate at a great disadvantage. The vast majority of defendants cannot afford to hire a team that matches what the prosecution has at its disposal—such as investigators to hit the streets and interview all the witnesses, and unlimited "experts" from a state crime lab to analyze the evidence and come up with seemingly slick CSI-type theories to support their theory of the case. The most that the typical defendant gets is an attorney—often appointed by the court—with little funds for bells and whistles like investigators or experts. At trial, the defense attorney usually has to take the prosecution's evidence at face value, without building his or her own case to challenge the prosecution's theory, and is limited to cross-examining the prosecution's various witnesses. Money for experts is granted to defendants by the courts in some cases, but funds are limited in each jurisdiction and funds for investigators are even more difficult to come by. Thus, defendants are often at a competitive disadvantage unless they are very wealthy. And the one thing defendants *are* always given—an attorney—is too often an overworked and underpaid public defender or appointed counsel who has so many cases she can't possibly give each client a fair shake.

The result is a system that is structurally imbalanced in favor of convictions.

JUDGES

I've told some stories above about judges who appear too close to law enforcement to remain fair and neutral, but one doesn't have to believe me to see that elected judges too often lose their objectivity and become part of the prosecution team. And I'm not just talking about the highly publicized incidents where judges are caught doing such things as text messaging helpful tips to prosecutors during a trial.[1] Indeed, the evidence is everywhere. If you live in any of the thirty-nine states where judges are elected, you will see the evidence on your television screen during election years.[2] In Cincinnati, where I live, if one judged only by the commercials in judicial election seasons, one would not be aware that our Constitution separates the judicial and the executive branches so that they can provide checks and balances on one another. My county prosecutor is the most sought-after endorser of judges and would-be judges, appearing on commercials and fly-ers of his preferred candidates running for judge and touting them as "tough on crime" in emotional pleas. One radio ad in the 2015 election cycle, for example, had our county prosecutor exclaiming over serious-sounding background music that a particular candidate "squared off against the worst criminals in Cincinnati as a prosecutor," and assured the public that this candidate wouldn't be afraid to do it again as a judge.

Many judicial candidates cozy up with the local prosecutor, and want his or her endorsement, for a reason: because it works. It's important politically for the candidates. And if a judge makes a decision on the bench that will cause him or her to lose the prosecutor's endorsement in the next election, that can be tantamount to political suicide. As former Justice Oliver Diaz of Mississippi admitted, "Judges who are running for reelection do keep in mind what the next 30-second ad is going to look like."[3] Even U.S. Supreme Court justices have recognized the political realities elected judges face that can lead them to align with their local prosecutor in order to appear tough on crime, noting that statistics show a correlation between election periods and case outcomes favoring the prosecution.[4] One Supreme Court opinion quotes an elected judge acknowledging this problem: "Let's face it. We're human beings."[5] And former chief judge of the Alabama Supreme Court Sue Bell Cobb agreed, saying, "Judges would have to be saints to ignore the political reality. And judges aren't saints."[6]

A recent Arkansas Supreme Court electoral race is illustrative. An ad praised appellate Judge Robin Wynne for "refusing to allow technicalities to overturn convictions." Another attacked Wynne's opponent, defense attorney Tim Cullen, by claiming that he had called child pornography "a victimless crime," which was a distortion of one of Cullen's defense briefs in a case. Over ominous footage of an empty playground, a mother's voice said, "Tell that to the thousands of victims robbed of their childhood." Cullen lost. He later opined, "If I were a criminal defendant, I would be concerned about Justice Wynne's fairness based on campaign ads that he benefited from."[7]

In a 2015 segment on HBO's *Last Week with John Oliver,* host John Oliver played some clips from the election cycle that year in which various judicial candidates flexed their pro-prosecution muscles.[8] An ad from the campaign of North Carolina Supreme Court Justice Paul Newby, for example, had actors in black cat-burglar outfits running from Newby's election signs while a man played a banjo and sang, "There's a judge they call Paul Newby, he's got criminals on the run. Paul's steely stare's got 'em running scared, and he'll take 'em down one by one. . . . Paul Newby (*strum, strum strum*) . . . tough but fair . . . (*strum, strum, strum*) . . . Paul Newby (*strum, strum strum*) . . . criminals best beware."

Next, Oliver screened an ad for former Alabama Judge Kenneth Ingram, which touted his tough-on-crime credentials and boasted how he came down hard on a particular murderer, while a voiceover exclaimed: "Without blinking an eye, Judge Kenneth Ingram sentenced the killer to die." Next up was a reelection commercial for Michigan Judge Paula Manderfield, which reenacted a courtroom scene where she sat at her bench, looked out at the camera with a steely gaze, and said, "My privilege is to sentence you to life in prison without the possibility of parole," and then harshly banged the gavel. Host John Oliver appropriately quipped, "Wait. It's your privilege? At best it's your duty! There are some jobs where that kind of occupational relish is inappropriate." Oliver next aptly commented: "The problem with an elected judiciary is that sometimes the right decision is neither easy nor popular. And yet campaigns force judges to look over their shoulder on every ruling. And while political attack ads can be aggressive, judicial attack ads can be downright horrifying."

He then played an attack ad against Illinois Justice Thomas Kilbride in which dark silhouettes of three imprisoned convicts (played by actors) were shown. Each convict took a turn stepping forward and talking about his crime. The first said, "I was convicted of stabbing my victims with a kitchen knife." The next said, "Of shooting my ex-girlfriend and murdering her sister in front of our child." The third said, "Of sexual assault on a mom and her ten-year-old daughter." He then chuckled and added, "Then I slashed their throats." While Justice Kilbride's picture appeared on the screen overlaying the image of the three criminals, the first convict said, over ominous background music, "On appeal, Justice Thomas Kilbride sided with *us.*" The second convict then added, "Over law enforcement or victims."

Oliver noted that none of the three inmates were actually set free by Judge Kilbride but that Kilbride merely had had, on appeal, the audacity to question the procedures used in their trials, which was his job. But, as Oliver went on to point out, there is no room for nuance in judicial campaigns, which is why, he added, you don't see judicial bumper stickers that say things like: "Justice is complicated, requiring a sublimation of our basic instincts that, while difficult, is the only thing that separates us from the anarchy of beasts. KILBRIDE 2015!!" Norman Reimer, executive director of the National Association of Criminal Defense Lawyers, has observed, "Constitutional rights of the accused persons are often the road kill in these judicial campaign wars. Our freedom and our constitutional rights depend on judges who have the courage to be fair and impartial. It's a real problem if they know every ruling is likely to become fodder in a campaign."[9]

. . .

Numerous studies show that judicial elections force judges to favor the prosecution in courtroom cases in order to appear tough on crime come reelection time. Trends in given jurisdictions are relatively easy to track. In past decades, judicial campaigns were low-budget, low-profile affairs, with attack ads—or advertising of any sort—fairly uncommon. But Supreme Court decisions loosening the ethical rules on judicial campaigning and deregulating campaign contributions in the last two decades have increasingly turned judicial elections into expensive and politically charged affairs.[10] Money spent on advertising, bringing with it the attack ads and pro-prosecution commercials we see today, has increased gradually in the past twenty years, to the point where these ads are now a ubiquitous part of the election landscape. And one can track the trends in judicial rulings as judicial elections have become more politicized and judges or would-be judges have been forced to fret about how their tough-on-crime credentials will play out in television ads and mailed flyers.

A 2013 study from the Center for American Progress, a nonpartisan think tank in Washington, focused on thousands of judicial rulings in four states: Illinois, Washington, Mississippi, and Georgia. The study found that as more campaign cash flowed into the judicial election process in these states, which resulted in ads like the ones discussed above, judicial rulings clearly trended in favor of the prosecution. The most evident bumps came in election years. The report concluded that as "campaigns become more expensive and more partisan, the fear of being portrayed as 'soft on crime' is leading courts to rule more often for prosecutors and against criminal defendants."[11]

In 2015, the Brennan Center for Justice, an institute at NYU Law School, issued a report entitled *How Judicial Elections Impact Criminal Cases.*[12] The report analyzed decades of data and synthesized findings from ten prior empirical studies on the same subject matter from various institutes and scholars. Thus, the Brennan Report is the most comprehensive paper to date on the impact that the judicial election process is having on the criminal justice system. The report starts by noting that 94 percent of felony cases—and 99 percent of rape cases and 98 percent of murder cases—are prosecuted in state as opposed to federal judicial systems. Eighty-seven percent of state judges across the country face judicial elections, which occur in thirty-nine states. Thus, the vast majority of persons charged with felonies in this country—well above 90 percent—have their cases adjudicated by judges facing reelection campaigns if they wish to continue on the bench.

The Brennan Report points out that television advertising has "become a staple" in judicial elections, and that most of this advertising focuses on criminal justice, either portraying the candidate as tough on crime or his or her opponent as soft on crime. In the 2013–14 election years, 56 percent of all judicial advertising fit this model, up from just 33 percent a few years earlier. Notably, the ads were often misleading. The report's finding includes the following observations:

- As television advertising increases in a given jurisdiction, rulings in favor of criminal defendants decrease.

- Elected judges hand down stiffer sentences in serious cases as they get closer to election day.

- Over the previous fifteen years, death sentences were overruled on appeal 26 percent of the time in jurisdictions with appointed judges, but only 11 percent of the time in jurisdictions with a competitive judicial election process.

In his segment on HBO, John Oliver noted another important aspect of all of this: much of the funding for judicial campaigns that are making judges increasingly pro-prosecution is supplied by big business or super PACs, rather than by people who have a stake in the criminal justice process, like prosecutors or police unions or representatives of crime victims. The commercial with the banjo player supporting North Carolina Judge Paul Newby was sponsored by a super PAC that is funded by, among others, tobacco company RJ Reynolds. And the attack ad against Illinois Justice Thomas Kilbride featuring the three convicts bragging about their heinous crimes was sponsored by a super PAC funded by corporations like Coca-Cola and John Deere.

Coca-Cola and RJ Reynolds do not, of course, particularly care if a judge they support is tough on crime or not. These companies want judges on the bench who will favor their business interests and who will know when these corporations' cases come before them that they owe their jobs and their future reelections to these corporations and super PACs. In other words, the corporations just hope to influence the judges for their business interests. But they also know that crime is what sways the public, so they use criminal justice themes to support judges they want on the bench, or to drive off judges who won't sufficiently further their corporate interests.[13]

Without a doubt, running for judicial election is highly political, and success depends acutely on fundraising and, for many judges, portraying themselves as "tough on crime." As Ohio Supreme Court Justice Paul Pfeifer candidly admitted to the *New York Times*, "I have never felt so much like a hooker by the bus station in any race I've ever been in as I did in a judicial race."[14] Former Texas Supreme Court Chief Justice Wallace Jefferson told *The Atlantic* shortly after leaving the highest judicial position in the state of Texas: "It is a broken system. We shouldn't have partisan elections. . . . I think fundraising undermines the confidence in a fair and impartial judicial system. So I would change it completely if I were king."[15]

Judges who got on the bench by cozying up to the local police chief or prosecutor for those all-important endorsements know that if they do anything on the bench that seriously ticks off the police and prosecutors, they risk losing those endorsements at reelection time. But more important, judges know that if they issue a ruling that can be spun during a later election as "soft on crime" in a misleading sound bite, they are giving ammunition not just to their election opponents but to the big money and super PACs if these deep pockets decide that some other candidate would do a better job of supporting business interests.[16] And even judges who sit on lower courts, like trial courts, where big money and super PACs tend not to focus so much, know their decisions will be subjected to scrutiny and attack if they are ambitious and ever want to move up the ladder to play on the fields where the corporations and big money routinely play.

Now, not all elected judges seem to be influenced by elections. Some have a reputation for being entirely independent. I could name several in Ohio, such as Michael Donnelly in Cleveland and Steven Dankof in Dayton, who eventually took over Dean Gillispie's case from the aforementioned judge who stepped down to run for mayor of Dayton. After taking over, Dankof courageously stood up to pressure from local prosecutors and tossed out Dean's case. But even judges who have ruled in favor of inmates making postconviction innocence claims have made interesting comments that reflected their awareness of this problem. An attorney who worked for another innocence project told me that she ran into a judge in the hallway of the courthouse after he ruled in favor of her client, and the judge purportedly made a comment to the effect of, "I already got a call from the media about this, because the prosecutors have gone on the offensive. I can't talk to the media, but when they call you you're going to explain why this was the right result, aren't you? You've got my back, right?" I ran into another judge at a social event while my client's motion was pending before him. I didn't discuss the case with the judge, but he looked at me at one point and said, "You know, they're going to try to hang me if I rule for your guy." This judge ended up ruling for my client regardless of his fear of being hanged, and in doing so demonstrated quite a bit of courage. These comments show, however, that even some judges who resist the pressure to rule for the prosecution are aware at some level that doing so puts them in an awkward position that is against their self-interest.

Talk to any criminal defense lawyer in a state with elected judges, and unless he or she is one of the defense lawyers who have lain down and become part of the political process, the lawyer will tell you stories of cases where the judge, seemingly because of the political realities, walked in lockstep with the prosecution to furnish the conviction the prosecution wanted. In fact, it's sadly considered the norm. When I have a new innocence case in a distant part of the state of Ohio, I always ask local defense attorneys from that part of the state about the judge assigned to my case. Defense lawyers know how to describe a biased judge, because it's the same routine most of the time and they're used to talking about the bias in the system. It's part of the common language. "Your judge is unfortunately like most of the others," is the typical response. "You're not going to get anywhere if the prosecution opposes your motion." They know this before they even hear about the details of my case. And then I go on to experience the judge firsthand, and inevitably learn why the defense attorneys had that opinion.

When a judge is considered fair and neutral, on the other hand, it's spoken with hushed excitement by the defense lawyer: "Actually, you know, she's a pretty fair judge. She actually tries to be neutral. She'll actually read your briefs. She's pretty independent of the prosecutor and is not afraid to do the right thing. You got real lucky with her." The lawyer telling me this will inevitably sound like I just found a four-leaf clover! He or she is excited to tell me how I hit the defense lawyer jackpot—a fair judge who will actually study the briefs, look at the case objectively, and rule according to the law and facts, even if it upsets law enforcement in the process. What a rarity! What a treat! The public undoubtedly thinks that having a fair and neutral judge would be expected—the norm—and not like finding the proverbial needle in a haystack. But that, unfortunately, is not the case.

I recently gave two out-of-state speeches to large audiences in which I mentioned the possible effect that the election process could have on judges. After each speech, I was immediately confronted by an angry elected judge waiting to speak to me the second my speech ended. The first judge was so upset that she started talking before she even reached me, yelling out to me from down the hallway as she approached, "How about a fair presentation, professor!!" When I asked her what she meant, she said she was very offended by my comment that elections could cause judges to bend toward the prosecution. She said, "I had my whole staff with me here today, and that was embarrassing. And it's not true." I chatted with her for a good fifteen minutes, and by the end got the sense that she was offended because she really does try to be independent and not allow such factors to sway her. She gave several examples in which she had ruled for a defendant despite feeling intense pressure from the prosecution and public. I told her that my comment was not meant to apply to every judge, and that if it's not true, as she claimed, then elected judges have a perception problem, because most defense attorneys believe it is true. I told her that I've even had conversations with federal judges who have scoffed at the notion that elected state judges are not influenced in favor of the prosecution. It seems that everyone believes this but elected state judges and prosecutors.

After my next speech in another state a week later, a judge came up to me and was so angry he was literally shaking. It looked like his head was going to explode. He strode up to me aggressively, wagged his finger in my face, and threatened, "You better be careful." I was taken aback at being confronted in such a combative manner by someone I didn't know, and didn't even know was a judge, and asked what he was talking about. He said angrily, "Your comments about elected judges were not well taken by me and the other judges in the audience. They were not at all appreciated." I was confused when he said this, because I didn't remember even mentioning elected judges in my speech. It certainly wasn't in my outline for the speech. But then I remembered that I had been asked by a member of the audience whether elections affect judges, and I had said, "Yes, in many instances I think they can—judges have to worry about the next election and many need to have the endorsement of law enforcement." That had been the extent of my comments on the subject. I tried to engage this judge in the same type of conversation I had had with the judge the week before, but he was too angry to even converse. Afterward, I wondered why he was so sensitive. After all, I thought, I'm just a law professor. And I'm from another state. Why does he care so much about what I think? And my comment was so innocuous. But I no doubt had touched a very sensitive nerve with this judge.

Maybe these judges were so upset because they truly weren't swayed by elections and were sick of hearing that they're biased. Or maybe they were so upset because my allegation was true—they "doth protest too much, methinks," as Shakespeare wrote in *Hamlet*. It's admittedly hard to tell just how much facing reelection causes judges to favor the prosecution. While defense attorneys report a general bias toward the prosecution in most cases, and I have seen it close-up many times myself, sometimes to ridiculous extremes, such bias could stem from other sources. Most judges were prosecutors before going on the bench and thus often have a prosecutorial mentality by nature.[17] Judges can also suffer from confirmation bias and tunnel vision just like other actors in the system. They are often in denial about the problems in the system, and have been part of the system for so long that they can't even see the problems. But even if a judge doesn't care about political realities, or is so entrenched that he or she doesn't really need to worry about reelection, they've often become hardened and biased through time. That's the way the system seems to shape many of them.

POLICE AND PROSECUTORS

Most prosecutors in this country, and most sheriffs, are elected. Thus, they face the same pressure as elected judges to appear tough on crime. Studies have shown that the desire to appear tough on crime for the sake of reelection affects the decisions prosecutors make on a daily basis,[18] as their decisions have "politically charged ripple effects."[19] But police and prosecutors have additional layers of pressure that judges don't feel. Office politics, and the desire for internal advancement, create a pressure to solve cases and convict. And the more difficult the case—in other words, the more that evidence of innocence exists for a defendant to exploit at trial—the more a conviction serves as a feather in the police officer's or prosecutor's hat. "Wow," their colleagues say when a detective or prosecutor wins a tough case, "He even won *that* case. That was a tricky one." All police officers and prosecutors naturally want to be the heroes in their offices.

Police and prosecutors also have budgetary pressures. In many police and prosecutors' offices, the budget for the following year depends in part on the number of arrests and convictions they obtained the preceding year. So running up the numbers ensures that their budget will increase—or at least not be cut—in the following year.

And police officers and prosecutors frequently suffer from confirmation bias and tunnel vision. The "competitive enterprise of ferreting out crime," in the words of the U.S. Supreme Court, would naturally cause any person to lose objectivity at times. Both office and political pressures contribute to this mindset, and move police and prosecutors to take on a "tough on crime" persona, pushing aggressively toward convictions in cases where a calmer, more objective approach might be better advised.

. . .

I know the internal pressures on police and prosecutors all too well, having spent many years in a prosecutor's office. Simply put, there is great atmospheric pressure to win cases and to appear tough and aggressive. Everyone in my office was ambitious and competitive. Everyone wanted to look good. Everyone cared about his or her reputation. Everyone wanted to advance. If you loafed around and were not aggressive with your cases, you would not gain a reputation for being a strong "prosecutor's prosecutor." If you lost a case, people would talk. If you lost more than a case or two in a short time period, people would start questioning your competence or dedication. So we all did our best to make sure that didn't happen.

The pressure to look good created a catchphrase, fashioned after a former prosecutor in my office whom I'll call "Schmidt." The legend was that before each of his trials, he would tell everyone in the office how the evidence in his case was weak, and how winning would be a longshot. He would appear stressed out and in agony over this awful upcoming trial that he was sure to lose. He would go on and on about the strength of the defense witnesses, and how he had so little to work with. In reality, he made these claims even when his evidence was strong. He did this, the legend goes, so that when he won everyone would think he had pulled a rabbit out of a hat. Everyone would think he must be some highly skilled wizard of a prosecutor to have won such a tough case.

So when any prosecutor in my office started talking about how the evidence in his or her upcoming trial was weak, or how the defense's evidence of innocence was strong, they would be accused of "Schmidting" their case. This reflected the competitive nature of the office, and how the cases where the defense had a lot of evidence of innocence in its favor—the tough cases—were the cases prosecutors wanted to win the most so they would look good in front of their colleagues.

If someone lost a trial—meaning, God forbid, the defendant was acquitted, which didn't happen very often—it was spoken about in hushed terms behind closed doors. Everyone wanted to know, "Did she screw up?" "What happened?" It was embarrassing to the prosecutor. I was once asked by my supervisor to take over a case from another prosecutor and try it before a jury just a few weeks before the trial was to start because the prosecutor on the case had just lost a jury verdict in another case. Her looming trial was seen as particularly difficult, with a risk of acquittal. My supervisor asked me to take it over from her because he thought that losing two cases in a row might devastate her self-esteem and could even cause her to leave the office. He needed to give her something easy—a sure thing—to help her "get back on the horse." I was instructed not to tell anyone why I was taking over the case, and an excuse relating to scheduling conflicts was made up for office consumption.

In other words, the pressure to win was so high that losing two in a row was understood as potentially a morale crusher. As Daniel Medwed, a leading scholar on the psychological pressures faced by prosecutors, notes in his book *The Prosecution Complex*, prosecutors may "treat their win-loss record as a sign of self-worth," and "become dependent on those [win] outcomes to bolster their confidence."[20] Medwed observes more broadly:

> A host of institutional, political, and psychological forces converge to pressure prosecutors to strive for convictions at trial. In an occupation where job performance is difficult to gauge, prosecutors are often evaluated based on their individual conviction rates. Stories abound of supervisors using motivational devices to push trial prosecutors to secure convictions. Examples include publicizing individual conviction rates in the form of batting averages or listing attorneys on a bulletin board with stickers next to each name, green for wins and red for losses.[21]

Medwed points out that one prosecutor's office offered financial bonuses for high conviction rates, and another required written reports to supervisors in the case of an acquittal explaining "what went wrong."[22]

. . .

In the prosecutor's office where I worked, as in many others, our budget each year was determined in part by the number of indictments we handed down the year before. I started in the office around the end of July, and our fiscal year ended on September 30. I was told when I started that new prosecutors like myself had one primary job until that date: indict as many cases as we could to improve our statistics by then. But since none of us new prosecutors had our own cases yet, we were handed files from more senior prosecutors to indict their minor cases that otherwise might not be indicted because the more senior prosecutors were too busy. And many of these cases were passed down to us for no reason other than that an additional indictment would give our stats a boost.

For example, if a senior prosecutor had a major case involving some serious crime, and the defendant fled the jurisdiction after the charges were brought and was on the lam, we would be handed the file to indict him again on what's called "bail jumping"—failing to show up in court and fleeing instead. But there was no real need for this. If the guy was eventually caught, he would still have to face the music on the murder charge or whatever his original serious charge was for. The bail-jumping indictment would be so minor in comparison that it might be ignored or negotiated away once he was caught. But indicting him for bail jumping helped our stats.

And if veteran prosecutors had other cases that they hadn't gotten to in the fiscal year because they were too busy with more important cases, or because the cases were weak and kept being pushed to the back burner in favor of stronger cases, we would indict those cases too if we thought we could get them past the grand jury and eventually get convictions. Thus, in the months of August and September, my office created an indictment machine, where we would push as many cases as we could from senior prosecutors down to junior prosecutors, and then through the grand jury—not because they really needed to be indicted for policy reasons but because we needed the stats. Simply put, if it weren't for the stats, I believe many of these cases likely would never have been indicted. It's not that decisions were made to indict people who we thought were innocent. That's not it at all. But some indictments that probably would never occur in the regular course of business were made to happen because of stats. People got indicted, or had extra charges added, for what amounted to budgetary reasons in the end.

So I spent my first two months in the prosecutor's office presenting case after case to the grand jury and getting my indictments like I was on an assembly line. I was new to the job and wanted to impress, so I did as I was told and pushed through as many indictments as I possibly could.

At one point in the aftermath of my indictment mania, I realized that I had messed up one of the cases. To the best of my recollection, I missed the deadline on the statute of limitations by a day or two, meaning the charge was defective and couldn't be corrected. But I remember that after I realized my mistake and knew I was going to have to dismiss the charges, I spoke to one of my supervisors and told him about it. (I had several immediate supervisors, several assistant criminal division chiefs who acted as supervisors, and other supervisors for some specific cases.) The supervisor in question told me to write a memo outlining my mistake and why the charges had to be dismissed. The memo had to be approved by various supervisors up the chain and ultimately by the U.S. attorney, our boss. I wrote the memo and apologized for my mistake, and in part to provide an excuse for myself, I said in the memo that I had made the mistake because I had indicted the case during the crazy "September indictment crunch," when I was handed so many cases to indict that I couldn't be as careful as I ordinarily tried to be.

A few days later, I was called into the supervisor's office. On his desk sat my memo, and I could see that someone—presumably one of the supervisors up the chain who had to approve the dismissal of charges—had circled where I had written "September indictment crunch." This person had also written a note in the margin next to that circle that said, "???! Talk to me about this." The supervisor asked me, "Why did you write this?" I said because I indicted this case during the time when I was given a million cases and told to indict as many of them as I possibly could. He said, "That's not true. There is no indictment crunch around here. You weren't told that." But I knew that he had told me that himself many times. And it wasn't just me. It was apparent that all the new prosecutors who had started in the summer like me had been instructed to do the same thing. In fact, the "September indictment crunch" was so well known and understood in our office at the time I was there that I had written those words innocently, not knowing it would cause a problem. I was new, and the last thing I wanted to do was get on someone's bad side.

I just said, "OK, I'm very sorry, I didn't know," and left the room. But I got the message. And the message was clear—we don't talk about any "indictment crunch," or any pressure to improve our stats, and we certainly aren't stupid enough to put something like that in writing.

. . .

But the reality is that stats are an ongoing pressure for many police and prosecutors. A 2015 lawsuit filed by several NYPD police officers against their department alleged that, although the NYPD claimed publicly that arrest statistics were not part of an officer's performance evaluation, the NYPD was nevertheless informally keeping statistics and basing requests for things like vacation-time approval, shift changes, and even promotions on these "arrest quotas." The lead plaintiff discussed the pressure to make arrests that this policy created, saying, "When it comes to the end of the month, and I need that number . . . Dude, it's your neck or mine."[23] That "dude" being the person who was arrested. Another NYPD officer, who was not part of this lawsuit, told the media: "Our primary job is not to help anybody, our primary job is not to assist anybody, our primary job is to get those numbers and come back with them." He added, "I'm not going to keep arresting innocent people, I'm not going to keep searching people for no reason, I'm not going to keep 'writing' people for no reason, I'm tired of this."[24]

And it's not just New York City where this practice exists: it is part of the police landscape across the country, even though many departments deny it.[25] In response to the above lawsuit, the NYPD denied it kept arrest stats, despite what its officers were claiming. My prosecutor's office would likely have denied the pressure to make indictments as well, or at least would probably have given some politically attuned answer, if questioned about it. But even in a police department or prosecutor's office that doesn't have an official policy of keeping stats, there is no question that those who bring in a large number of arrests or convictions are viewed more favorably. And those who routinely do it in the "tough" cases are viewed the most favorably. The pressure is always there, regardless of whether a tally sheet is distributed at the end of the month.

· · ·

And then there are pressures to toe the party line due to fear of harming personal and professional relationships. Police officers and prosecutors are of course friends with others in law enforcement. Close relationships develop over time. Standing up and confronting someone who you feel is not doing the right thing can lead to personal and professional repercussions. In the Gillispie case, discussed in the last chapter, the detective who refused to sign an affidavit exposing the misconduct of a fellow officer cited this very reason. I remember he said at one point something to the effect of: "This past weekend I was at a barbecue. Everyone there was in law enforcement. They are my best friends. My wife is best friends with the wives of the other officers. If I sign an affidavit like this, that's all history." I understood what he meant.

There were two occasions in my prosecutorial career when I said "no" to a fellow law enforcement officer on an important matter, and I suffered both times. The first was when I declined a case from the DEA because I felt that they had violated the Fourth Amendment in stopping and searching a suspect. (They ended up finding drugs during the search.) I declined the case not out of some sort of philosophical support for the Fourth Amendment, or because I was worried about the drug dealer's constitutional rights, but because I felt that any judge would throw the case out and I didn't want to waste my time working on a guaranteed loser. The DEA agents disagreed with my analysis and threw a fit. They went up the ladder and had their boss complain to my boss, and then asked for a meeting with my boss to see if they could get my decision overruled. But my boss agreed with me. (This may have been, in part, because she also felt pressure to "have the back" of one of her prosecutors.)

After that, the agents from that division of the DEA tried to make my life hell in any way they could. Petty stuff. Like once when I was on trial and had been too busy to sign subpoenas that the DEA agents wanted me to sign, one of them came into the courtroom while I was questioning a witness on the stand and waved the unsigned subpoenas around in the air while pointing at them and making angry faces. The judge was legally blind and couldn't see what was going on. But it was obnoxious and a huge distraction. The jury stopped listening to me and started watching the DEA agent, trying to figure out what was going on. The FBI agent working on the trial with me had to stand up and escort the DEA agent out of the courtroom. He later joked that he wished he could have punched the DEA agent in the face right then and there. That's just one example. The DEA agents from this particular unit continued to pull stunts like that throughout my prosecutorial career because I had had the audacity to decline one of their cases.

In another case, a federal agent who had become a very good personal friend over the years because we worked on several difficult cases together brought a new case to me that he had worked on very hard for a long time. He had excitedly talked to me about the case for months before our meeting, as he was building the case, and I knew he was proud of his work on it. The case involved my friend going undercover, with some degree of danger involved, and recording conversations between himself and a suspected Mafia goon. Eventually, my friend recorded the Mafia goon agreeing to commit a crime. So we had potential conspiracy and attempt charges against him.

When I listened to the taped conversations between my friend and the Mafia goon, however, I got a sick feeling. It was clear to me that the goon, if arrested, would have a very strong entrapment defense. Entrapment is when a defendant can prove that the undercover agent pressured or talked him into committing the crime. And when I listened to the tapes, that's what I heard. So I knew I had to decline the case. Not because I was worried about the Mafia goon's rights, but once again, because I wasn't about to put months and months of work into a case that I was bound to lose. And with the entrapment defense, a judge can't dismiss the case before trial. Rather, it is up to the jury to decide if a defendant was entrapped. This meant that if I approved my friend's case I was going to have to go through all the work of preparing for and putting on a trial, likely only to lose.

I mulled it over and procrastinated as long as I could but eventually had to deliver the bad news. I told my friend I was declining the case due to possible entrapment. He was furious and stormed out of the room. Once again, his agency tried to get my decision overruled by my superiors, but I prevailed. To make a long story short, my friend not only stopped bringing cases to me but he never spoke to me again. Ever. The friendship was over. Period. That was, needless to say, a very painful experience. He had been one of my best friends in law enforcement.

I tell these stories to illustrate that personal relationships and peer pressure play a role in compliance. A twenty-five-year veteran of the Philadelphia PD has written: "Peer pressure will often trump common sense. This was why cops, just like crime organizations, protected their own by keeping their mouths shut. If you want to be a part of 'the team'; if you want to feel safe and know that you have support in dangerous situations; if you want to feel secure in your job and not have supervisors and commanders harass you; then you keep your mouth shut no matter what indiscretion you witness or hear about other officers."[26] A law enforcement official must think long and hard before standing up to someone else in law enforcement about an important matter when personal and professional relationships are on the line. Although I can name two occasions in which I said "no" anyway, I have no doubt that such relationships at times cause law enforcement officials to agree to things they shouldn't. It's human nature.

. . .

Some might be surprised to learn that I have generally found Republicans to be easier to work with on innocence matters than Democrats. This goes for judges, prosecutors, and legislators alike. I'm painting with a broad brush here, and of course there are exceptions to the rule. But the two county prosecutors who have fought back the hardest in our innocence cases, and who have exhibited the most close-minded vitriol time and time again, are Democrats from heavily Democratic counties. The prosecutor who has been the most reasonable to work with is Ron O'Brien, a Republican from Columbus, Ohio. Some of the most reasonable judges my office has appeared before have been Republicans. Many of the most unreasonable, like the trial judge in Dean Gillispie's case mentioned earlier, were Democrats.

From about 2007 until 2010, I spent a significant percentage of my time in the state capital of Columbus educating state senators and representatives about the need to pass our innocence reform bill, which finally became law in 2010. This bill had many components, including expanded access to DNA testing for inmates claiming innocence, eyewitness identification reforms, police interrogation reforms, and a requirement that the police save and properly preserve the DNA collected from crime scenes in certain cases like murder and rape cases. I generally found the strongest supporters for our bill among the Republican ranks. Those who held up the bill at various stages, on the other hand, and who tried their best to defeat it, were Democrats.

My theory is that Democrats are generally viewed by the public as "soft on crime" and thus have a Napoleon complex about crime issues. They feel they have to go above and beyond to show the public how tough they can be on crime issues. Republicans, on the other hand, have fewer insecurities about the matter. The public gives Republicans the benefit of the doubt on issues relating to crime, and thus Republican politicians feel they can be more reasonable as they have less to prove. Whatever the reason, I'm not the only one in the innocence movement who has noticed this discrepancy. Many innocence leaders from other states have reported to me the same observation.

DEFENSE ATTORNEYS

It is not uncommon for a murder prosecution to cost the state millions of dollars.[27] While other types of cases often cost the prosecution less, the state has nearly unlimited resources at its disposal to prosecute its cases, with a host of investigators and state crime labs to help it. But when it comes to funding the cost of a proper defense, the reality tends to be quite different. The public often sees only the celebrity trials, where defendants like Michael Jackson or O.J. Simpson are able to hire an expensive defense team that allows them to wage a somewhat fair head-to-head match with the prosecution. But that kind of defense rarely occurs in the real world. Most criminal defendants are given a public defender, or court-appointed attorney working on contract with the local public defender's office, who is grossly underpaid and so overloaded that he or she has little time to devote to any given case.

The Netflix docu-series *Making a Murderer* did an excellent job depicting this problem. One of the two defendants in the case of the murder of Teresa Halbach, Steven Avery, was able to afford two top-notch defense attorneys who were on top of the case from start to finish, and who assembled an impressive team of experts and investigators, because Avery had recently settled a civil case for $400,000 for his wrongful conviction of the rape of Penny Bernstein. He was able to dump that money into his defense in the Teresa Halbach case. But the other defendant in the Halbach case, Brendan Dassey, had no money and was left with a court-appointed attorney, Len Kachinsky, who sold him down the river by assuming his client was guilty and admitting as much to the media before doing any investigation or even bothering to meet his new client. Kachinsky then allowed his sixteen-year-old cognitively impaired client to be interrogated by the police without him being present in the interrogation room. The difference in the quality of representation for the two defendants was striking. While the rare criminal defendant who has significant wealth is able to mount the type of quality defense that many in the public believe is routine, many of the rest are left with the Len Kachinskys.

The structural imbalance between the prosecution and the defense bar has been widely reported. In any given year, one can find media reports from all across the country in which public defenders, who represent 80 percent of those charged with crimes in this country,[28] complain that they simply are unable to do their jobs due to underfunding and overloaded dockets.[29] In fact, in several jurisdictions the ACLU has filed suit against public defender offices because they are unable to operate effectively, depriving their clients of their constitutional right to adequate counsel. These lawsuits, or threats of such lawsuits, are common.[30] But nothing ever changes. In Missouri, the state's head public defender became so exasperated by the governor's refusal to adequately fund his department that he used an obscure law to appoint the governor, a licensed attorney, to represent an indigent defendant.[31] Of course, the governor refused the assignment. But this maneuver reflects the frustration that public defenders feel around the country.

Many public defenders are forced to carry dockets two or three times the number of cases that the American Bar Association recognizes as the maximum.[32] In New Orleans, for example, public defenders are so overloaded that they are able to devote an average of just seven minutes of work on each misdemeanor case.[33] Seven minutes! In 2016, the public defender's office in New Orleans had the courage to refuse to take new felony cases for serious crimes, as the lawyers were so overloaded that they simply didn't have time to provide an appropriate defense in each case.[34] In 2017, five pubic defenders from New Orleans appeared on a segment of *60 Minutes* and declared their belief that they have represented innocent clients who have gone to prison because they lacked the time and resources to defend them properly.[35]

But this problem is not limited to New Orleans. It occurs across the United States on a daily basis.[36] One court-appointed public defender in Detroit, Bob Slameka, has made no bones about giving his clients only what the state pays for. Because he is not reimbursed for accepting collect calls from his clients in prison, he simply doesn't accept them. "My God, [the collect calls] run about how much money and you don't get paid for that stuff. Nothing," he said. He has been reprimanded sixteen times by the Michigan Supreme Court for failing to perform his minimum duties, but the courts continue appointing him to cases. One of his clients, Eddie Joe Lloyd, was later proven innocent and exonerated after spending seventeen years in prison for a crime he didn't commit. Slameka admitted he never even met with Lloyd or accepted his calls, explaining, "I did the best I could given what I had. That's all I could do."[37]

Many public defenders in this country work on a freelance basis. They are independent contractors who accept appointments from the local public defender's office or the courts. But because the pay is so low for each case, they are forced to take on a great number of cases to keep their practices afloat, or to spend more of their time on their privately retained cases, which pay much better. But because they can't possibly handle a huge number of cases in a professional manner, or can't afford to spend too much time on their low-paying appointed cases, they convince their indigent clients to plead guilty early on to get as many cases out of the way as possible, and do little to no work on the rest. It's a volume business, one where the indigent defendants are often deprived of the attention of an attorney.[38]

I know this firsthand. My wife is a contract public defender in Cincinnati. For felony cases, she is paid $45 an hour. For any felony case where the client pleads guilty, her fee is capped at ten hours, or $450. If a plea occurs after some litigation takes place, like an evidentiary hearing to suppress evidence, then the cap is fifteen hours, or $675. If she takes a case to trial, her fee is capped at around $1,200. Her basic office expenses and overhead at her office downtown, when she had one, were what you would expect. To cover this overhead and make a profit that would net her a livable income— say $60,000 a year—she would have to take so many cases that she couldn't possibly afford to do much work on any of them. One complicated felony case, if it goes to trial, should take months of an attorney's full-time attention to properly and fully prepare. And when retained cases come in the door, business interests require the attorney to give those cases priority and push the low-paying appointed cases to the back burner.

But because I make a livable income sufficient for both of us, and because my wife is passionate about the problem of indigent defense in this country, she decided to do it the right way—to give each client the best defense she could muster. So after a few years of renting office space downtown, she downgraded her office space and started taking only the small number of cases each year that will allow her to do thorough legal research and fully understand each case before she goes to court. She gives each client her full attention and builds the best defense she possibly can, although, except in rare cases, she still does not have funds for experts or investigators, which of course are a necessary part of a good defense.

As a result, she has made not much more than the cost of her overhead expenses, like liability insurance, office supplies, and courthouse parking. So she essentially makes an unlivable wage but chooses to do so because she is passionate about the cause and is fed up with the inequities in the system. I don't know any other defense attorney who does this. But her example shows that if an attorney wants to provide the appropriate attention to each case, and will not accept doing less, then it will be difficult for him or her to stay afloat under the current system unless he is one of the lucky few who have a booming business of rich retained clients, or who is married to someone who earns a living wage. So many attorneys in her shoes do what Bob Slameka in Detroit does—take the number of cases needed to make a living and then fail to provide every client with a proper defense.

This is the reality for most appointed public defenders, the norm.[39] And it's not any better for attorneys who work full-time in a public defender's office for a set annual salary. They are handed so many cases that they simply can't do an adequate job. As one public defender recently wrote in the *Washington Post:*

> It's impossible for me to do a good job representing my clients. . . .
> Because we don't have enough lawyers on staff, the week I passed the bar in 2013, I began representing people facing mandatory life sentences on felony charges. . . . An unconstitutionally high caseload means that I often see my clients [only once]. It means that I miss filing important motions, that I am unable to properly prepare for every trial, that I have serious conversations about plea bargains with my clients in open court because I did not spend enough time conducting confidential visits with them in jail. I plead some of my clients to felony convictions on the day I meet them.[40]

JURIES

Juries are not the great equalizer. Even when the defendant is innocent, jurors often see a trial that is one-sided because the prosecution has all the resources, has the access to all the evidence, and holds all the cards. Also, the jurors come to the courtroom with their own biases. Although there is a theoretical presumption of innocence, jurors typically think, "The police, the prosecutors, and all these fancy experts know a lot more than me. This is what they do for a living. Why would they waste all this time if the guy didn't do it? And the prosecution is adamant that this guy did it. I'm just a person off the street. Who am I to question these good, hardworking professionals?"

Professor Keith Findley, a leading criminal justice scholar, has opined:

> The presumption [of innocence] is under constant assault from jurors' natural assumption that if someone is arrested and charged with a crime, he or she must have done something wrong. It is also vulnerable to the media frenzy around high-profile cases, the fear-driven politics of crime, and the highly punitive nature of our culture and the innate cognitive processes that produce tunnel vision and confirmation bias.
>
> Indeed, research suggests that the presumption of innocence exists more in theory than reality. In studies, mock jurors predict a 50 percent chance of voting to convict—before hearing any evidence. Other research shows that while simulated jurors initially assign low probabilities of guilt, they abandon the presumption of innocence promptly as prosecution evidence is introduced.[41]

And then there's the natural human reaction, particularly when dealing with heinous crimes, to think: "If the guy *probably* committed this rape, even if there is some doubt, how can I possible let him back on the street to do it again? I'd be responsible for his next victim. I couldn't live with myself. Someone I know could be his next victim, and then what? And the prosecution is sure he did it, and they know more than me. Plus, an acquittal would devastate this poor victim and her family. She was so distraught during her testimony and her entire family was in agony throughout the trial. What about justice for them? How can I possibly acquit this guy when it looks like he *probably* did it? It's better to be safe than sorry."

Veteran federal appellate Judge Alex Kozinski, appointed by President Reagan, agrees that the presumption of innocence is a myth: "Juries are routinely instructed that the defendant is presumed innocent and the prosecution must prove guilt beyond a reasonable doubt, but we don't really know whether either of these instructions has an effect on the average juror. Do jurors understand the concept of a presumption? If so, do they understand how a presumption is supposed to operate? Do they assume that the presumption remains in place until it is overcome by persuasive evidence or do they believe it disappears as soon as any actual evidence is presented? We don't really know."[42] Judge Kozinski suggests that, from his many years on the bench, it does not appear to him that jurors truly embrace the presumption of innocence. This is partly due to psychology, he suspects. It is well understood in the psychological literature that "whoever makes the first assertion about something has a large advantage over everyone who denies it later." Because the defense presents its case after the prosecution—often days or weeks after the prosecution in longer, more complicated felony trials—it may be that "jurors start forming a mental picture of the events in question as soon as they first hear about them from the prosecution witnesses," Kozinski writes. "Later-introduced evidence, even if pointing in the opposite direction, may not be capable of fundamentally altering that picture and may, in fact, reinforce it," due to the confirmation bias that has set in by that time.

And in many cases, Kozinski points out, the defense doesn't put on its own case, as it's not required to do so. Yet, "when accusations or assertions are met with silence, they are more likely to feel true." He concludes: "It may well be that, contrary to instructions, and contrary to their own best intentions, jurors are persuaded of whatever version of events is first presented to them and change their minds only if they are given very strong reasons to the contrary."

When I was a prosecutor in Manhattan, our jury pools were selected from all counties within the jurisdiction of our federal district, which was known as the Southern District of New York. Some of these regions are urban, like Manhattan and the Bronx. Others are suburban or rural, like Westchester, Rockland, and Putnam counties. But our juries for each case were all from a single county—the counties were not comingled. When a trial commenced, therefore, you learned that you had a jury from the Bronx, for example, or perhaps a jury from Rockland County. And the county from which you drew your jury completely affected your view of the case. Juries from the rural or suburban counties were known to be pro–law enforcement; juries from Manhattan and the Bronx more sympathetic to criminal defendants and sometimes suspicious of the police. Prosecutors would groan if they drew a Bronx jury but sigh in relief if they drew a Putnam County jury. In a tough case that drew a Bronx or Manhattan jury, therefore, a prosecutor was more apt to offer a better pretrial deal to the defendant than she might if she drew a jury from a rural or suburban region. While this is perhaps not surprising, it demonstrates the degree of arbitrary variance in attitude from jury to jury.

And juries, unfortunately, do not always take their jobs seriously or understand the meaning of proof "beyond a reasonable doubt." In the Dean Gillispie case, for example, discussed throughout this book, the jury voted 8-4 in favor of acquittal on a Friday afternoon and reported to the judge that they were deadlocked. After being told they would have to work through the weekend if they didn't reach a resolution, they came back with a guilty verdict shortly thereafter. God forbid, they couldn't miss their golf outings or soccer carpools on Saturday morning. Gillispie's convictions were later tossed out and he was freed, but only after he spent twenty years in prison.

That said, I have told many that in postconviction innocence cases like Clarence Elkins's or Gillispie's, where new evidence proves my client innocent after he has served many years in prison, I would much rather have a jury decide my client's fate than an elected judge. Jurors get the human emotion and deeply feel the unfairness. They are not jaded by politics or hardened from years on the bench. At trial, I think the jurors' bias works in favor of the prosecution, as I have said, where the crime is fresh and raw and jurors think, "Why would the prosecution and police waste their time on an innocent person?" But in the postconviction context, the sympathy factor for someone who has already been in prison for many years and now has strong evidence of innocence, I believe, would often work in favor of the defense. By the time of a postconviction innocence motion, the crime and all the emotion it brings with it are now often decades in the past, and the public has seen and cheered for the many exonerated men and women the media has documented walking out of prison in the past few decades. Unfortunately, I do not have the option of choosing a jury, as the law says that these exoneration motions must be decided by the same elected judge who convicted my client years earlier. Convincing an elected judge to admit that a terrible mistake happened in his or her courtroom is usually a steep hill to climb.

4.   Blind Bias

At a surface level, we are all aware that our preconceived biases affect how we view the world. In 2000, I remember being with a good friend, who happened to be on the opposite end of the political spectrum, while we watched the presidential debate between Al Gore and George W. Bush. I thought that, without a doubt, my candidate appeared more presidential, intelligent, and honest, whereas it was obvious that my friend's candidate was being evasive. By the end, I knew that even my friend would have to admit that his candidate had hardly answered a single question, and when he did, it was with a jargon-filled catchphrase meant to appeal to his base. There was no substance there.

But when we discussed the debate afterward, my friend fervently thought the opposite. My candidate, he said, hadn't answered a single question all night; whereas his candidate addressed the problems head-on, gave details and specifics, and appeared more presidential. Our contrasting reactions reflected national surveys. Democrats thought Gore appeared more presidential and honest, and gave more specific, concrete answers, while Republicans thought the same about Bush. The American public, my friend and I included, saw what we wanted to see. We had preconceived biases, and we focused on only those pieces of evidence that confirmed them. Evidence that contradicted our biases did not register.

This phenomenon is known as "confirmation bias." The psychological definition of confirmation bias is "the seeking or interpreting of evidence in ways that are partial to existing beliefs, expectations, or a hypothesis in hand."[1]

Human susceptibility to confirmation bias is pervasive in our lives and society, and has been demonstrated in studies time and time again since the concept was first introduced into the psychological literature more than fifty years ago. In one study, for example, subjects watching a videotape of a child taking an exam who were able to see the answers provided by the child were far more likely to rate the child's answers as "above grade level" when told beforehand that the child was from a high socioeconomic background, and "below grade level" when told the child was from a low socioeconomic background.[2]

In another study, therapists watched a videotape of a man responding to personal questions asked by another person. When the therapists were told that the man was a job applicant who was responding to these questions as part of a job interview, they tended to label him as "well-adjusted." But when told he was a "patient," thus implying he was seeking psychological help, they were more likely to label him as "disturbed." Even though the two groups watched the same videotape, those who believed they were observing a job applicant described him with terms such as "responsible," "bright," "pleasant," and "attractive," while those who believed they were watching a "patient" described him with adjectives such as "defensive," "passive-aggressive," "repressed," and trying "to seem brighter than he is."[3]

Studies show that when people are given evidence that is contrary to a theory they support, they tend to stick to their beliefs despite the evidence.[4] Interestingly, when they are later questioned about the contradictory evidence, they fail to remember it, or they remember it in a distorted manner that merely confirms their preexisting beliefs.[5] Another study showed that jurors tend to make up their minds about a case fairly early on in a trial, and then, after trial, remember only those pieces of evidence that confirmed their initial instincts. They are unable to recount the conflicting pieces of evidence, or they remember the evidence in an inaccurate manner that simply confirms their initial beliefs.[6]

In a nutshell, studies reveal that the human mind is wired to confirm rather than disprove its initial suspicions. One of the first clinical studies designed to explore confirmation bias, known as the Wason Rule Discovery Test, after its creator, Dr. Peter Wason, asked subjects to identify the rule that applied to a series of three numbers.[7] They were given the series 2-4-6 as the starting point. To decipher the rule and test their hypothesis, subjects could suggest other number sets; they were told "yes" or "no" as to whether their number sets followed or violated the rule. When the subjects were confident that they had discovered the rule, they were told to stop and announce it.

Given the numbers 2-4-6, most subjects came up with the same initial hypothesis: that the rule was a series of increasing *even* numbers. Thus, the vast majority of subjects suggested triplets of numbers that complied with that rule, such as 4-8-10 or 2-6-8, and were told that those suggestions complied with the rule. After a few attempts to confirm their initial hypothesis, and after receiving positive feedback, most subjects announced that they were confident they had discovered the rule—a series of increasing even numbers. But they were wrong. The rule was simply "a series of increasing numbers." Thus, odd-numbered series, like 3–5-7, or sets mixed with increasing odd and even numbers, would have also satisfied the rule. But very few subjects attempted to disprove their first hypothesis. Odd numbers did not occur to them, given their initial hypothesis. They set out to confirm the hypothesis, and thus obvious and simple number sets like 3-5-7 that might disprove their hypothesis simply did not register as possibilities.

Confirmed in various contexts, Wason's Rule Discovery Test stands today for the widely accepted psychological phenomenon that the human mind works only to confirm its initial suspicions. It does not set out to falsify its own theories and thus does not explore contradictory avenues that, with hindsight, should have been fairly obvious.

The mind's vulnerability to confirmation bias has been so widely studied in a variety of contexts that even the Wikipedia definition of the term references nearly 150 studies confirming its existence in many different contexts. The prominent psychologist Raymond Nickerson of Tufts University, founder of the *Journal of Experimental Psychology*, has written that confirmation bias is so "sufficiently strong and pervasive that one is led to wonder whether the bias, by itself, might account for a significant fraction of disputes, altercations, and misunderstandings that occur among individuals, groups and nations."[8] He writes:

> Can anyone doubt that whenever one finds oneself engaged in a verbal dispute [confirmation bias] becomes very strong indeed? In the heat of an argument people are seldom motivated to consider objectively whatever evidence can be brought to bear on the issue under contention. One's aim is to win and the way to do that is to make the strongest possible case for one's own position while countering, discounting, or simply ignoring any evidence that might be brought against it. And what is true of one disputant is generally true of the other, which is why so few disputes are clearly won or lost. The more likely outcome is the claim of victory by each party and an accusation of recalcitrance on the part of one's opponent.[9]

Nickerson goes on to discuss how confirmation bias infiltrates not just our personal lives but also various fields, including medicine, science, and law. It has contributed to societal problems ranging from the wholesale rejection of compelling new ideas (like Galileo's theories or groundbreaking concepts like continental drift) to great tragedies like the Salem witch trials and the Holocaust.

. . .

This book cannot tackle all the ways that confirmation bias affects us unnoticed in our daily lives. But by demonstrating how confirmation bias contaminates the criminal justice system in ways unknown to the general public—and how these biases result in great injustices—one can begin to understand how this phenomenon might wreak havoc in other parts of our lives as well.

Indeed, the criminal justice system is saturated through and through with confirmation bias. For example, detectives tend to believe witnesses who tell them stories that confirm their own beliefs about a case. Witnesses who give contradictory information are seen as lying or mistaken and are often pushed to the wayside.

But perhaps the best way to understand how confirmation bias affects outcomes in the criminal justice system is to study how it operates in the forensic sciences. Crime scene investigation (CSI) experts in their white lab coats are held up by our society as bastions of neutrality. Theoretically at least, they have no stake in whether a criminal defendant is convicted or acquitted. They often have fancy degrees and operate in a world of cold, hard, objective science. But once we understand how easily even forensic scientists succumb to confirmation bias, we can begin to see how police officers, prosecutors, defense attorneys, judges, and even witnesses succumb as well, skewing the facts and bringing about grave injustices.

. . .

The discovery of hundreds of wrongful convictions by the innocence movement in the past two decades has exposed deep problems in our forensic sciences. In fact, inaccurate forensic science testimony was a contributing factor in 154 of the first 325 DNA exonerations in the United States, second only to mistaken eyewitness identifications. In other words, 49 percent—nearly half—of those convictions involved bad forensics.[10]

With this knowledge, social scientists began asking: Why are we getting all these wrongful convictions based on inaccurate scientific testimony? Why did the forensic expert in this case testify that he microscopically compared the defendant's pubic hair to one left by the rapist at the crime scene and concluded that they matched, when DNA testing of the hairs has now told us that they're not a match? Why do we keep seeing flawed scientific testimony in case after case?

When an innocent person is wrongfully convicted as a result of flawed forensic testimony, one of two possible phenomena, or both, may be at play. First, some of our forensic sciences are now known to be nothing more than theories or speculation without sufficient grounding in actual science or scientific method. In other words, the method used to analyze the evidence and reach a conclusion is untested with no known accuracy rate. When this problem contaminates a case, it was not necessarily the expert who testified that was the problem; rather, it was the weaknesses in the method she was trained to use. The second phenomenon that can lead to flawed scientific testimony is the confirmation bias of the expert who analyzed the evidence. This bias can skew the results in a case even if the scientific principles underlying the expert's conclusions are generally sound.

Contrary to popular belief, many of the "CSI sciences" that experts describe in court are not based on objective, hard facts immune to manipulation or misinterpretation. Instead, experts typically analyze patterns, or compare images, to determine if the pattern or image matches or is "consistent with" something else. Does the defendant's tire tread match the tire tread left in the mud when the perpetrator peeled out and fled from the robbery? Do the microscopic grooves on the bullet found at the crime scene match imperfections in the barrel of the suspect's gun? Were the drops of blood found on the suspect's clothing consistent with examples of high-velocity blood spatter? Does the handwriting on the demand note used in a bank robbery match samples of the defendant's handwriting? Do any of the suspect's fingerprints match the fingerprint found on the bloody knife? Does the bite mark on the victim's body match the plaster impression of the suspect's teeth?

In other words, many forensic sciences are subjective processes of comparing and matching rather than purely objective exercises. That is where human error can enter the equation. And in the wake of the innocence movement, with the scads of cases uncovered in which experts have given inaccurate courtroom testimony that led to a wrongful conviction, social scientists have performed a variety of experiments to see if and how confirmation bias of the expert might skew results and lead to these injustices.

Dr. Itiel Dror, a leading researcher from the University College London, has been at the forefront of this research. In 2005, Dror and his colleagues performed an experiment using five experienced fingerprint experts.[11] They asked the experts to make a comparison between two prints, one of which belonged to a suspect and the other of which came from a crime scene. They informed the experts that the prints were from a case in which many now believed that the fingerprint expert had made a mistake and incorrectly concluded that the prints were a match, leading to a wrongful conviction. Thus, Dror provided the fingerprint experts with background and context in an attempt to create a preexisting bias that the fingerprints likely would not match. Dror told the experts, however, to ignore this contextual information and to perform an independent examination to determine for themselves whether the fingerprints matched or not.

Unbeknownst to the fingerprint examiners, Dror and his colleagues did not actually supply the experts with a set of fingerprints from another case where an error had likely occurred, but instead provided each with a set of fingerprints that that particular expert had previously concluded was a match in a prior case. (Fingerprint experts look at thousands of fingerprints each year, and likely cannot remember a set of fingerprints they examined even a week before.) Although each of the experts was unknowingly examining a set of prints that he or she had personally called a match in a prior case, four of the five reversed their conclusions and now gave a different answer. Three of the five determined that the fingerprints did *not* match, while one said that the answer was inconclusive. Only one fingerprint expert stuck to his original conclusion of a match. Thus, 80 percent of the fingerprint experts changed their answer as a result of being given a context that created a preexisting belief about what the right answer should be.

A follow-up study involved forty-eight different trial samples.[12] It demonstrated once again that fingerprint experts were highly susceptible to suggestion of either a match or a nonmatch depending on the context provided (for example, "he confessed to the crime" vs. "he has a strong alibi"). And confirmation bias swayed the results even in fairly obvious cases where there were strong similarities or discrepancies between the fingerprints.

This is shocking from a forensic science that has long held itself up as "infallible,"[13] and boasted that errors are "virtually impossible."[14] These studies show how subjective the process really is and how easily fingerprint experts can produce flawed results that are skewed by their preexisting beliefs about what the "right" answer is supposed to be. But Dr. Dror and his colleagues have gone beyond the world of fingerprints, revealing the presence of confirmation bias in areas such as anthropology (determining the gender of skeletal bones),[15] handwriting analysis,[16] and DNA test result analysis,[17] among others.

· · ·

The high-profile case of Brandon Mayfield provides a perfect example of how this confirmation bias plays out in the criminal justice system.[18] In 2004, a series of bombs exploded in four commuter trains in Madrid, Spain. The authorities immediately suspected a terrorist attack, perhaps by Al

Qaeda, which spurred an international investigation, including heavy involvement by the FBI. A fingerprint was found on a plastic bag that had contained explosives used in the attack. The FBI ran the print in the AFIS database (which includes fingerprints taken from arrestees in the United States), and the computer kicked back several fingerprints from different Americans as possible matches. The FBI then examined those fingerprints more closely to see if one of them was a perfect match to the one retrieved from the bomb packaging. One of the individuals connected to a fingerprint on the list immediately raised serious suspicions. He was Brandon Mayfield, a lawyer from Oregon, who was on an FBI terrorism watch list in part because he was married to a Muslim Egyptian national and had recently converted to Islam himself. With the belief that Mayfield was by far the best suspect of the group, a series of FBI fingerprint examiners independently compared Mayfield's print to the print from the bombing and concluded that it was a definitive match. Mayfield's fingerprint was on the bomb package. No question. So Mayfield was arrested.

After his arrest, Mayfield asserted his innocence and had a defense-hired expert examine the fingerprints, too. Mayfield's expert confirmed what the FBI already knew—it was without question Mayfield's print on the bomb package.

Two weeks later, Spanish authorities linked the fingerprint in question to an Algerian national named Ouhnane Daoud. The FBI ultimately conceded that the fingerprint did not match Mayfield. He was released from jail, awarded $2 million in compensation from the government, and received a formal, written apology.

Later, the FBI acknowledged that confirmation bias played a role in the misidentifications. Indeed, three different FBI fingerprint examiners—*and Mayfield's own defense expert*—may have succumbed to the bias and erroneously declared a match as a result. This happened despite clear discrepancies between Mayfield's print and the bomber's, ones obvious to the Spanish experts.[19] The biases of the American experts did not allow them to see those discrepancies. The experts saw only what they expected to see, and their minds did not register anything else.

Please take about ten seconds to complete the following test (without looking at the answer below).

How many letter Fs are in the following text?

FINISHED FILES ARE THE RE
SULT OF YEARS OF SCIENTI
FIC STUDY COMBINED WITH
THE EXPERIENCE OF YEARS . . .

If you answered six, you are in the minority who got it right.[20] Typically, about 75 percent of people in this experiment answer three, leaving out the Fs that appear in the three uses of the word "of." Why do most answer three? Because the mind is so accomplished at reading that it no longer needs to analyze or register the word "of." The mind has deemed it a waste of time, so it creates a shortcut, causing most readers to miss those three Fs.

By analogy, when experts—or anyone for that matter—expect a particular result, their minds naturally create shortcuts to help them see only what they need to see. There were many discrepancies between Mayfield's fingerprint and the bomber's, but the experts did not see them or register them because of confirmation bias. Likewise, Dror's experiments demonstrate how common it is for expert witnesses to miss discrepancies and call two fingerprints a match when confirmation bias tells their minds not to see the differences.

. . .

But fingerprint comparisons, unscientific though they are, are actually far less subjective and open to interpretation than many of our other forensic sciences. Bite mark comparisons (comparing a bite in the victim's skin left by the perpetrator to the suspect's dental impression), microscopic hair comparisons, tire tread comparisons, ballistic fingerprinting, blood spatter analysis, and a host of other forensic disciplines are equally, if not more, subject to skewed results from confirmation bias.

The problem is compounded by the fact that, when making such determinations, experts are usually not working with clear, easy-to-read images. While a plaster cast of the suspect's tire tread made in a police impound lot may be fairly clear, rarely is a tread left by the perpetrator's car when peeling out and away from a crime scene clean and easy to decipher. It may be filled with gravel, distorted from the sideways spinning of the car, or left in wet mud that immediately began to change shape from gravity and moisture. While a suspect leaves clear fingerprint images in a police station booking room, where an officer dips his fingers in ink and carefully rolls them on a fingerprint card sitting on a stable surface such as a desk, murderers rarely dip their fingers evenly in blood and carefully roll each finger across the knife they just used to murder someone.

The plaster dental impression made of a suspect's teeth by a forensic odontologist is often an accurate reconstruction of the suspect's teeth. But a bite mark on a victim's body, often made through layers of clothing, is created while significant movement and sliding are likely occurring during a struggle, and on a surface—skin—that has varying degrees of elasticity and is overall a poor substance on which to record and retain an accurate image.

To demonstrate this point, perform the following experiment. Turn your arm so that the inside is facing you (so you can see the blue veins in your wrist). With your other hand, place your thumb and index finger in pinching position, one of them on either side of your arm just below the elbow (the side of the elbow toward your hand). Now squeeze the skin toward the middle of your arm and examine the amount of skin you are able to pinch. Next, attempt to gather skin from your arm in the opposite direction. Place your index finger toward your hand and your thumb toward your elbow, and attempt to pinch inward. You will see that it is nearly impossible to grasp much skin when pinching in this direction. This is because skin, in different parts of your body, is elastic in some directions but not in others.

Thus, parts of a curved bite might impact skin that is quite elastic and moves from that pressure when the bite takes place, while another part of the same bite may impact skin that holds firm. The result is a distorted image that does not accurately reflect the position of the biter's teeth. This is just one factor, in addition to movement and sliding from the likely struggle and the layers of clothing in between the teeth and the skin, that may cause a bite mark on a body to differ significantly from the shape of the biter's teeth.

In sum, experts often make comparisons by examining one clean image—the suspect's image taken at a police department under controlled conditions—against a distorted or smeared image left at the crime scene. This opens the door even more to human interpretation, confirmation bias, and error. Evidence examined by forensic scientists is not cold, hard data immune to human interpretation. Rather, it is somewhat like a Rorschach inkblot. Different people see the evidence in different ways, and what they see in an image can be skewed by what they expect to see.

· · ·

In my days as a prosecutor, we routinely told experts examining our evidence what outcome we needed. That may seem shocking to some readers, but it was run-of-the-mill for us. If it were a ballistics test, we might say, "Confirm that the bullets came from the defendant's gun," or, "We believe these are from the defendant's gun, so please run the test to confirm." When we used the word "defendant," it meant that he was already arrested and we were trying to solidify our case. Even if the word "suspect" was used, it was, in hindsight, a loaded term that told the expert that we had gathered enough evidence to move forward, and that he should expect a match.

Typically, we even supplied the experts with a likely trial date and corresponding deadline before trial by which we needed their written report. This sent the message, of course, that we thought this defendant did it (and that we had enough evidence already to have made an arrest and gotten an indictment from the grand jury), but that we needed more evidence to nail him.

Some experts developed reputations in my office for being "good," meaning that they gave you the results you wanted. I prosecuted many white-collar crime cases, which usually involved a lot of documents, and thus I had a frequent need for a handwriting expert. The first time I needed one, I did what everyone in the office did—I asked around the office for recommendations. I received several. One prosecutor gave me the name and number of an expert and told me, "He always gets back to you quickly and he's not a wimp—he's not afraid to call a match a match."

I used this particular handwriting expert numerous times in my prosecutorial career. On one occasion, I needed droves of documents that I believed the defendant had signed to be analyzed in a very short period of time. The trial was starting, but I did not receive these documents until the eve of trial. I shipped the documents to the expert overnight and asked him if he could give me an answer on them as quickly as possible, because my trial was starting. I also sent the defendant's handwriting exemplars (samples of his signature that were not disputed), so the expert could make the appropriate comparisons.

Two days later, I got a package back in the mail from him. He confirmed that all of the signatures had been made by my defendant. Given that it would have taken him overnight to ship the package back to me, it's clear that he had analyzed all of the signatures—perhaps hundreds of them—in one day.

In my prosecutor's office, we not only routinely told forensic scientists what answer we sought from their analysis and the time by which we needed it, but in some instances indicated that it was important because a "match" would be crucial to getting a conviction. This no doubt put great pressure on the forensic scientists to confirm our theories of the case, and created strong confirmation biases. In the example above, I told the handwriting expert that I needed him to confirm that the signatures on all the documents matched the defendant's, and I made clear that this was important because trial was starting and I needed the answers ASAP.

Experts who were too technical, and too worried about nuance rather than the big picture (the big picture of course being that a match existed between the defendant and the crime scene evidence because the defendant was clearly guilty), were considered an aggravation, too academic, and prone to miss the forest for the trees.

At the time, I, and I believe others in my office, felt that there was nothing wrong with this practice. I was completely unaware of the effects of confirmation bias, as most prosecutors and police officers remain equally ignorant today. And we all believed that our defendants were 100 percent guilty. We *knew* that the signatures were made by the defendant even *before* we had an expert examine them. And in a ballistics case we believed that *of course* the bullet came from the defendant's gun. Perhaps in many cases we believed this simply because we were correct. But perhaps we also had our own ingrained confirmation biases and suffered from tunnel vision. My bias explained why I did not question how the handwriting expert could have possibly been careful when he analyzed hundreds of signatures in a single day. It was a formality. Experts were there to confirm what we already knew, and to provide a form of evidence that would convince the jury.

But it was not just my prosecutor's office that created confirmation bias in expert witnesses. Figure 2 shows a actual submission form sent in 2008 from a detective to an expert witness requesting forensic analysis.[21]

Note that in the "Summary of Case" in the middle of the document, the detective effectively told the expert that he should expect to find the suspect's fingerprint because the suspect "reportedly drove" the car prior to the shooting and others in the car had already been eliminated as sources of the fingerprints. In the "Remarks" section toward the bottom, the detective tells the expert that the suspect is a murderer (he "pulled the trigger"), then puts great pressure on the expert, who is a fellow state employee, by saying that she is "making every effort to place [the suspect] in the truck," and that a fingerprint match from the expert is crucial because the "one witness riding in the truck was too drunk to make an identification." In other words, the detective is telling the expert that he should expect to find a match and that this is very important for nailing a murderer. This intake form is not an aberration. It is typical of how we communicated with experts in my office, and I believe typical of how it is done today all across the country.[22] One-third of forensic scientists in the UK who responded to a 2012 survey from *New Scientist* magazine admitted that they have felt pressured by law enforcement to reach results helpful to the prosecution in their cases.[23] In my opinion, if one-third *admit* to being pressured by law enforcement, the actual percentage who have actually been pressured is likely higher, as this is something that many would be loath to admit. And of course, short of outright pressure, confirmation bias is still created whenever a forensic

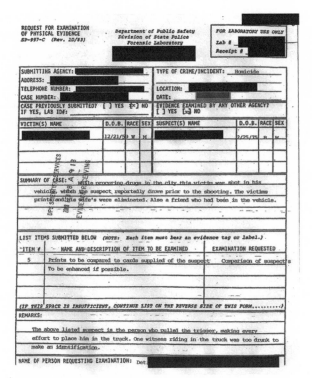

FIGURE 2.   Form submitted by detective to forensic
expert in 2008 for forensic testing. Received by author
from Dr. Itiel Dror, which he obtained from a case file
during his research. Reproduced with permission of
Dr. Dror.

scientist is told the expected "right" answer before he or she begins their
analysis.

In the Netflix docu-series *Making a Murderer,* which America binged-
watched in 2015 and 2016, several examples of this phenomenon were clearly
depicted. In that case, Steven Avery had been charged with the murder of
Teresa Halbach. The police believed that Avery killed her in his garage, where
they found a bullet on the garage floor. On cross-examination, it was revealed
that when the police sent the bullet to a state lab for DNA testing they
told the lab, "We need you to place Teresa Halbach in Steven Avery's
garage." In other words, the DNA lab technicians were told even before com-
mencing their testing that the "right" answer would be an opinion that
Teresa Halbach's DNA was on the bullet. Further cross-examination

revealed that even though the results of the test should have been ruled inconclusive under the lab's own protocol, the lab technicians went against that protocol to render an opinion that Halbach's DNA was on the bullet.

Another dispute in the case was whether Halbach's bones, found near Avery's home, had been moved to that location after they were burned. If so, it would support Avery's theory that someone had framed him. The prosecution put a forensic anthropologist on the stand who, it became clear, had been told by the prosecution before she began her assessment what answer she was supposed to give—that the bones hadn't been moved. And, of course, that was the opinion she ultimately gave in her testimony. However, on cross-examination, the defense was able to show not only that her opinion differed from that of the defense's expert witness, but that her opinion had no basis in science and, even worse, contradicted common sense. The forensic anthropologist ultimately seemed to back off from her opinion on cross-examination, admitting, once its fallacies were exposed, that she couldn't really give an opinion either way as to whether the bones had been moved.

In *Making a Murderer,* the way the forensic experts had been preconditioned by the prosecution to give answers that confirmed the prosecution's theory of the case brought to the public's consciousness what those of us in the innocence movement had known for years: that confirmation bias is a problem in our criminal justice system, and that it affects even supposedly neutral scientists.

In some jurisdictions, it gets even worse—lab technicians are not only told the "right" answer before they begin, but they have a financial incentive to provide that answer to law enforcement. Indeed, some jurisdictions provide the lab with an additional fee—taken out of the defendant's court costs!—which kicks in only if the defendant is convicted.[24] In others, forensic scientists receive formal "kudos" within their department for helping the police and prosecutors get convictions, as reflected in the minutes of crime lab meetings in Houston.[25]

A lab technician in Ohio, whose work may have led to several wrongful convictions, including the conviction of my client James Parsons, favored the prosecution so much that her personnel file even contained comments to that effect written by her supervisors. In my opinion, if a lab supervisor actually *puts in writing* that a lab technician goes too far to help the prosecution, it has to be bad. Really bad. Indeed, she was even overheard on the phone asking cops, "What do you need the evidence to say?"[26] Cops and prosecutors loved her, though. One thank-you note in her personnel file, among many others of equal enthusiasm, said, "If you were here right now,

I would give you a heartfelt hug and kiss for Valentine's Day. . . . You helped me more than you will ever know."[27]

. . .

In 2009, the National Academy of Sciences (NAS) issued a report entitled *Strengthening Forensic Science in the United States: A Path Forward.* The NAS is a private, nonprofit agency of scholars "dedicated to the furtherance of science and technology." Congress chartered it during the Lincoln administration, with a mandate to advise the federal government on scientific and technical matters. *Strengthening Forensic Science* was initiated by a 2005 act of Congress, which required the NAS to examine the state of forensic science in the United States and make recommendations for improvement.

The NAS held hearings throughout 2008, taking testimony from federal agency officials; academics, and research scholars; private consultants; federal, state, and local law enforcement officials; scientists; medical examiners; a coroner; crime laboratory officials from the public and private sectors; independent investigators; defense attorneys; forensic science practitioners; and leadership of professional and standard-setting organizations. Between hearings, the NAS reviewed the literature on forensic science—reports, studies, and so on—to aid its inquiry.

The NAS also considered what the innocence movement had taught about the state of forensic sciences in this country. It invited Peter Neufeld, cofounder of the Innocence Project (based at Cardozo Law School in Manhattan), to testify. The work of the innocence movement was noted in the NAS report.

Strengthening Forensic Science was released on February 18, 2009. In the introduction, the NAS declared, based on what it had heard from those who testified: "The forensic science system, encompassing both research and practice, has serious problems that can only be addressed by a national commitment to overhaul the current structure that supports the forensic science community in this country. This can only be done with effective leadership at the highest levels of both federal and state governments, pursuant to national standards, and with a significant infusion of federal funds."[28] *Strengthening Forensic Science* reveals the problematic state of forensics in this country. Ironically, at a time when the public watches *CSI* and believes that forensic scientists are performing scientific miracles to catch bad guys, the report demonstrates that reality is far from this Hollywood myth.

Strengthening Forensic Science explicitly acknowledges the role that confirmation bias plays in causing error in the forensic sciences. Indeed, Dr. Dror testified before the committee, and his groundbreaking work was cited throughout the report. The NAS recognized that the prevalence of confirmation bias in the forensic sciences is partly a result of the close relationships between forensic scientists and law enforcement. It made two significant recommendations. First, it advised that Congress create a National Institute of Forensic Science (NIFS) to oversee forensic scientists in order to "remov[e] all public forensic laboratories and facilities from the administrative control of law enforcement agencies or prosecutors' offices." Second, it recommended that the NIFS "develop standard operating procedures . . . to minimize, to the greatest extent reasonably possible, potential bias and sources of human error in forensic practice. These standard operating procedures should apply to all forensic analyses."[29]

Strengthening Forensic Science was welcomed by all in the innocence movement. The report not only recognized that confirmation bias distorted expert conclusions and testimony, but recommended that forensic scientists be entirely independent of prosecutors and police. Leaders in the movement who had been trying to raise awareness of this problem for many years, in an effort to push through reforms, got little to no traction. Finally, a prestigious independent agency that advises Congress had recognized the depth of the problem and urged Congress to make sweeping changes to improve the system.

Yet, more than eight years later, little to no reform has taken place. I frequently speak about the innocence movement across the state of Ohio and around the country. Prosecutors and judges are often in the audiences. From talking to them and answering their questions, I am under the impression that, even today, very few know anything about *Strengthening Forensic Science*. Many have not even heard of it.

As a result, many of the forensic disciplines that were identified as problematic in the report are still being used without any significant modifications or improvements in courtrooms across America. Indeed, in 2016, the President's Council of Advisors of Science and Technology issued a report echoing *Strengthening Forensic Science*, concluding that many forensic disciplines still in use are based on "scant scientific underpinnings" and need additional support to be considered valid and reliable. In response, U.S. Attorney General Loretta Lynch issued a statement saying her department "believes that the current legal standards regarding the admissibility of forensic evidence are based on sound science and sound legal reasoning." She concluded by adding, "the department will not be adopting the recommendations related to the admissibility of forensic science evidence."[30]

One recommendation from *Strengthening Forensic Science* that was adopted, however, was the Department of Justice's creation of the National Commission on Forensic Science to implement some of the suggestions from the report. Shortly after it began its work, however, Donald Trump was elected president, and his administration promptly killed it.[31]

The beat goes on.

. . .

Cases where the confirmation bias of a forensic scientist contributed to a wrongful conviction are plentiful. Ray Krone's case in Arizona is a notorious example.[32] On the morning of December 29, 1991, the body of a thirty-six-year-old female bartender was found in the men's bathroom of the bar where she worked. Krone, a regular patron, became a suspect because he had helped the victim close up the night before. Because the victim had been bitten during the attack, and bite marks were found on her body, the police had Krone bite into a Styrofoam cup to take an "impression" of his teeth. Several experts for the state then compared the impression to the bite marks on the victim's body and declared them a definitive match.

Krone's teeth were particularly crooked, and he became known in the media as the "Snaggletooth Killer." At his trial, the forensic experts told the jury that Krone's distinctive teeth—and *only* Krone's teeth—could have made the bite marks on the victim's body. The prosecution played up the power of this CSI-type evidence in its closing arguments. And, of course, with such seemingly ironclad evidence, the jury convicted. Krone was given the death penalty and sent to death row.[33]

Ten years later, Krone became the hundredth person exonerated and freed from death row in America. DNA testing of the saliva from the bite marks and blood left by the perpetrator proved that Ray Krone was not the killer. Rather, a man named Kenneth Phillips, who had been convicted of a sexual offense and lived near the bar, was identified as the true killer. Krone later received a $4.4 million settlement from the state of Arizona, and is "snaggle-toothed" no more after getting his teeth reconstructed on the TV show *Extreme Makeover*.

Krone's case begs the question: How could several forensic odontologists have taken the stand, looked the jury in the eye, and told them that Ray Krone's unique teeth—and only Ray Krone's teeth—could have made the bite marks on the victim's body? Were they intentionally lying to frame an innocent man? Of course not. The state's scientists were given a job to do—

match Krone's teeth to the bite marks on the victim's body. Before they even started their analysis, they believed Krone's teeth would match because he was the person held up by the police as "the guy who did it." With a task as subjective as comparing a bite mark in malleable skin to a bite impression on a Styrofoam cup, it is easy for an expert to see what she expects to see. Simply put, Krone was convicted not on the grounds of cold, hard, neutral science, as the jury believed, but as a result of confirmation bias.

The Larry Pat Souter case out of Michigan is one of many that highlight how pressure from prosecutors and police to solve a crime and help nail their prime suspect can lead forensic scientists to view evidence in a skewed way.[34] In August 1979, Kristy Ringler was found unconscious on a highway in White Cloud, Michigan. She died shortly thereafter. An autopsy concluded that she died from two blows to her head that could have been caused either by homicide or by being struck by a car.

When police arrived on the scene where Ringler's body had been spotted, a crowd of people had already started to gather. The group told the police that Ringler had been with them at a nearby party earlier that night, and that they had come down the street to see what had happened. Larry Pat Souter was at the scene, and he told police that he had met Ringler at a bar earlier that night and that she had accompanied him to the party. Souter admitted to police that at one point during the party he and Ringler had gone outside together, and that she had said she was going home and then began walking along the highway. Souter claimed that he had followed her a short distance trying to convince her to get a ride rather than walk, but then gave up after a few minutes and went back to the party.

The next day, police found a whiskey bottle near the spot where Ringler's body had been found. A trace of blood was found on the label. A lab determined that it was the same blood type as both Ringler's and Souter's. Souter admitted that the bottle was his, explaining that he had discarded it on the way to the scene. But he insisted that he had nothing to do with Ringler's death. He told police that the blood on the bottle had come from a cut on his finger from earlier that night.

Police also recovered particles of glass from Ringler's clothes that the lab determined were not from a car's headlights. Nevertheless, a forensic pathologist consulted by the police told them that, in his opinion, Ringler's injuries were a result of being struck by a car. At that point, the local county prosecutor decided that there was not enough evidence to charge Souter or anyone else.

The investigating police officer on the case, however, had an ongoing suspicion that Ringler had been murdered. He speculated that Ringler could not have been hit by a car because her body appeared to have been placed in the road, and no blood or debris was found on her clothing. A few years later, he presented the case to the county medical examiner, who concluded that the whiskey bottle belonging to Souter *could* have caused Ringler's injuries. But the local prosecutor again decided that there was not enough evidence to charge Souter.

More than a decade after Ringler died, a newly elected sheriff, who had run on a promise of solving old homicide cases, including Ringler's, took over the investigation. With renewed vigor, his deputies reinterviewed many of the old witnesses from the case in an attempt to jump-start the investigation, but they discovered no new leads. In this pressure-filled atmosphere, the sheriff asked the medical examiner to review the evidence again, and this time—miraculously—the medical examiner concluded that Ringler's injuries were caused by a blow from Souter's whiskey bottle. In 1991, more than twelve years after Ringler's death, Souter was arrested for her murder.

At Souter's trial, in 1992, several forensic pathologists working for the state testified that Ringler's injuries were consistent with being struck by the whiskey bottle. Souter claimed innocence, and explained his blood on the whiskey bottle by presenting the testimony of the owner of the house where the party took place, who told the jury that Souter had asked her for a bandage that evening because he had cut his finger on a broken door handle. Another witness testified that when Souter returned to the party, he was not acting abnormally, sweating, or breathing hard, and that there was no blood visible on his clothing. Still, Souter was convicted and sentenced to twenty to sixty years in prison.

In prison, Souter continued proclaiming his innocence. Eventually he and his supporters were able to amass substantial new evidence demonstrating his innocence. The most compelling was a statement from a woman who had read about Souter's possible wrongful conviction, and came forward and provided police with evidence that her father had been involved in a hit-and-run on the same night and highway where Ringler was killed. Ultimately, a federal appellate court found that Souter had presented compelling evidence of innocence, and a federal district court reviewed that evidence and tossed out Souter's conviction. He was released in December 2005 after serving thirteen years for a crime he didn't commit.

Notice that in Souter's case the changing opinions of the state's forensic scientists depended on how fervently the state believed at the time that Souter had killed Ringler and how much pressure the authorities were under to obtain a conviction. When the medical examiner got the message that the authorities believed Souter did it—and wanted his conviction—

suddenly, after more than ten years had elapsed, the whiskey bottle with Souter's blood on it matched the injuries on Ringler's head and became "the murder weapon."

Some may say that the fix was in on this case, and that the forensic scientists knew there was no match between the whiskey bottle and the injuries, but simply rubber-stamped the sheriff's request. But, after seeing this phenomenon in case after case, I believe the problem is subtler. In cases where scientists provide slanted reports to assist the prosecution, I think they usually deeply believe their flawed conclusions. Because scientists are human, and humans tend to see what they want to see when the pressure is on, most of these scientists simply convince themselves that the wrong answer is correct. In other words, rather than trying to shoot an arrow at a bullseye on the side of a barn, they shoot the arrow first and then paint a bullseye around wherever it lands. What they come to believe as the "right" answer causes them to see things, honestly see things, they didn't see before.

Take the Robert Lee Stinson case in Wisconsin. Confirmation bias caused two forensic odontologists to call Stinson's teeth an "identical" match to a bite mark on the victim "with no margin of error," even though Stinson was missing a tooth where the perpetrator clearly had a tooth.[35] DNA evidence later conclusively proved Stinson innocent, and a panel of odontologists who reviewed the case easily identified this obvious discrepancy that the state's experts at trial had overlooked. Stinson served two decades in prison for a murder he didn't commit, before he was released in 2009.

In another case, in Mississippi, a forensic odontologist provided testimony for the state that bite marks matched a number of different suspects, resulting in a series of possible wrongful convictions. And in at least two of the cases where DNA testing later cleared the defendants after years in prison, it was determined that the marks on the victims' bodies weren't even bite marks at all but had been made by insects and other animals after the victims had been killed and left outdoors.[36]

A particularly extreme example of confirmation bias skewing a result—so extreme that it may approach outright forensic fraud—comes from the Missouri case of George Allen. Allen was convicted in 1983 of murdering and raping a woman in her apartment. The crime occurred before there was DNA testing, and a forensic serologist testified that blood typing of the semen found on the victim's clothes could not exclude Allen as the perpetrator.[37] In closing arguments at trial, the prosecutor hammered home this evidence, stating that if Allen had been excluded as a source of the semen, "We wouldn't be here. We'd know that he couldn't have [done it]. But it's consistent."

Years after he was convicted and imprisoned, Allen's attorneys found notes from the forensic serologist, which had not been previously disclosed, indicating that he had initially concluded that the semen from the crime scene contained an antigen that excluded Allen as the source. But the serologist had crossed out that finding and changed it to a finding consistent with Allen's culpability after learning of Allen's blood type. When he later typed up his formal report for trial, he revealed only that the semen was consistent with Allen. Years later, after all of this came to light with Allen's exoneration, the serologist explained in depositions that after he learned from the authorities that Allen was the culprit, he assumed that his initial result excluding Allen must have been a result of lab error. So he just changed it.

Allen was freed in 2012 after serving thirty years in prison for a crime he didn't commit. Again, the "right" answer—the one that the scientist deemed "must" be true given the state's theory of the case—rather than objective science, dictated the result. The scientist in Allen's case believed so strongly in the state's evidence against Allen that it caused him to conclude that his initial finding exonerating Allen *must* have been a mistake.

Lest the reader think that confirmation bias leading to skewed expert results has only occurred in a few random cases around the country, let me say directly: that would be a serious misimpression. Any attorney who, like me, does postconviction innocence work in any state in this country can tell story after story about cases where forensic experts provided tenuous conclusions that did nothing but confirm the preexisting beliefs they had developed from their friends in the police department or prosecutor's office. It is a very common occurrence. And one does not have to dig very deeply into the files of any organization like mine, the Ohio Innocence Project, to see plenty of examples. It's like shooting fish in a barrel.

My office represented Walter Zimmer, who with his co-defendant, Thomas Siller, was exonerated and received a six-figure settlement from the city of Cleveland after spending thirteen years in prison for a murder he didn't commit.[38] The true killer, Jason Smith, had initially been caught red-handed because his fingerprints were all over the home of the victim, an elderly woman who had been tied to a chair and beaten to death in her living room. Smith cut a deal with prosecutors, however, receiving what a court later called a "breathtakingly favorable deal" to testify against Zimmer and Siller, whose fingerprints were also present in the victim's home. Zimmer and Siller were contractors who had done extensive work there.

At trial, Smith testified that he was present when Zimmer and Siller beat the victim to death, but witnessed the crime from a distance inside the house. Zimmer and Siller asserted their innocence. They argued that Smith committed the crime alone and implicated them simply to save his own skin. Pants worn by Smith on the night of the murder were analyzed by the state's forensic scientist, who testified initially that he did not find a single drop of blood on them, thus corroborating Smith's story that he was not the killer. Later, the scientist modified his conclusion, admitting that he found one drop of the victim's blood on Smith's pants. Although Smith's pants had numerous small brownish stains on them, the scientist said that he had not performed tests on those spots to determine if they too were the victim's blood because he could tell from their appearance that the stains were not blood. The prosecutor maintained in closing arguments that the single drop of the victim's blood likely got on Smith's pants when he rubbed up against Zimmer or Siller—who would have been soaked in the victim's blood if they'd committed the murder—and that the absence of a large amount of blood on Smith's pants corroborated Smith's story.

But DNA testing performed after Zimmer and Siller had already served years in prison demonstrated that Smith's pants were, in fact, covered with the victim's blood. Those brownish spots that the scientist had concluded could not be blood were indeed blood, and not just any blood, but blood that DNA testing confirmed belonged to the victim. Zimmer and Siller were exonerated, and Smith got five years in prison for perjuring himself against the pair to reduce his own culpability. In the expert's mind, the spots weren't blood since he believed that Smith was not the killer, and hence that's what he saw. Zimmer and Siller spent a combined twenty-six years in prison as a result. They were declared innocent and compensated by the state of Ohio.

In the Ohio murder case of Bob Gondor and Randy Resh, the authorities theorized that the two men killed the female victim and then put her body in the back of Gondor's pickup truck so that they could dispose of it in a nearby pond.[39] The state's experts analyzed marks and cuts on the victim's face and body, and concluded that they were made from the body bouncing on the pieces of wood found in the back of Gondor's truck, and from gravel near the pond, as the defendants had allegedly dragged the body into the pond where it was later found. Years later, after substantial evidence of their innocence was amassed, an expert from Minnesota re-analyzed the marks. The expert, hailing from a state full of ponds and lakes, was very familiar with bite marks left by turtles on dead bodies found in water, and she testified that the marks on the victim's face and body were textbook turtle bites. Gondor and Resh were released and declared innocent by the state of Ohio after spending sixteen years in prison for a crime they didn't commit. The state's expert had analyzed the body under a belief that Gondor and Resh had carried it in a truck full of wood and then dragged it through gravel, and—presto—saw wood and gravel marks on it. This conclusion was presented at trial as a high-tech CSI revelation, when in reality it simply confirmed a preexisting belief.

In the Ohio Innocence Project case of James Parsons, the authorities believed that he had killed his wife with a large tool that had the brand Craftsman embossed on the side in raised letters.[40] The supposed expert who testified for the state claimed that she had analyzed the sheet that was over the victim when she was attacked, and, from her extensive experience, was able to see some of the letters from the word "Craftsman" in the bloodstains on the sheet. She claimed that she could see the letters only under special conditions in her lab that could not be reproduced at trial. And she failed to photograph the incriminating images that she alleged she had been able to produce in her lab. Later, when the Ohio Innocence Project took the case back to court to try to exonerate Parsons, and exposed this junk science in the process, OIP was able to obtain this lab technician's personnel file. It contained notations indicating that she often slanted her lab results in favor of prosecutors.[41] Parsons' conviction was overturned after this junk science was exposed in postconviction litigation—but only after he had spent twenty-three years in prison.

In another Ohio Innocence Project case, one that is no less disturbing, two victims had been murdered in a bar, and the perpetrator had then used a crowbar to rip open the cigarette machine to take the coins inside.[42] When Ed Emerick later became a suspect, a forensic expert analyzed Emerick's crowbar and testified that it—to the exclusion of every other crowbar in the world—had made the scratches on the side of the cigarette machine. Emerick's attorney, to his credit, questioned the state's expert during trial about the possible effects of confirmation bias. He got the expert to admit on the stand that he knew what the "right" answer was before he even began his analysis. The expert countered by arguing that his supervisor had performed an independent examination of the crowbar after he reached his conclusion and reached the same conclusion. The defense attorney then got the expert to admit, however, that the supervisor was only asked to "confirm" the results of an initial analysis if a match had been made by the first expert. Thus, the supervisor had the same preexisting bias as the first expert and knew that his underling had already called Emerick's crowbar a match. To this day, Emerick remains in prison.

If all that isn't scary enough, consider the Ohio case of Ryan Widmer, which I helped litigate. The state theorized that Widmer drowned his wife in their bathtub, while Widmer maintained that his wife suffered from a medical condition that caused her to lose consciousness in the tub and drown.[43] The police found large body marks on the sides of the tub. Such marks can be left by parts of a human body, such as arms and legs, touching the tub and leaving an oil mark much as when a fingerprint is left. The state's expert claimed to be able to identify certain marks on the tub as a "male forearm" and a "female hand." Moreover, his identification of the gender and body part of each mark corroborated precisely the state's theory as to how Widmer pushed his wife into the tub to drown her.

In the Parsons, Emerick, and Widmer cases, the state's expert testimony was not grounded in any sort of actual science. There is no accepted scientific principle that allows an expert to conclusively identify letters from a tool in a bloody sheet that no one else can see. There is no scientific principle that allows an expert to determine that Emerick's crowbar—to the exclusion of every other crowbar in the world—left the scratches on the cigarette machine. There is no scientific principle that allows an expert to identify body-oil smudges on the side of a tub as a male forearm or a female leg. Rather, in each of these three cases, a forensic scientist simply saw what he expected to see as a result of confirmation bias, and then presented that conclusion to the jury under the guise of scientific infallibility.

The cases I've recounted here are from my own case files. Other similar cases from my files are too numerous to even mention. Again, any attorney doing postconviction innocence work in this country can literally tell story after story of individuals being convicted based on unscientific speculation by experts stemming from a desire to confirm the prosecution's theory of the case. This goes on every day.

5. Blind Memory

In 1979 in Georgia, a woman was raped by an intruder in her home. She told police that her attacker had a round face and stocky build.[1] Several weeks after the rape, the police had her look at suspects in a live lineup (see fig. 3).

All five suspects in the lineup are quite thin with narrow faces, except the man on the far right. The man on the right seems to be the only one who fit the physical characteristics of the rapist described by the victim. Nevertheless, the victim selected the man in the middle, John Jerome White. After she identified him again at trial, White was convicted and spent more than twenty-two years in prison before DNA testing exonerated him.[2] The testing further proved, however, that the man on the far right, James Parham, was the actual rapist.

Why did the victim erroneously choose White when the real rapist was right in front of her? Because a few days before the live lineup, the police had her look at a photo spread, which included a photo of White but not Parham. The victim selected White because out of the choices given to her that day, he looked the most like the rapist. Her selection of White, however, placed White's face in her memory as the face of the rapist, overpowering her original memory of the rapist, and led her to select White again at the live lineup a few days later, even when the real rapist was present right in front of her nose! As I will explain, memory experts now understand that when a rape victim incorrectly selects the photo of an innocent person, the face in that photo often transplants the face of the real perpetrator, and the victim may no longer even recognize the actual rapist.

· · ·

I first became aware of the phenomenon of altered memory early in life, from two different events. The events remained a mystery to me, or perhaps

FIGURE 3.   Photo of live lineup in the case of John
Jerome White.

more accurately a curiosity, until later in life when I studied memory and
understood better what had happened. The first involved being bitten by a
dog as a small child, probably at age five or six. My neighborhood friend
named Keith had an aggressive, protective dog. Whenever I went over to his
house to play, the dog had to be locked away in the basement, where it
would bark violently whenever I walked by the basement door. On one
occasion, Keith and I were watching television in a room far away from the
basement door when the dog got free and came charging into our room,
jumped onto the couch, and bit me hard on the thumb through the nail and
down to the bone. The bite bled profusely and, of course, the whole event
was very traumatic. I had to go to the doctor, and the thumbnail eventually
turned black and fell off.

I was a frequent visitor to that house over the next decade, and on several occasions other kids from the neighborhood would arrive to play with
Keith when I was there. Keith's mother would have to explain the barking
dog to these kids and why it had to be locked away in the basement. Each
time this happened, she would tell the kids, in my presence, something like,
"Don't worry, the dog won't get you from the basement. Once when Mark
was really little he teased the dog through the door. I told him to stop, but
he was little and didn't listen and just opened the door instead, and of course
he got bit." "He learned a lesson about following instructions that day," she
would say laughing, patting me on the head. Sometimes she told me, "It's
okay, you were little and didn't know better." She would go on to assure the
new kids, "If you just stay away from the basement door, the dog won't
bother you."

As a child, I didn't have the courage to challenge her version of what had happened. I clearly had the impression, however, that each time she told that story she truly believed it.

The second event occurred when I was perhaps eleven or twelve years old. It involved the only childhood "fight" I ever had. I can no longer remember why the fight occurred, but it was with a childhood friend, who I'll call Dan, in his backyard. Several other neighborhood kids who were mutual friends of Dan and myself were present, as were some of Dan's siblings. I remember Dan was very angry over something that had occurred at school that day, and he began yelling at me. At some point Dan physically charged me. I was much bigger than he, and quickly wrestled him to the ground. I pinned his arms down without any of his punches landing, and tried to talk through whatever had happened at school to defuse his anger. After a while, I let him up, but he just charged me again, so I pinned him down again and continued trying to calm him down. This cycle of charging, wrestling, and pinning him down went on two or three more times until his mother, who was unaware of the scuffle, yelled out the window for the kids to come in for dinner.

At that point, the fight ended, with no punches ever landing. Dan, his siblings, and the neighborhood kids who had been rubbernecking followed me over to my bike as I left. As I hopped on, Dan said, "You won today, but this is not over and we're going to finish this tomorrow." His sister said the same thing, telling me I won "round 1," but that when it continued the next day with "round 2," Dan would fare better. Of course, nothing happened the next day, the whole thing blew over, and we soon resumed our friendship.

The curious thing for me, which always made me scratch my head, was that a few years later when we were in high school Dan and his sister brought up the "fight" during a conversation at their house, and their version differed drastically from mine. I was an athlete in high school, and the first time the fight came up was after I had won a wrestling match at school. Dan brought up my victory and said something like, "Remember when we were kids and I totally kicked your butt in the backyard? That's hilarious to think about now." I laughed and told him that was nonsense—that he and his sister had conceded at the time that I had won round 1, and that round 2 never took place. But then Dan's sister "remembered" the same version of the incident as Dan's, colored with a lot of detail about how Dan had given me a black eye and bloody lip. It was clear to me by the way they talked that Dan and his sister had discussed Dan's "victory" over me many times in the past.

Another friend was present for this conversation at Dan's house, and he had been at the altercation many years earlier. When we left Dan's house together that day, I asked him why he didn't back up my version of the story. He said something like, "It wasn't even a fight—you just pinned him down and that was it. It's not worth arguing about."

Dan and his sister brought up the fight a few more times in the remaining years of high school, but from then on I just let it slide and laughed it off. I agreed with my friend—it wasn't worth arguing over.

My memories of these events are as clear as they possibly can be. I am as confident about them as almost any other memory in my life. I can remember as clear as day watching television and seeing the dog charge into the room out of nowhere, jump up onto the couch, and bite me unprovoked. It happened so quickly I could barely react. I was not teasing the dog by the basement door on the other side of the house, and I did not ignore Keith's mother's request to stop teasing the dog. I was scared to death of the dog and never would have teased it or opened the basement door. Likewise, no punches were landed during my only childhood "fight." I did not get a black eye or bloody lip from Dan's punches. In fact, I never had a black eye as a child or at any other time in my life.

I look at these events now and think that Keith's mother, Dan, and his sister had modified their memories out of confirmation bias and cognitive dissonance—the human desire to remember life events in a way that comports with our positive self-image. The mother didn't want to be responsible for my bite due to her own negligence in not properly protecting me from the dog. She didn't think of herself as someone who would allow a small child to be violently bitten by a dog under her charge. As time passed, her memory changed to fall in line with her vision of how she protects her guests and small children. She needed to tell future guests that they were safe, and that her dog had *never, ever* hurt anyone who had listened to and followed her instructions. Likewise, Dan and his sister had twisted their recollections of the "fight" through time in a way that comported with Dan's self-image of his physical prowess. And it was clear to me that they honestly believed their memories wholeheartedly.

But despite the clarity of my memories of these events, I now know enough about human memory to realize that I might be the one with altered memories. Although I still believe that my memories of these two events are largely accurate, I am open to questioning. I may have my own reasons, perhaps subconscious ones, to have reshaped these memories in my mind. Or my memories about the "fight" could have been shaped through conversations with other kids who were present and were trying to boost my self-esteem (although, if so, I have long forgotten those conversations). It is possible that the truth might be the version of events told by Dan's family, or something in between my version and theirs.

In more recent years, I have experienced the phenomenon of altered memory numerous times. I tend to pay more attention to it now that I'm so keenly aware of it. I have attended meetings at work where several peers and I met with our boss, and where each person came out of the meeting with a different memory of what the boss said. Often, the impression that each person took away from the meeting reflected what they *wanted* the boss to say before the meeting started. If my coworker was pretty sure before we went in that the boss would not approve my idea, sometimes the coworker, in my opinion, twisted comments by the boss to support that notion, while forgetting the boss's comments that suggested she liked my plan. When I pushed the coworker on the discrepancy, I often became convinced that it was not just a case of my coworker intentionally twisting things, or lying, to further his own agenda, but rather his version of events had become a memory that he firmly believed.

I have gone into family meetings with a doctor about a terminally ill family member, where each family member had a different belief before the meeting started as to which medical treatment our ill family member should receive next. In their reports to the doctor, each person "remembered" the symptoms our family member had demonstrated since the last appointment in a way that increased the chances that their desired treatment would be approved. And often each family member came out of the meeting with the doctor "hearing" what they wanted to hear before they went in, and their version of events had already become steadfast memory as soon as the meeting ended. They recounted what the doctor said in a way that made me wonder if I was in the same doctor's appointment. Of course, confirmation bias may have led each family member to hear what they desperately wanted to hear, and then this altered version of events became their memory.

Again, I recognize in these instances that I could be just as guilty of having an altered memory as anyone else, so I try very hard to be as objective as possible. I cannot know what my success rate actually is. But because of confirmation bias and malleable memories, our reality—the "facts"—are often different to us than they are to other people. "He said / she said" is not always one person lying and the other telling the truth. Both people may be truthful about their memories and simultaneously baffled at the story told by the other.

The documentary film *Stories We Tell* (2012) is a fascinating exploration of this phenomenon. The film's director, actress Sarah Polley, grew up the youngest of several children. Sarah's mother died when she was young. After her death, the notion that Sarah had been conceived as a result of her mother having an extramarital affair became a family myth among the older siblings and her father; it was always cast as a light-hearted "inside joke" within the family. Sarah decided to investigate the myth, filming her efforts. She extensively interviewed all of her family members and her mother's friends about the myth and their memories of key events from the past, such as behaviors or comments by her mother that might suggest an affair. She also investigated past events that might shed light on who her mother might have had an affair with. The film culminates with Sarah performing DNA testing of the various male suspects that her investigation identified, revealing that she was, in fact, the product of an extramarital affair.

But by the time shooting wrapped up, the film had become something Sarah had not expected. Rather than being a "whodunit," the film's most compelling narrative was the drastic differences in memory among all persons who were interviewed. Each person conveniently "remembered" key events in ways that comported with their own theory as to whether their mother had an affair and, if so, with whom. The film was billed as exploring "the elusive nature of truth and memory . . . and how our narratives shape and define us as individuals and families." Polley explains:

> I think what kind of captivated me about what was happening in the aftermath of this story . . . was the way we were all telling the stories about it, and the way those stories were different from each other. There are these huge gaps between these stories we were telling, both in terms of the fact of them, but also in terms of the perspective and what we decided were the most important elements of it. I got really transfixed by this idea that it was so necessary for us to be able to tell this story to make sense of some kind of basic confusion we had in our life. I just started thinking of storytelling as a really basic human need.[3]

I do not believe that Sarah Polley's experience is unique. Anyone, if they become aware of this issue and start paying close attention to memory discrepancies in work and family situations, will probably report similar occurrences. Although most at first blush will say that others with different memories are "lying" or "twisting things" because they are "biased" and have an "agenda," the psychology of memory shows that is not always the case. Confirmation bias and cognitive dissonance exert powerful influences on our memories.

.   .   .

Most people recognize that human memory is fallible to some degree. We have all had the experience of forgetting a friend's birthday or searching for our car keys mystified at their disappearance. These types of memory lapses are common and widely understood as part of the human experience.

However, most people think of their memories as generally being fairly reliable. We may forget things here and there, but what we *do* remember we remember correctly. We think of memory as like a video recorder, accurately recording from the mind's eye what happens in our lives, with the events able to be played back later when the need to remember them arises. Or, if not a video recorder, then a hardbound encyclopedia or computer hard drive that encodes and stores the events from our lives verbatim as they happen. Occasionally, parts of our internal videotape or hard drive get erased as time passes, and sometimes we are too busy and distracted to even hit the record button. But if we think back about an event, the parts we remember we recall accurately.

Yet human memory is much weaker and more malleable than most people realize. Rather than acting as a hard drive or videotape, our memories are more like Wikipedia, a metaphor coined by the famous psychologist and memory expert Dr. Elizabeth Loftus. We constantly edit our memories subconsciously. And, just as anyone can edit a post on Wikipedia, other people can edit our memories as well, by the mere act of suggestion. We don't even realize it when external suggestions have altered our own memories. By the time we recall an event hours, days, weeks, or years later, frequently we or others have altered our memory. We may state our memory with confidence, and may truly feel confident about it, but it may be completely inaccurate. The videotape may have been edited, the code in the hard drive altered. Human memory is a bit like images, sounds, smells, and thoughts set in quicksand, always changing and shifting underneath us.

The scariest thing is that because we don't know when this has happened, we often cling to an altered or false memory with confidence, if not defensiveness, when someone contradicts our version of the facts: "You're wrong; that's not what happened." "No, *you're* wrong," the other person replies. While both people arguing over what happened may be confident that they are right, the truth is that we often can't know who is right, or if both are wrong. Indeed, if a third person joins the discussion, that person's memory might differ as well. But each person might be supremely confident about their memory.

Several cognitive problems cause altered memories. Misattribution occurs when our minds blend past memories together, or fill in gaps in our memories with information from other sources without knowing it. A common example of misattribution occurs when we learn a fact from a friend or a TV commercial but later think we learned it from a more reliable source, like a newspaper. Studies show that this type of misattribution is quite common, a daily experience.[4] In the criminal justice system, misattribution occurs when, for example, an eyewitness to a crime sees a mug shot of the alleged perpetrator on TV, notices that he has a mustache, and then later "remembers" that the culprit had a mustache, when in fact he was clean-shaven. This may cause her to select an innocent person from a lineup.

Confirmation bias frequently twists our memories as well. If we are told that someone we are about to meet is a successful doctor, we are more likely to remember her as well-dressed and smart than if we are told that she is a waitress.[5] Cognitive dissonance is also a powerful sculptor of memory. Leon Festinger's famous theory of cognitive dissonance holds that humans are uncomfortable with memories or facts that are inconsistent with their positive self-image or with their beliefs and behaviors.[6] As a result, we have an inner drive to bring our memories and attitudes into harmony. This causes us to engage in what is frequently referred to as "revisionist history," where we alter our memories to better fit our theories and self-images.

THE RESEARCH

While the weaknesses and malleability of human memory have not yet reached the public's consciousness, research by leading psychologists has demonstrated this phenomenon for decades. Dr. Elizabeth Loftus is probably the most influential psychologist in the field of human memory. Several of her studies have become the gold standard for demonstrating flaws in human memory. In her 1974 study "Reconstruction of Automobile Destruction: An Example of the Interaction between Language and Memory," subjects viewed an automobile accident and then attempted to reconstruct from memory what they saw.[7] Loftus noted that prior experiments and even courtroom cases had demonstrated how common it is for witnesses to have wildly divergent memories about such things as how fast cars were traveling before they collided, or how much time had passed between the sounding of the first car horn and the crash. In one study, for example, when subjects were told in advance that they would be asked how fast a car was moving, they later recalled speeds ranging from 10 mph to 50 mph, when the car in question was actually moving at 12 mph.[8] Loftus's study set out to determine how easily subjects' memories could be altered by the mere words chosen when questioning them about their memories of an event.

Loftus had forty-five subjects view seven films of automobile accidents, each five to thirty seconds in length. After each film, the subjects received

TABLE 1 Effect of Word Choice on Car Speed
Remembered

Term Used	Estimated Speed (mph)
contacted	31.8
hit	34.0
bumped	38.1
collided	39.3
smashed	40.5

a questionnaire asking them to recount what they had witnessed. The forty-five subjects were divided into different groups, but only one question differed from group to group. Some questionnaires started out by asking how fast the cars were going when they "contacted" one another, while others used increasingly loaded and suggestive terms in place of "contacted," such as "hit," "bumped," "collided," and finally "smashed." The more suggestive the term, the faster the subjects remembered the speed of the cars, as table 1 illustrates.

Thus, the mere use of the word "smashed" in the questionnaire caused subjects, on average, to remember the speed of the car as nearly 9 mph, or 27 percent, faster than when "contacted" was used. It may not be surprising that a change of words could cause subjects to remember the cars as traveling faster, since speed is a very subjective variable. But Loftus's follow-up study produced more startling results. She again had subjects watch an automobile accident on film and then answer questions about it from a written questionnaire.[9] Fifty of the subjects were asked, "How fast were the cars going when they hit each other?" Fifty other subjects were asked, "How fast were the cars going when they smashed?" Similar to the first study, when the word "smashed" was used, subjects remembered the speed as 30 percent faster than when "hit" was used.

But this time Loftus also had the subjects return one week later and complete a second questionnaire without rewatching the film. The critical question in this second questionnaire was, "Did you see any broken glass in the automobile accident?" The correct answer was no—neither of the cars depicted in the fender bender suffered shattered windshields, headlights, or taillights, in the slightest. But subjects who had been asked one week earlier "How fast were the cars going when they smashed" were *more than twice as likely* as those in the "hit" group to incorrectly answer that they had seen broken glass in the film the week before.[10] This proved to be true even for those subjects for whom use of the word "smashed" did not cause them to significantly inflate the speed of the cars. Thus, use of the word "smashed" as opposed to "hit" had the effect of both increasing the mean speed and causing subjects to falsely remember that they saw broken glass. But these two dependent variables were somewhat independent of one another—one effect could occur without the other. Of course, unlike speed, which is subjective and perhaps easy to manipulate in one's memory, whether or not there was broken glass in the film is a concrete fact.

If the mere use of the word "smashed" in a written questionnaire can cause witnesses to "remember" broken glass that wasn't there, imagine how a witness's memory might be altered when they feel intense pressure to help solve a terrible crime and a stressed-out police officer is repeatedly returning to questions like, "Are you sure he wasn't out of breath and acting nervous or flustered at all when he returned to the bar that night?" "And are you sure he returned by 11:00 P.M.? It could have been 11:30, couldn't it? How close were you paying attention to the clock when you were partying and watching the game? Other witnesses in the bar that night are telling us it was more like 11:30."

Another paper by Elizabeth Loftus, "The Formation of False Memories," delves further into how false memories can be created by information supplied to a witness after an event. She writes:

> For most of the century, experimental psychologists have been interested in how and why memory fails. As Green has aptly noted, memories do not exist in a vacuum. Rather, they continually disrupt each other through a mechanism that we call "interference." Virtually thousands of studies have documented how our memories can be disrupted by things that we experienced earlier (proactive interference) or things that we experience later (retroactive interference).
>
> Relatively modern research on interference theory has focused on retroactive interference effects. After receipt of new information that is misleading in some ways, people make errors when they report what they saw. *The new post-event information often becomes incorporated into the recollection, supplementing or altering it, sometimes in dramatic ways. New information invades us, like a Trojan Horse, precisely because we do not detect its influence.* Understanding how we become tricked by revised data about a witnessed event is central goal of this research.[11]

Loftus goes on to recount prior studies in which witnesses to an event, such as a horrible crime, were given incorrect written information about the event that they then incorporated into their memories. For example, if the color of the automobile fleeing from the scene was first reported by witnesses as blue, reading a report of the event in which the vehicle is described as white can cause a significant number of those witnesses—often as high as 30 or 40 percent—to remember the vehicle as being white. Similar studies show high rates of altered witness memories of such things as a clean-shaven man having a mustache, straight hair as curly, stop signs as yield signs, hammers as screwdrivers, and "something as large as a barn in a bucolic field" as a scene with no buildings at all.[12] All of these altered memories were created from having the witnesses read written reports, with no police officer or other person applying any type of stress or other pressure.

Loftus noted in these studies that witness memories were altered about events that actually happened. In her next study, however, she attempted to find out how easily false memories could be created about events that *never occurred*. Loftus told her subjects that she was studying "the kinds of things you might be able to remember from your childhood." An older relative of each subject was interviewed in advance to provide three real events from the subject's childhood. Each subject was then given materials that contained four stories about different childhood events that the subject was informed had been obtained from the subject's family. While three of these stories had actually been reported by the subject's family member, the fourth story, which involved the subject being lost in a mall as a child, was entirely made up by Loftus and her team. (Loftus confirmed with each subject's family that the subject, to the family's knowledge, had never been lost in a mall as a child.) An example of a false story, provided to a Vietnamese-American woman who grew up in the state of Washington, was as follows: "You, your mom, Tien and Tuan all went to the Bremerton K-Mart. You must have been 5 years old at the time. Your mom gave each of you some money to get a blueberry Icee. You ran ahead to get in the line first, and somehow lost your way in the store. Tien found you crying to an elderly Chinese woman. You three then went together to get an Icee."[13] The subjects were first asked to recall their memory of each of the four events in writing, and then were interviewed about their memories twice, once two weeks after completing the written document and again two weeks later. In their written responses, 29 percent of the subjects not only "remembered" the false event of being lost in a mall as child, but described it. (In the follow-up interviews, one of the subjects recanted her memory of being lost in a mall, bringing those who clung to the false memory down to 25 percent.) One subject, for example, used a full ninety words to describe the incident in her written response. The Vietnamese-American subject, for example, wrote, "I vaguely, vaguely, I mean this is very vague, remember the lady helping me and Tien and my mom doing something else . . . but I don't remember crying. I mean I can remember a hundred times crying. . . . I just remember bits and pieces of it. I remember being with the lady. I remember going shopping. . . . I don't remember the sunglasses part." She went on to remember the lady who rescued her as "nice" and "heavy set, older."[14]

At each interview, subjects were asked how confident they were in their memories of being lost in a mall. Interestingly, the confidence level of the subjects increased significantly between the first and second interviews, demonstrating that the more a person talks about a false memory, the deeper it becomes imbedded in his or her psyche.[15]

In a similar study reported by Loftus, one subject recalled additional "facts" in a second interview such as looking at puppies in the pet store when she became lost, and that the lady who rescued her was wearing a long skirt. The subject reported, "I do remember her asking me if I was lost . . . and asking my name and then saying something about taking me to security." She recalled that she didn't cry while she was lost, but cried once she was finally reunited with her parents. She remembered a feeling of "initial panic when you realize that your mom and dad aren't there anymore." After the second interview, when she was informed that the event never happened, the subject found it so hard to believe that she called both of her parents, who confirmed that it had never taken place and that they had worked with Loftus's team to construct the false story.

Psychologists have also reported success rates of 20 to 25 percent in implanting false memories of being at a wedding and spilling the punch bowl on the parents of the bride; having to evacuate a grocery store when the overhead sprinkler system malfunctioned, suddenly spraying everyone with water; being in a car in a parking lot and releasing the parking brake, causing the car to roll and crash into something; being rescued from a pool by a lifeguard; being bitten by a dog; and being hospitalized overnight with a high fever caused by an ear infection.[16]

For any reader wishing to hear more about the malleability of human memory, a great source is Elizabeth Loftus's fascinating seventeen-minute TED talk recorded in June 2013 and available online.[17]

MEMORY AND EYEWITNESS ERROR

Faulty eyewitness identification testimony—caused by errors in human perception and memory—is the single greatest cause of wrongful convictions. Of the first 325 DNA exonerations in the United States, 235, or 72

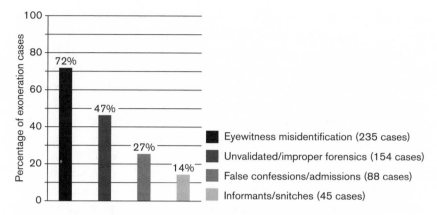

FIGURE 4. Contributing causes of wrongful convictions (first 325 DNA exonerations). Total is more than 100 percent because wrongful convictions can have more than one cause.

percent, involved mistaken eyewitness identification testimony.[18] This figure dwarfs the second leading cause, bad forensic testimony, which accounted for 154 cases, or 47 percent (see fig. 4).

The National Registry of Exonerations, which currently lists more than two thousand DNA and non-DNA exonerations in the United States since 1989 (with the number growing weekly), says that faulty eyewitness identification contributed to 30 percent of wrongful convictions.[19] These statistics do not include cases where a witness intentionally lied to frame an innocent person.[20] Rather, they encompass only those cases in which eyewitnesses testified in good faith—believed they were telling the jury the truth—but were simply wrong. Their memories failed them, causing an innocent person to be convicted.

When a person witnesses a crime, there are many things that can lead to inaccurate memory recall later in a courtroom. In fact, the psychological literature on eyewitness identifications is so rich that entire books have been dedicated to this issue.[21] Below I will provide just a quick overview, and then focus on a few specific subfacets of the problem that are both pervasive and preventable.

ENCODING, STORAGE, AND RETRIEVAL

In general, memory involves three stages: encoding, storage, and retrieval. Encoding occurs when the witness experiences the event. But, given limitations in our cognitive abilities, we simply cannot encode everything that we take in during an event, no matter how important the event is to us. Rather, "we integrate fragments of a new experience into memory by combining it with what we already know or what we are expecting in a situation," as one memory expert has noted.[22] In other words, the mind encodes some of the new information, but provides shortcuts for the rest, supplying information from previous memories or filling in the blanks with our assumptions. For example, if you go to a child's birthday party, you probably will not encode what the birthday cake looked like unless for some reason the appearance of the cake was particularly important to you. Instead, you may combine the image of the cake with preexisting memories of children's birthday cakes, and save the fresh encoding space in your brain for something that mattered most to you, like where the cake was purchased if the taste was particularly delicious, or the fact that your ex showed up at the party unexpectedly. The less important details surrounding the event, such as who else was at the party or the color of the balloons, may not have been encoded but combined with some previous memory or a bias as to who you *expected* or *assumed* would be at the party, or what you think balloons at a child's birthday party are *supposed to* look like.

In one sense, therefore, the brain helps us by not forcing us to encode everything that we encounter, allowing us to borrow from past memories and our expectations to create shortcuts. But, in another sense, the brain cheats us by creating inaccurate memories about many of the details we experience in everyday life. Sometimes details may seem minor or trivial when we experience them, like whether a person we barely know named Dave was at the birthday party, and thus we do not encode them cleanly. But this same fact can become very important later when we suddenly realize that our testimony as to whether Dave was present or not at the birthday party could mean the difference between whether he is convicted or acquitted of the murder of his wife, which occurred at the same time as the party. We may feel that we have a strong memory as to whether or not Dave was present, but in reality, unless our brain encoded that information correctly on that day, we cannot know if the memory is accurate.

Obviously, intoxication, or not wearing glasses, impacts our ability to encode, as does anything else that hinders our ability to perceive. Contrary to popular opinion, stress negatively impacts the encoding process as well. While many jurors believe a witness when he or she says, "As the crime happened, my adrenaline was pumping. . . . I became very awake and aware and paid close attention," the reality is that stress of this nature interferes with the encoding process and significantly reduces the reliability of the resulting memories.[23]

Studies show that when a crime occurs and the perpetrator brandishes a gun, victims and eyewitnesses tend to engage in "weapon focus," where they become intent on keeping an eye on the gun at all times to be ready should the perpetrator point it at them. In such situations, the eyewitnesses may "see" the hair color or other features of the perpetrator, such as whether he has a mustache, but will not encode them accurately; instead, they focus all of their brainpower on the gun. Later, when they are asked to recall the facial features of the perpetrator, their "memories" may be nothing more than a contaminated collection of past memories and expectations that their brain used to fill in the picture so that it could focus on more important things—like where the gun was pointed.[24] But the witnesses will not know that their memories are inaccurate.

The selective encoding process allows confirmation bias and cognitive dissonance to contaminate our memories. A story in the *Washington Post* about eyewitness accounts of a NYPD shooting of a hammer-wielding assailant illustrated this phenomenon.[25] Immediately after the incident, one eyewitness told a *New York Times* reporter that the deceased was fleeing when the police officer shot him. "He looked like he was trying to get away from the officers," the witness said. A second eyewitness was riding her bike when she saw the shooting. Shaken, she contacted the *Times* and told them that the man had been shot by the police in cold blood after he was already in handcuffs. "I saw a man who was handcuffed being shot," she reported. "And I am sorry, maybe I am crazy, but that is what I saw." Later, a surveillance video surfaced that showed that the police shooting was completely justified and both eyewitnesses were wrong. When contacted by the *Times* after the video was released, the second eyewitness said, "I feel totally embarrassed." Radley Balko of the *Washington Post* wrote:

> She now believes that she saw the initial encounter and then looked away, as she was on her bicycle. In that moment, the man began the attack, which lasted about three seconds until he was shot. "I didn't see the civilian run or swing a hammer," she said. "In my mind I assumed he was just standing there passively, and now is on the ground in handcuffs." "With all the accounts in the news of police shootings, I assumed that police were taking advantage of someone who was easily discriminated against," she added. "Based on what I saw, I assumed the worst. Even though I looked away." As the [*Times*] article points out, there's no reason to think that [this eyewitness] was lying. False memories can seem just as real as real memories.

The next stages of memory after encoding are storage and retrieval. These stages influence each other. Several factors at the storage and retrieval stages often affect the reliability of memories. Two changes happen. The first is that our memory of the encoded event weakens as time passes. Memory does not improve over time.[26] One study has shown, for example, that an eyewitness's ability to correctly identify the perpetrator from a photo lineup is no better than chance after eleven months have passed from the day of the crime, even if the witness accurately encoded many details on the day the crime occurred.[27] This is due to the passage of time, which severely weakened the encoded information. In the meantime, the second change occurs: weakened memories are supplanted with false information that the witness saw on the news about the case (like a picture of the suspect who was arrested), or contaminated by what the police or others tell her about the case. Or her memory could be contaminated by her biases, assumptions, expectations, and personal desires about the case. When she picks someone from a lineup eleven months later, studies show that her identification should be handled with great caution, even though she may feel highly confident in her memory.

Dr. Charles Goodsell described the contamination of memory by extraneous information and biases as an expert witness in my Ohio Innocence Project case of *Ohio v. Douglas Prade*, which involved very shaky eyewitness identifications made after significant time had passed and the witnesses had seen my client's mug shot on the television news:

> A suggestion by another person (e.g., another witness, the police, or the media), or an inference made by the witness, can modify or influence a memory. . . . There are countless studies that demonstrate this phenomenon. . . .
>
> Most do not realize that memories are the result of a constructive process whereby we combine specific elements we can recall from an event, along with general knowledge and assumptions or expectations of what should have happened. *Each time you recall (think about) some memory, that memory is altered.* There is opportunity to add, change, or omit elements of that memory as you store that latest instance of the memory. New information that is received or belief about what probably happened can be added in, or information that now doesn't seem consistent or accurate can be omitted or changed.
>
> In short, the memory possessed by the witness at some later point (e.g., when the witness testifies in court) can be quite different from the memory he or she formed at the time of the event. Longer retention intervals (the time between witnessing and recall of an event) result in a greater likelihood of forgetting and incorporation of inaccurate information. This new, but inaccurate, information can get incorporated into the person's memory of the original event, thereby increasing memory distortion.[28]

Dr. Goodsell noted that because the eyewitnesses had seen my client's photo on the news prior to selecting his photo in a lineup, we cannot know whether they did so as a result of an accurate memory or contamination. DNA testing later suggested that my client was innocent.

CONTAMINATION AND MISATTRIBUTION

Countless wrongful-conviction cases demonstrate the phenomenon discussed by Dr. Charles Goodsell. Eyewitnesses see an innocent suspect's picture on the television news, where he's presented as the man just arrested for committing the crime, and then they "remember" that face as the face of the perpetrator instead of the face they actually saw when the crime occurred. Or the police may ask a witness a question suggesting that the perpetrator's mustache was bushy or trimmed, and the witness suddenly "remembers" a mustache on the clean-shaven perpetrator that he saw the week before. This is called memory contamination or misattribution.[29] The study by Loftus mentioned previously, where subjects incorrectly remembered broken glass in the film showing an automobile accident simply because the loaded word "smashed" was used to describe the accident, is a perfect example of memory contamination in the clinical setting.

In these examples of misattribution, the subjects' memories became contaminated by outside influences even though they had no internal motive to alter their memories. In the examples I gave at the beginning of this chapter from my childhood, however, the witnesses had a motive to alter their memories. The mother with the dog that bit me had a strong internal motive, stemming from cognitive dissonance: she wished to assure visitors that her home was safe and that her dog had never bitten anyone who followed her instructions. She did not want to think of herself as a dog owner who would allow a small child under her care to be bitten. It did not comport with her self-image.

Make no mistake: in criminal investigations, motive is a powerful influence on perceptions and behavior. When a crime happens, the victim, the eyewitnesses, the police, the prosecutor, and the public all want it solved and solved quickly. They want retribution, and they want the bad guy off the street. Thus, eyewitnesses and players in the criminal justice system are subconsciously more likely to integrate outside information or suggestions into their memories if it helps move the case in the right direction. Any lawyer like myself who specializes in wrongful conviction cases can provide dozens of examples where the witnesses changed their stories—their memories— over time to keep the train moving toward conviction. I frequently saw this process at work when I was a prosecutor as well. Because we do not collectively appreciate the dangers of memory malleability, altered memories are ingrained in the system.

Numerous eyewitness identification studies have shown this phenomenon at work. The following framework has been employed. Subjects are shown a surveillance video depicting a convenience store robbery and then a photo lineup that does *not* include the actual perpetrator. They are asked if they see the perpetrator in the lineup. Among those who select a photo, some are told that they made the right choice and some are given no feedback. The subjects who selected a photo are asked to complete a questionnaire requiring them to rate such things as how confident they are that they selected the right person, how closely they paid attention to the video, and how willing they would be to testify in court.

These studies produce similar results regardless of the age of the subjects or other factors.[30] When witnesses receive positive feedback about their identification, it significantly increases their confidence level. They also report that they viewed the crime more carefully and are more willing to testify at trial. Outside influences have contaminated their memory. Instead of going to court and testifying that the defendant "looks like" the perpetrator, or "I'm only 75 percent sure it is him," for example, witnesses who receive confirmatory feedback will often come to court and testify that they are 100 percent certain that they saw the defendant commit the crime. And they will testify that they paid very close attention to the perpetrator's physical features. Yet their confidence—which can easily lead to a wrongful conviction—was simply manufactured by the confirmatory feedback, without the witness even being aware of it.

Confirmatory feedback can take various forms. When a police officer says, "You picked the suspect," that, of course, is a clear example of confirmatory feedback. But when a witness goes to the police station, picks a photo, and then learns from the TV news that the man she picked has been arrested by the police, that is another form of confirmatory feedback. So is hearing on the news that "several" witnesses identified the suspect as the culprit. Another example, which is also not uncommon, is making a selection from a photo lineup and hearing the police officer sigh in relief, then watching him excitedly put away the photo lineup while he says, "Thank you. We will be in touch very soon."

The American public saw an example of the effects of confirmatory feedback in *Making a Murderer,* the Netflix docu-series that explored Steven Avery's conviction for murdering Teresa Halbach, as well as his earlier wrongful conviction for the rape of Penny Beernsten. Avery was later exonerated of Beernsten's rape by DNA testing. But after Beernsten had incorrectly chosen Avery as her rapist, the police told her that she had selected their suspect. Beernsten later told *Dateline NBC* that this confirmatory feedback greatly boosted her confidence.[31] From that point on, she was confident in her memory. And when she remembered the attack, she saw Steven Avery's face "like a photograph."[32]

When I was a prosecutor, an FBI agent and I worked on a case for a long time and finally developed some evidence against a particular suspect. Our ability to bring charges against the suspect hung on the ability of the crime victim to identify him from a photo lineup. When she arrived at my office, the FBI agent and I were very nervous. We had put a lot of work into the case, believed our suspect was guilty, and desperately wanted the victim to select his photo. When she selected him, the FBI agent and I quickly left the room into the hallway and excitedly started discussing what to do next, just around the corner from where the victim was sitting. In fact, when we first left the room, we did little "touchdown dances" and gave each other high fives. There is no doubt in my mind that the victim—the lone eyewitness to the crime—knew from our reactions that she had picked the right person. She could also tell that this was a big deal to us, and that it would be important to keep moving forward with the case. After seeing how we reacted, she would surely have known that she would be disappointing us tremendously if she ever expressed doubt about her identification. I, like many prosecutors and police officers today, had no idea how this behavior could alter the testimony of an eyewitness.

EYEWITNESS MISIDENTIFICATION CASES

With eyewitness error so common and human memory so malleable, it should come as no surprise that in many cases multiple eyewitnesses—in one case, even ten—can all be dead wrong.[33]

Raymond Towler

I represented Raymond Towler, who was convicted in Cleveland in 1981 of raping a young girl in the woods of a public park. A few weeks after the rape, Raymond, who had just successfully completed a stint in the military and was going to the park to relax and meditate, was pulled over by a park ranger. He was stopped presumably because he was African-American, like the rapist, in a park surrounded by an affluent, white neighborhood. The ranger took Raymond's picture and identification information and let him go. Later, the rape victim, her older brother, and two adult eyewitnesses all identified Raymond from his picture in a photo lineup as the rapist. At trial, all four eyewitnesses again identified Raymond as the rapist, and they expressed great confidence in their identifications. Raymond was convicted. After serving twenty-nine years in prison, he was exonerated by DNA testing and freed in 2010. The four eyewitnesses were all dead wrong.

Dean Gillispie

I have talked at length about Dean Gillispie's case, in which three different eyewitnesses identified him as the perpetrator of rapes that occurred in 1988. In that case, a police officer created a photo lineup that was highly suggestive.[34] All of the photos had a glossy finish and a blue background, except Dean's, which had a matte finish and a yellow background. Also, the rapist had been described as having a wide face, so Dean's face appeared close to the camera—his face took up the entire square in the photo—while the other individuals in the lineup were much further away; their photos could be characterized as torso shots. Many years later, the *Dayton Daily News* aptly characterized Dean's photo as "all but circled and starred."[35]

Dean's case involved gross examples of confirmatory feedback by the police officer. The witnesses were not shown the photo lineup until twenty-two months after the crime, which, as we've seen, studies have shown renders the reliability of their identifications close to nil and their memories highly vulnerable to alteration through suggestion. Indeed, the eyewitnesses admitted on the stand at trial that after they selected Dean from the photo lineup, the police officer told them that they had selected the right person. Such statements, of course, grossly inflate eyewitness confidence and can alter memories, implanting the face of the man in the photo in witnesses' minds as the face of the perpetrator.

In addition, Dean's hair was brown and peppered with a lot of gray, but no red, while the eyewitnesses had described the rapist's hair as brown with a reddish tint but no gray. At trial, when Dean's defense attorney cross-examined one of the eyewitnesses about the discrepancy between Dean's hair color and how she had previously described the hair color of the rapist, she responded something to the effect of, "He has colored his hair." The surprised defense attorney then inquired further of the witness, and the witness admitted that the police officer in question had told her before trial that Dean would not look like the rapist because he had colored his hair and tried to alter his appearance for trial. Though Dean's attorney called Dean's hair stylist to testify that his hair had been gray for many years and had never been dyed, and several witnesses testified to Dean's alibi, the jury convicted him. This is not surprising: it is a rare jury that will not convict, despite such discrepancies and an alibi, when three separate eyewitnesses take the stand, cry, and state with emotion that they are "positive" this man was the rapist. Jurors naïvely tend to accept the testimony of eyewitness as gospel, despite the limitations in human memory.[36]

To this day, the three eyewitnesses still believe that Dean was the rapist. That, too, is not uncommon in wrongful conviction cases. Once a false memory is created, and a conviction is obtained as a result of it, confirmation bias, cognitive dissonance, and a desire to avoid confronting the possibility that your mistake put away an innocent man for twenty years tend to fortify the falsely created memory. Penny Beernsten, the rape victim who incorrectly identified Steven Avery as her rapist, before DNA testing proved that her attacker was actually Gregory Allen, described this phenomenon well: "I've seen a picture of Gregory Allen and he doesn't look real to me. I would swear I've never seen him before in my life. I look at his picture, I can't feel angry, I think he could walk in the room and my blood pressure wouldn't even go up. I still see Steven Avery as my assailant."[37]

Ronald Cotton

Jennifer Thompson was a twenty-two-year-old college student in North Carolina when, on July 28, 1984, a man broke into her house and raped her.[38] During the half-hour she spent with her attacker, she took great pains to study and memorize his face. The detective in charge of the case later recalled that Jennifer's first comment when she arrived at the police station was, "I'm gonna get this guy who did this to me. I took the time to look at him and I will be able to identify him if given an opportunity."

She was shown a photo lineup and selected the photo of a young man named Ronald Cotton. A few days later, she also identified Cotton from a live lineup. The detective told her that Cotton was the same man she had selected from the photo lineup. Later, Jennifer explained that when she heard this she felt a sense of relief. "Bingo . . . I did it right . . . I did it right," she thought to herself. She subsequently testified with certainty and confidence at Cotton's trial. And, of course, Cotton was convicted.[39]

After Cotton went to prison, he saw another inmate who looked like the composite sketch Jennifer had made of her attacker after the rape. He was in for rape. Cotton approached the inmate, who he later learned was Bobby Poole, and asked him where he was from. Poole said that he was from the same town in North Carolina as Jennifer and Cotton. Cotton's lawyers later won a new trial so that they could argue that Bobby Poole, a known rapist from the same area, was the actual perpetrator. At the new trial, Poole was brought into the courtroom for Jennifer to view. She stated that she had never seen Poole in her life. She later recounted that she felt intense anger at the defense—"How dare you question me. How dare you paint me as someone who could have forgotten what my rapist looked like—the one person you would never forget." Ronald Cotton was convicted again, and this time he was given two life sentences.

Seven years later, back in prison, Cotton was listening on his radio to the O.J. Simpson trial, and he learned about DNA testing. He wrote to his lawyer, saying he wanted DNA testing in his case. The testing proved what he had been maintaining all along: not only was he innocent, but Jennifer Thompson's rapist was Bobby Poole. Cotton was released after serving ten years in prison for a rape he didn't commit.

Thompson, when she learned the news, was initially incredulous. But eventually she accepted the truth, saying that she felt "suffocating, debilitating shame." But, like Penny Beernsten, when she thought or dreamed about the rape, she still saw the face of the wrongly convicted man. Her false memory of Cotton had been contaminated and then reconfirmed for so many years that it couldn't be easily broken. The memory expert Dr. Elizabeth Loftus later explained on a *60 Minutes* episode about the Cotton case that once an eyewitness like Jennifer or Penny picks an innocent suspect, that face replaces the face of the attacker in the eyewitness's memory.[40] It is now a false memory, and one very hard to ever shake.

Jennifer ultimately asked to meet Cotton, to whom she apologized, and a friendship eventually developed between the two. Together, Jennifer and Ronald wrote the book *Picking Cotton*, which became a *New York Times* bestseller.

But Jennifer and Penny, both of whom openly acknowledged their mistakes, are the exception rather than the rule. In my experience, eyewitnesses—and police and prosecutors—are often unable to ever fully embrace the truth that their mistake may have put an innocent man in prison. The witness's false memory, now hardened by time, confirmation bias, and repeated confirmatory feedback, and a desire to avoid coming to terms with their error, often causes the witness to dig in deeper. This is, of course, a natural human reaction. In fact, Jennifer later stated that when she saw Bobby Poole in the courtroom at the second trial, there wasn't even a "flicker" of recognition, so hardened was her false memory of Cotton. Jennifer once told me that memory is not like beef stew, where you can pick out and separate the potatoes, carrots, and beef, but more like beef stew after it's been put through a blender. Once memory is contaminated, you can't tell which recalled memories are real, and which ones are the result of outside influences and other forces. Just like beef stew put through a blender, it can never be put back together as it was.

Knowing what I now know about human memory, I think it was naïve of Ronald Cotton's lawyers to think that when they brought Bobby Poole before Jennifer Thompson during the second trial there was any chance that Jennifer would say, "Oh, that's him. I made a mistake." It would virtually never happen. And it only happened later in Cotton's case because of the DNA testing that conclusively matched Bobby Poole, and the remarkable courage, open-mindedness, and humility of Jennifer Thompson.

Damon Thibodeaux

In 1997, Damon Thibodeaux falsely confessed to the rape and murder of his fourteen-year-old stepcousin, Chrystal Champagne.[41] Champagne had gone missing on July 19, 1996, and her body was found the following evening along a levee in Bridge City, Louisiana. She had been strangled and badly beaten, as well as partially disrobed, leading investigators to believe that she had been sexually assaulted.[42]

Damon was one of many people questioned about Chrystal's death the day after the murder. At first, Damon denied involvement and agreed to take a polygraph test. Afterward, he was told that he had failed. He was interrogated for eight and a half hours, less than an hour of which was recorded.[43] Eventually, he gave the police a detailed false confession by incorporating crime facts he had learned from them during the interrogation.[44] He was then arrested and charged.

Following his arrest, two eyewitnesses came forward claiming that they had seen a man pacing near the levee the day of Chrystal's murder. The eyewitnesses identified Damon in a photo array and then in court at trial.[45] Damon was convicted of capital murder and rape on the basis of the eyewitness identifications and his confession. He received the death penalty.[46]

A decade later, the Innocence Project and the Jefferson Parish District Attorney's Office joined forces to reinvestigate Damon's case.[47] After a five-year investigation they jointly reached the conclusion that Damon's confession was false and that he had been misidentified by the eyewitnesses who testified at his trial.[48]

Why did they misidentify Damon? Prior to identifying him from a photo array, both witnesses had viewed his photograph on television during a news segment that identified him as the alleged culprit.[49] As Elizabeth Loftus explained on the *60 Minutes* episode about the Cotton case, witness identifications are easily contaminated by prior exposure to a suspect's image in a news segment. After seeing Damon's picture on television, their memories were altered, and they replaced the face of the man they'd seen with Damon's face without even knowing it.

Damon's confession was determined to be entirely false, a conclusion supported by common sense, logic, and DNA evidence. Nearly everything in his statement was at odds with the rest of the case.[50] Damon's descriptions of the crime did not match the crime scene and conflicted with other evidence.[51] Furthermore, while none of the DNA found at the scene belonged to Damon, the DNA of an unknown male was discovered on the cord used to strangle the victim.[52] The DNA tests also disproved the theory that the victim had been sexually assaulted.[53]

In September 2012, a Louisiana state judge vacated Thibodeaux's conviction, and he was released after sixteen years of incarceration, fifteen on death row. He was the three hundredth person in the United States to be proven innocent through DNA testing.[54]

FALSE MEMORIES AND FALSE CONFESSIONS

False confessions are another leading cause of wrongful convictions, and perhaps, at first glance, the most counterintuitive. Of the first 325 DNA exonerations in the United States, 88 cases, or 27 percent, involved a false confession by an innocent defendant.[55] Of the more than two thousand wrongful convictions identified by the National Registry of Exonerations, 12 percent involved a false confession by an innocent defendant.[56]

Psychologists have identified three types of false confessions. Voluntary false confessions occur when, without any police prompting, an innocent person decides to falsely confess to a crime he or she didn't commit. These cases usually involve the mentally ill. A typical scenario can be found in the U.S. Supreme Court case *Colorado v. Connelly*,[57] where a mentally ill man walked up to a Denver police officer and out of the blue confessed to a murder. Another example, one that received national media attention in the 1990s, is the voluntary false confession of John Mark Karr for the murder of child beauty pageant queen JonBenet Ramsey.[58]

Coerced-compliant false confessions occur when a suspect falsely confesses to a crime under police pressure despite knowing he is innocent and without constructing false memories during the interrogation. This type of suspect usually confesses because extreme police interrogation tactics—for example, fabricated stories by the police that his DNA or fingerprints have been found at the scene—ultimately convince him that his situation is hopeless, that he will be convicted, and that the only way he can get the interrogation to end and minimize his punishment is to tell the interrogators what they want to hear. This type of confessor comes to rationally believe that confessing is his only option, the lesser of two evils. While many people believe they would never confess to a crime they didn't commit, this type of false confession occurs surprisingly often. An excellent discussion of coerced-compliant false confessions can be found in Dr. Richard Leo's book *Police Interrogation and American Justice*, and compelling examples can be found in Tom Wells and Richard Leo's book *The Wrong Guys* and John Grisham's *The Innocent Man*.[59] The documentary film *The Central Park Five*, which recounts the false confessions of five boys who were falsely convicted of the violent rape and assault of a female runner in the "Central Park jogger case," provides another excellent account of coerced-compliant false confessions.[60]

The third category of false confessions, coerced-internalized ones, occurs when suspects come to actually believe, as a result of police pressure, that they committed a crime they did not commit.[61] The police pressure makes them doubt their memories, and they ultimately start to "remember" the crime, constructing the facts from information supplied by the police. The false confession expert Dr. Saul Kassin writes that "coerced-*internalized* false confessions are statements made by an innocent but vulnerable person who, as a result of exposure to highly suggestive and misleading interrogation tactics, comes to believe that he or she may have committed the crime—a belief that is sometimes supplemented by false memories."[62]

I have had two innocent clients who falsely confessed in this last way, but both involved special circumstances that make them atypical. Chris Bennett, discussed earlier, was convicted of vehicular manslaughter after the police charged him with being the intoxicated driver in an accident that killed Chris's best friend. But Chris suffered a head injury in the crash and was diagnosed with amnesia. He could not remember anything about the crash, or the events preceding it, including whether or not he had been driving. He came to believe from the police officers and others who told him that he had been the driver, however, that he must have been the driver, and he agreed to plead guilty. Later, in prison, Chris's memory started to return in snippets, and he eventually realized that his deceased friend had been driving and that he had been in the front passenger seat. Through DNA testing of the bloodstains left by the impact of the occupants on the windshield, and the discovery of a new witness who placed Chris in the passenger's seat, we were able to get Chris's conviction overturned, and he was freed after four years in prison.

Ohio Innocence Project client Glenn Tinney was exonerated after being convicted due to a false confession of murdering a waterbed salesman in his store. But Tinney is severely mentally ill, which caused him to crumble under police questioning and believe what they were telling him rather easily.

SEVENTY PERCENT OF COLLEGE STUDENTS
CONSTRUCT DETAILED, FALSE MEMORIES
OF CRIMES THEY DIDN'T COMMIT

Before you say, "I would never confess to a serious crime I didn't commit," consider this. In 2015, psychology professors in Canada, simulating typical interrogation methods used by the police, got 70 percent of their college student subjects to create false memories of having committed an assault, assault with a weapon, or theft that was entirely fictitious.[63]

The researchers contacted each of the seventy subjects' parents or other prior caregivers to confirm that none of the subjects had ever been arrested or had any sort of criminal background. They also obtained details about a true event that had happened to each subject between the ages of eleven and fourteen. In the first interview with them, the researchers told the subjects that they were studying memory-retrieval methods, and asked the subjects to recall two events that happened to them between the ages of eleven and fourteen. Subjects were told that the researchers had learned about both events from interviewing their caregivers. Unbeknownst to the subjects, the second event was a false story of having committed a crime that had been manufactured by the researchers.

In the first round of interviews, the subjects generally could recall the true event but none could recall the false story about having committed a crime. Before leaving, each subject was told that if they tried hard enough, they could remember details about the criminal activity, and they were asked to try visualizing the crime each night before coming back for the second interview.

In the second and third interviews, researchers employed tactics commonly used by the police in interrogations. They told the subjects that there was incontrovertible proof that they had committed the crime, in the form of detailed statements about the crime from their caregivers, and that "most people are able to retrieve lost memories if they try hard enough." The researchers mentioned "facts" that would make the subjects believe the researchers knew intimate details about their crime, like the name of a friend who they had allegedly committed it with, and a specific, familiar location in their hometown where the crime allegedly occurred.

By the third interview, the vast majority of the college students admitted that they had committed the crime, and were able to tell a detailed story about how they did it. Yet their stories were all based on constructed false memories of facts that had been supplied by their interrogators. At the end of the process, the subjects were asked if they truly believed they had committed the crime or whether they had merely gone along with what the interrogator told them without really believing it. Seventy percent reported that through the memory-retrieval process employed by the researchers they had retrieved a true memory, and now believed that they had committed the crime.

The psychologists who performed this experiment concluded: "This study provides evidence that people can come to visualize and recall detailed false memories of engaging in criminal behavior. Not only could the young adults in our sample be led to generate such memories, but their rate of false recollection was high, and the memories themselves were highly detailed. Additionally, false memories for perpetrating crime showed signs that they may have been generated in a way that is similar to the way in which memories for noncriminal emotional memories are generated. False memories for committing crime also share many characteristics with true memories."[64] Dr. Saul Kassin notes that police interrogators create an atmosphere conducive to false memory construction—far more intense than the atmosphere created in this study—by "exhibiting strong and unwavering certainty about the suspect's guilt, isolating the suspect from all familiar social contacts and outside sources of information, conducting sessions that are lengthy and emotionally intense, presenting false but allegedly incontrovertible proof of the suspect's guilt, offering the suspect a ready physical or psychological explanation for why he or she does not remember the crime, and applying implicit and explicit pressure on the suspect, in the form of promises and threats, to comply with the demand for a confession."[65] An interrogation conducted in such an intense manner, for a lengthy period of time, can produce a "trance-like state of heightened suggestibility" so that "truth and falsehood become hopelessly confused in the suspect's mind."[66]

Peter Reilly

Young Peter Reilly came to believe, through such police pressure, that he committed a crime he didn't commit. One night in September 1973, his mother, Barbara Reilly, was brutally beaten and stabbed to death in her home.[67] Three hours after discovering her body, Peter, eighteen, was hauled off to the police station for questioning. An eight-hour interrogation consisting of four rotating officers moved him from denial to confusion and self-doubt, and finally to acceptance of his alleged culpability. Reilly ultimately confessed to his mother's murder. He had become convinced of his guilt.

Years later, Reilly, speaking at a conference, explained a bit disjointedly what led to his false confession:

To be kept awake for many hours, confused, fatigued, shocked that your only family was gone, in a strange and imposing place, surrounded by police who continue to tell you that you must have done this horrible thing and that nobody cares or has asked about you . . . assured by authorities you don't remember things, being led to doubt your own memory, having things suggested to you only to have those things pop up in a conversation a short time later but from your own lips . . . under these conditions you would say and sign anything they wanted.[68]

Reilly served two years in prison before his conviction was tossed. His mother's murder remains unsolved.

Michael Crowe

Michael Crowe was only fourteen years old when overzealous detectives persuaded him that he had killed his younger sister.[69] On January 21, 1998, twelve-year-old Stephanie Crowe was found murdered in her bedroom in San Diego. Michael eventually confessed to the killing after a series of brutal interrogations. He at first adamantly maintained his innocence—which would later be proven through DNA testing—but by the end of his final interrogation, he was convinced of his guilt. His belief persisted for two weeks while Michael was held in juvenile hall awaiting trial. But by the end of the two weeks, he had come to realize that he had falsely confessed to a crime he did not commit.

Michael, too, had been told he failed a lie-detection test and that there was evidence implicating him in the crime. To help him reconcile his memory with the events envisioned by the police, the interrogating officers suggested that he had a split personality. The so-called bad Michael murdered his sister but the good Michael could not remember bad Michael's actions. The officers then pushed Michael into a corner, insisting that if he had not committed the crime someone else in his family did. Faced with no option but to accept guilt or lay blame on a family member, Michael confessed. "You keep asking me questions I can't answer," he said at one point. "I'm not sure how I did it. All I know is I did it . . . I don't remember details."

After being charged and arrested, Michael spoke to his parents on the phone from juvenile hall, admitting that he must have committed the crime. But his parents never believed it.

Before the case could reach trial, the charges against Michael were dropped. The DNA testing proved that the perpetrator was a mentally-ill drifter named Richard Tuite. Tuite was tried and convicted of manslaughter in 2006.

Bill Wayne Cope

In 2001, Billy Wayne Cope falsely confessed to the murder and sexual assault of his twelve-year-old daughter, Amanda, after police convinced him of his guilt as well. He had denied killing his daughter more than 650 times.[70] But after police berated him unmercifully and told him he had failed a lie-detector test, he confessed. Cope had come to believe that the police were right.

At trial and after retracting his confession, Cope testified that the supposed polygraph results had caused him to distrust his memory:[71]

> I started to doubt myself . . . I thought I knew better. I thought I knew different and I knew that I didn't do nothing to Amanda. But then he kept saying . . . Mr. Cope, you did and even pictures don't lie. . . .
>
> [I] started to formulate all these images in my head . . . I started to doubt myself. I felt weak. I felt maybe I did . . . I really did not know. . . . And I started to doubt everything that I had been telling him. I felt vulnerable. I listened to what he said. I trusted the machine. It said I was a liar. . . .

Cope was so convinced that he had committed the crime, he felt relief upon confessing: "I truly did. I thought I had done it . . . I was relieved I had gotten it out and now my daughter's death could be avenged . . . I was glad to get . . . the images out of my head." Although semen and saliva collected from the crime scene matched the DNA profile of a local sex offender named James Sanders, as of 2017 Cope remains in prison and continues to fight his conviction today.[72]

SYNTHESIZED TESTIMONY

Criminal investigations and prosecutions often rely for their success on altered witness memories that have been subtly changed by police and prosecutors. This pernicious problem has not received as much attention as it deserves.

When I became a prosecutor, I learned that it was common for the various witnesses to a crime to have contradictory stories of what happened. Some witnesses might give statements helpful to the prosecution, and others might give statements helpful to the defense. Through leading questions, we would often "correct" the statements of witnesses helpful to the defense so that they were more in line with our theory of the case. For example, if the crime happened at 11:00 P.M., and a witness said the suspect left the bar at 10:30 P.M. and returned at 11:30 P.M., we would "test" the memory of a second witness who claimed that the suspect was in the bar at 11:00 (thereby providing the suspect with an alibi) by grilling him on what we believed was his "obviously faulty" memory. Through our questioning, and even sometimes our implicit hints that other witnesses or other evidence contradicted him, his statement would often change. Indeed, it doesn't take much in the way of repeated questioning and exasperated responses for a witness to get the message that his memory on a certain point must be wrong, and that he ought to dig deeper and think about it some more. And the "correct" answer was always obvious from our questioning.

Eventually, the witness might come to say, "You know, the more I think about it, you're probably right. He probably left earlier than that." He then might suddenly "remember" that the football game playing on the bar's TV ended around 11:00, and that the suspect had certainly left well before the end of the game. By the time this witness testified at trial, he might be certain that the witness left the bar at 10:30, before the end of the game, and that he didn't return until much later. And if the witness had earlier said that he noticed nothing out of the ordinary about the suspect when he returned to the bar, with enough pointed questions he might eventually agree that the suspect appeared disheveled, distracted, or agitated when he got back. These are very helpful statements for a prosecutor who thinks that the suspect committed a murder before he returned to the bar.

Psychologist Dan Simon calls this "synthesized testimony."[73] Two factors contribute to it. First, witnesses often want to please law enforcement and help the police catch the "bad guy." If they pick up from the questioning what the police want them to say, and what the "right" answer is, some witnesses are apt to assume they are wrong and to go along with what the police think happened. When I was a prosecutor, I recall an FBI agent coming back from a witness interview that had taken place at the witness's home. I asked him, "How'd it go? Did he tell us what we expected?" The FBI agent answered, "He's a buff." I asked what that meant. He said, "We get these people who are big FBI fans—buffs. And they're so excited when an FBI agent knocks on their door that they tend to cooperate and give us whatever we want." I imagine the same holds true, albeit perhaps to a lesser degree, when any kind of detective or official investigator knocks on the door of a law-enforcement buff.

Second, memories, as we've discussed, are quite malleable. Thus, witnesses can be made to question their memories, and then ultimately adopt, and even come to believe, a statement that is quite different from their original statement. Based on my experience as a prosecutor, and what I have seen as an innocence lawyer, I know that synthesized testimony is a common occurrence in our criminal justice system. And it's not only inappropriate, but it can lead to wrongful convictions.

When we engaged in this practice in my prosecutor's office, we didn't feel we were unethically altering witness testimony. Because of tunnel vision, cognitive dissonance, and other human factors, we were always certain that we *knew* what had happened, even though of course we weren't there when the crime happened. There was never a doubt in our minds that we had the right guy. So if a witness suddenly uttered that the suspect was still in the bar at 11:00 P.M., and that didn't fit with what we knew, then this witness *had* to be wrong. And it was our job to help him remember correctly. After all, it would be an outrage for a suspect to get off scot-free because of the sloppy recollection of a single witness who obviously wasn't paying close attention, or was not trying hard enough to remember correctly, and who spouted answers to our questions before really thinking them through. By prodding the witness on points that he was "obviously" wrong about, we were helping him make his testimony more accurate and truthful, we believed. Or so we told ourselves.

In fact, when I was hired as a prosecutor, one of the first things I was told was not to write down the parts of a witness's statements that I believed were incorrect until he had "come to Jesus" and told the "truth." If we wrote down an early version of the witness's recollection when he still might be "confused," it would later have to be turned over to the defense attorney, and that witness would be torn apart on cross-examination for changing his story. The defense attorney might even suggest to the jury that we had told the witness what to say and coaxed him into changing his story. That, of course, is arguably what we had done in reality, but we didn't see it that way.

So we considered a witness's initial answers to our questions, if they were incorrect, to be preliminary thoughts or off-hand comments. A statement was not an official "statement" that needed to be written down until the witness had time to collect his thoughts, hear our questions and prodding, had time to focus, and get his memory straightened out. Once he had "come to Jesus" and given us what we wanted to hear, then the statement became official, and could be written down. After that, if we were worried about the witness wavering or going back to his original story at trial, we would have him testify in the grand jury to "lock in" the statements that were helpful to us. Indeed, after a witness has testified in the grand jury under oath, there's no going back. If he tries to change his story later, we can remind him that he already testified to the contrary under oath, and thus that changing his story could result in a perjury prosecution. "Locking in" witness statements was so common that everyone knew what you meant when you said, "I'm going to put this witness in the grand jury to lock him in."

What I was taught is, apparently, not uncommon in prosecutors' offices around the country. A survey of federal prosecutors nationwide found that it is "office lore" in many places not to "take notes until you have enough of the truth."[74] Its status remains as "office lore" because a prosecutor's office could never enact this practice as an official policy and put it in writing (as it violates the constitutional *Brady* doctrine!).

As Dan Simon has expressed:

> Courtroom testimony is usually proffered months, sometimes years, following the criminal event. Moreover, the investigation itself can induce erroneous testimony. Over the course of the investigation and preparation for the adversarial contest, the evidence often undergoes editing, embellishment, and alteration. Thus, by the time the memorial account is presented at trial, it has both decayed and been subjected to conditions that are conducive to contamination. The transformation of evidence also guts some of the traces of accuracy that occasionally accompany the testimony. Determining the facts accurately from this *synthesized evidence* is a daunting task. This is one of the most serious impediments to accurate factfinding in the criminal justice process.[75]

I was also told when I started as a prosecutor not to make the various witness statements *too* in line with one another. If we did, it would give the defense attorney ammunition at trial to claim that we were telling the witnesses what to say. So we would intentionally include in our notes incorrect information supplied by the witnesses on minor points—points that didn't matter to the case—to show that we weren't coaching them. If an accusation of coaching was made at trial, we could point to these discrepancies and say, "See, they didn't all tell the same story—look at these differences! If we were telling them what to say, their stories would all be the same."

While the vast majority of the time we probably *were* dealing with guilty suspects and helping witnesses "correct" faulty memories or initial attempts to hide the truth, this practice manufactures evidence and can lead to wrongful convictions in cases where the suspect truly is innocent. And if such a questioning process did help a witness remember more accurately, the change in story should be disclosed to the defense attorney so that she can question the witness about it on cross-examination. If the change was innocent, the witness should have to explain as much to the jury.

When I say "we" did this in my prosecutor's office, I cannot speak for every prosecutor. There was no office-wide training on these issues, and no official policy. Rather, each new prosecutor learned the customs and practices from the senior prosecutors who were assigned to supervise them, and to "second chair" or mentor them during their first three jury trials. It was "office lore." And I at times did it myself, convinced that I was doing the right thing by helping witnesses to properly refresh their memories. But, again, I cannot speak for every single prosecutor in the office, although I believe this practice was fairly widespread.

When I look back on the cases of the individuals the Ohio Innocence Project has exonerated and freed, I am struck by my first meetings with my clients in prison—before we had the evidence proving them innocent. A common comment I heard from them in these initial meetings was, "How did the prosecution get the witnesses to say all these things that weren't true?" My client Clarence Elkins was wrongfully convicted of killing and raping his mother-in-law and assaulting and raping his niece. When I first met him in prison, he said, "They took all these innocent interactions I had with my mother-in-law before she was murdered and made them look sinister. Witnesses testified that at certain parties and gatherings I had appeared angry with her, and I had said hateful things to her. But I was in a good mood at those parties. I wasn't angry with her at all. That stuff didn't happen." Other innocent clients reported similar occurrences. Another client told me that witnesses testified at his trial that he was angry with the victim at a child's birthday party shortly before she was murdered, and that he left in a huff. But in reality he had been in a good mood at the party and nothing like that had actually occurred. Rather than leaving early in a huff, he'd even stayed late after the birthday party to help clean up.

Now that we know these clients are innocent and were wrongfully convicted on false evidence, it is easy for me to see how such testimony may have been synthesized. After a murder has occurred, and the community is outraged and filled with hatred toward the person the police think did it, it is not a stretch for witnesses to suddenly "remember" social interactions in a way that favors the prosecution's case. Particularly when the police are asking them pointed questions suggesting the "correct" answer. Just as all the family members in Sarah Polley's film *The Stories We Tell* remembered social interactions in a way that confirmed their beliefs about whether or not her mother had an affair, witnesses to criminal activity often fall prey to memory alterations when they're asked by the police, "Was he angry with her or did he act strange toward her at all in the weeks leading up to the murder? Are you sure? Think hard."

My office represented Dewey Jones, who was eventually exonerated by DNA evidence and freed after spending nineteen years in prison for a murder he didn't commit. At trial, several witnesses identified Jones as the culprit, but only after their statements had been synthesized or manufactured by the police. Robert Strittmatter, for example, testified at trial that he had seen Jones standing outside the victim's house on the day he was murdered. What the jury didn't hear, however, was that Strittmatter had made multiple contradictory statements before eventually identifying Jones. Indeed, when first interviewed by the police, Strittmatter said that he knew Dewey as a frequent visitor to the victim's house but that Dewey was *not* the man whom he saw outside the victim's house on the day of the murder. When shown a photo lineup, Strittmatter selected the picture of a man named Terry Bowers as that man. Shortly after the first interview, the police went to Strittmatter's house again, this time with thirty photographs, including a photo of Dewey. This time, Strittmatter selected the photo of a man named Bill Wilson as the man he saw outside the victim's house that day. He also picked up the photo of Dewey and said that he knew Dewey as a frequent visitor to the victim's house, but that it wasn't Dewey whom he saw on the day of the murder.

Several weeks later, the police went to Strittmatter's house again to talk about the murder. They brought up Dewey Jones as a suspect again. But Strittmatter continued to insist that Bill Wilson was the man he had seen outside the victim's house, and again stated that it wasn't Dewey Jones. A few months later, the police returned to Strittmatter's house with a five-person photo lineup that included a picture of Jones. Strittmatter again stated that he recognized Dewey as a man who frequented the victim's house, but that Dewey wasn't the man he had seen on the day of the murder. The police then showed Strittmatter a single photo of Jones, and Strittmatter finally gave them the answer they had been looking for—that Dewey was the man outside the victim's house on the day of the murder. Later, the police returned to Strittmatter's house with a new photo array that contained Dewey's picture, and Strittmatter formally identified Dewey again and signed the photo lineup with his selection.

Another eyewitness, Charles Hughley, received similar "corrections" from the police. Hughley first identified a man named Larry Hayes from a photo lineup, but after repeated attempts by police to get him to identify Jones, he eventually succumbed and identified Jones.

None of these discrepancies came out at trial. Why? Because the police reports containing the witnesses' prior statements had been improperly hidden from Jones's defense attorney. We found out about them only years later, after Dewey had already spent nearly two decades in prison.

It is interesting to me that the early, inconvenient versions of Strittmatter's and Hughley's statements were even written down by the police, since early versions of statements are often not written down if they are not helpful to the prosecution. Although the jury didn't know how the police had manufactured a case against Dewey through synthesized testimony, we fortunately found the reports years later and were able to exonerate him with these reports and the results of DNA testing on the crime scene evidence.

. . .

In a study in 2016,[76] researchers set out to determine whether witnesses could be made to falsely accuse others through a typical police interrogation process. Thirty college student subjects signed up to take what they believed would be a logic test. When they arrived, one at a time, they were placed in a room with another person, who was unknown to the subject and who was also set to take the same test. After the administrator distributed the tests and provided basic instructions, she left the room. A few minutes later, she returned and told the test takers that she had left her cell phone in the room, and she asked if either had seen it. In reality, the administrator never even had a cell phone.

Later, the subjects were interrogated for thirty minutes about the missing cell phone. Interrogators told the subjects that the other test taker had stolen the phone and that they needed the subject to cooperate and tell what they saw. Pressures typical during police interrogations were used on the subjects, such as expressing disbelief when the subject stated he had not seen the cell phone, and in some instances the administrators interrogating them even threatened the subjects with disciplinary action at their universities if they did not cooperate. After only thirty minutes of such discussion, five of the thirty college students stated that they had seen the other test taker steal the cell phone. Each of the five even provided a narrative story about what they had witnessed.[77]

If five out of thirty college students will make up a false story—a complete fabrication, concocted out of whole cloth—to implicate an innocent person under such prodding in an experimental setting after only thirty minutes, it's not hard to understand how a much higher percentage might be willing to blur a few edges when it comes to helping the police catch someone they think is a dangerous criminal. And when dealing with more subjective and ambiguous details, such as what time the suspect returned to the bar, or whether he appeared shaken up or agitated when he returned, malleable memories begin to play a bigger role. When a police officer asks enough times, "Are you sure he didn't appear agitated or angry?" and the witness grasps what the officer wants and adopts the statement, the witness often believes it by the time he testifies at trial.

Another recent study also demonstrates how synthesized testimony can be elicited through supplied information.[78] In this study, subjects were left alone in a room with another person, who was a confederate of the researchers, and asked to perform some tasks with this person. The purported purpose of the experiment was to study human problem-solving abilities when working alone versus when working in pairs. While the pair were working together, several $20 bills were visible in an open moneybox sitting on a desk in the room. After working on tasks together for a while, the pair were moved to another side of the room behind a cubicle wall, and asked to perform tasks individually. From that point on they could no longer see the money.

A short while after the subjects were moved, they were informed that, after they had moved behind the cubicle wall, the cash had been stolen. Because the subjects were together at all times behind the cubicle wall, however, and could either see or hear each other at all times (the confederates in the study had been told to shuffle papers or otherwise make noise when they were not in the subject's line of vision), the subjects theoretically should have been able to provide an alibi for the participants and vice versa.

As expected, when interviewed by the researchers, more than 90 percent of the subjects initially provided an alibi for the confederate they were paired with, stating that they could see or hear the confederate at all times and that this person could not have returned to the other side of the room and stolen the money. But upon being shown an "incident report," which said that the confederate had confessed to stealing the money, but had then recanted his or her confession and claimed he or she was innocent, 55 percent of the subjects who initially provided an alibi backed off their alibi (even though the alibi was true) and were no longer willing to assert that the confederate remained behind the cubicle wall at all times. When the researchers went a bit further and exerted some pressure on the subjects, by suggesting that they could be implicated in the theft if they continued to "cover" for the confederate, 80 percent of the subjects backed off their alibi.

Subjects in this experiment who abandoned their alibi statement reported that they believed in the guilt of their partner, and questioned their own memories, once they learned of his confession.

This study shows, again, the extent to which witness statements, and often their memories, can be influenced by how they are questioned and what they are told during an investigation. The results of this experiment comport with my own experience as a prosecutor, having seen witnesses frequently change their testimonies in response to pointed law-enforcement questioning. And I believe that most of the time when this occurs, the witnesses end up believing their new statements, either as soon as they utter them or, at a minimum, by the time they testify later at trial.

Synthesized testimony was apparent in the docu-series *Making a Murderer* with respect to the case against Steven Avery for the murder of Teresa Halbach. According to police reports, a young man named Michael Osmundson told the police during the initial investigation that, after it became public that Halbach was missing, he and Avery's nephew Bobby Dassey had joked with Avery about whether Avery had Halbach locked in a closet somewhere, and that Avery joked back that he needed help hiding a body. If this conversation occurred, it was crude and insensitive but would not be considered incriminating since it was known publicly by that point that Halbach was missing and had possibly been abducted and killed.

At Avery's trial, however, prosecutor Ken Kratz did not call Osmundson to testify, but instead called Bobby Dassey. In response to leading questions from Kratz, Dassey agreed with Kratz that Avery was the one who brought up the subject of Halbach's disappearance—by asking Dassey and Osmundson if they could help him hide her body. Dassey further testified, or rather agreed with Kratz's leading questions, that this conversation occurred a week earlier than what Osmundson had told the police. The date of the conversation was crucial, because Dassey's version placed the conversation at a time when it was not yet publicly known that Halbach was missing. If Dassey's testimony were true, it would be highly incriminating evidence against Avery, because only the murderer would have known at that point that Halbach was missing and dead.

At a press conference following Dassey's testimony, reporters expressed shock that Dassey had given testimony that contradicted the only police report on the matter. They accused prosecutor Kratz of suggesting the date of the conversation in his questions to Dassey in a leading fashion, rather than letting Dassey answer the questions on his own. They also asked Kratz why there were no police reports backing up Dassey's testimony, and how Kratz was able to obtain such incriminating testimony on the eve of trial. Kratz responded that Dassey provided the incriminating date and details of the conversation during a pretrial preparation session only a few days before the trial. In response, the reporters expressed concern because the leading way in which Kratz had directed Dassey to the "correct" date at trial raised serious questions as to whether Kratz had put words in Dassey's mouth—in other words, whether he had synthesized Dassey's testimony on this point. Given what I routinely saw as a prosecutor, and the leading way Kratz questioned Dassey at trial, I share the reporters' concerns.

THE PUBLIC'S MISCONCEPTION OF MEMORY

The public believes that memory is reliable. When an eyewitness testifies that she is positive the man on trial is the man who raped her, jurors tend to think, "Why would she lie? What does she have to gain by lying? She was there. She would know." And when the prosecution introduces evidence that the defendant confessed to murder, and signed a written confession, jurors think, "Why would he confess to murder if he didn't do it? I would never do that unless it was true. There's no way."

In a survey of prospective jurors in Washington DC, three-quarters reported that their memories were "excellent."[79] My guess is that the quarter who admitted to not having a perfect memory did so because they are aware of being forgetful at times, *not* that they think they have false or inaccurate memories of events they actually remember. And almost half of those taking the survey agreed with the statement that memory is like a tape recorder that can be recalled as if it had been "imprinted or burned onto one's brain." Again, I suspect that those who disagreed with this statement did so because they acknowledge that they are forgetful, but they are unaware of the malleability of their own memories and the extent to which they likely hold false memories of their own lives. Police officers have given similar responses about human memory. A survey of British police officers found that three-quarters believed that eyewitnesses are rarely wrong.[80]

Even judges are often ignorant of the problem. In several of my cases involving false confessions, judges have made comments like, "Why in the world would he confess if he didn't do it?" Comments like this serve as an important reminder of the work that needs to be done to get the judicial system to understand modern advances in memory science.

The public reacts with scorn when someone in the public spotlight is exposed as having a false memory, as if their error must have been intentional. NBC news anchor Brian Williams had a false memory of being in a helicopter that was shot down when he covered the war in Iraq. The public reacted with outrage, and he was suspended for sixth months for the transgression.[81] Mitt Romney, a presidential candidate in 2012, got in trouble for claiming on the campaign trail that he vividly remembered when he was four or five years old attending the "Global Jubilee," when three-quarters of a million people gathered to celebrate the fiftieth anniversary of the automobile.[82] The event was notorious because it was the last public appearance of Henry Ford. The problem, however, was that Mitt Romney had not yet been born when this event occurred. Romney's running mate, Paul Ryan, got in similar hot water for claiming that he had once run a marathon in less than three hours.[83] He later explained that his memory had simply failed him. But both were lambasted for their memory transgressions.

President George W. Bush gave three contradictory accounts as to how he learned of the 9/11 terrorist attacks. He even claimed to have seen television coverage of the plane hitting the first tower at the World Trade Center at a point in the day when no footage of it yet existed, even for the president.[84]

Misattribution about where you were, or what you were doing, when you learned of a famous event, such as the Pearl Harbor attack, the Kennedy assassination, or the Challenger space shuttle explosion, is actually quite common and called a false "flashbulb memory." My sister recently recounted a vivid memory of when she lived in a particular home for several years in the 1990s. She woke up one morning, put on her bathrobe, and retrieved the newspaper on her doorstep, only to learn that Princess Diana had died the night before in an automobile accident. When we argued over what year it was that Princess Diana had died and then looked it up to resolve the dispute, she realized she had been wrong and that, in fact, she no longer lived in that particular home on the date Princess Diana died. Even after knowing that she had experienced a false flashbulb memory, when she thought about learning of Princess Di's death, she could picture only being in the home in which she was no longer living at that time.

Such is the terrible unreliability of human memory.

6. Blind Intuition

Our criminal justice system rests on the widespread belief that human intuition allows us to know when a witness is telling the truth or lying. As recently as 1998, the U.S. Supreme Court stated that it is a "fundamental premise" of our system that the "jury is the lie detector," and that "determining . . . the credibility of witness testimony" is the jury's job because they are "fitted for it" due to their "practical knowledge of men and the ways of men."[1] Accordingly, jurors are formally instructed in nearly every courtroom in America that detecting the truthfulness of witnesses is a primary—if not *the* primary—reason they are there. They are routinely told to analyze the "demeanor" of each witness on the stand and their "manner of testifying" to resolve who is lying and who is telling the truth, and to render a verdict accordingly.[2]

This belief that humans are lie detectors is not limited to the criminal justice system. Popular culture is saturated with supposed experts who analyze the demeanor of celebrities or politicians caught in scandals, and who opine with confidence as to whether the public statements of these notables demonstrate truthfulness or deceit. The American Amanda Knox, for example, gained international celebrity when she was wrongfully convicted and imprisoned for several years in Italy for allegedly murdering her roommate, only to be eventually exonerated by the Italian Supreme Court. After her first interviews on national television in the United States, which aired prior to her exoneration, "experts" lined up to analyze her facial movements and voice, and render opinions as to whether she was innocent or guilty.[3] When these supposed experts published their opinions in articles on the Internet, members of the public filled the comment boxes with their own strong opinions about whether or not Knox was telling the truth. These lay experts seemed supremely confident in their abilities to divine the truth from gestures like Knox's eye movements and the way she held her mouth when listening to a question. It was almost comical.

In the Steven Avery case, depicted in the Netflix docu-series *Making a Murderer*, a local Wisconsin politician decried the public support for Avery's possible innocence after the show aired, writing, "I will never forget the look in Steven Avery's eyes when he was being brought into the courthouse. . . . I know a person cannot be convicted based on that, but I made up my mind that day. Avery was guilty."[4] Wow.

Although the public and our judicial system have yet to recognize it, we now know that this confidence in human lie detection is misplaced. In reality, we are pretty bad at measuring truthfulness from watching another person's demeanor or listening to their voice as they recount their story. The things we accept as barometers of truthfulness, such as steady eye contact and confidence, are simply not good barometers. And things we accept as indicators of dishonesty—appearing nervous, fidgeting, a lack of eye contact, or a cracking voice—are not great indicators of lying. These are just notions we have been taught and have accepted as they have been handed down for centuries—folklore—that are now refuted both by new understandings of human psychology and by the simple facts about human error brought out through the innocence movement. While human intuition should not be completely ignored, it is not something that should ever be taken to the bank. We must fight hard against coming to conclusions based solely on "gut feelings" or intuition, or placing so much confidence in our intuition that it clouds our view of the objective facts.

I learned this lesson the hard way. One of my first cases as a prosecutor involved a bank robbery in which the FBI agents investigating the case believed that a particular teller had been involved. This teller had taken an extra $10,000 from the vault and placed it in her cash drawer shortly before the robbery occurred. When the robbers approached her teller station with guns drawn, she gave them all the money in her drawer, including the extra $10,000. When questioned after the robbery, she claimed that she had retrieved the $10,000 from the vault because a gentleman had come in a few minutes earlier to cash a $10,000 check but had forgotten his ID and said he would return a few minutes later to complete the transaction. The FBI agents found this answer suspicious, and from this fact alone concluded that this was an "inside job" and that the teller must have been involved in planning the robbery.

I was assigned the case, and for months the agents and I couldn't crack it. The teller was our only lead, as the robbers had been wearing masks, and so for months the agents dogged her. They brought her to the FBI headquarters over and over and aggressively interrogated her for hours each time. But she stuck to her story and never wavered. And she was convincing. I was present for one of these interviews, along with two interns who I brought along with me, where she started crying and pleading with the FBI agents to leave her alone and stop ruining her life through their constant harassment. She explained how the stress from their harassment had carried over to her family, and how her young son was now struggling in school because of his mother's stress and depression. Her gaze was steady. Her voice was sincere and emotional. She was adamant and confident. She seemed to me to be a woman clearly suffering badly from false accusations. I started feeling uneasy, and before long the two interns were staring at me as if to say, "I hope they leave this poor innocent woman alone." I was convinced by the end that she had nothing to do with the robbery.

The investigation went cold for several more months, until another woman was arrested on an unrelated charge. In order to work a deal, this woman told the arresting officers that she had information about my unsolved bank robbery case. When the FBI agents and I interviewed her, she said that her good friend—the bank teller—had been involved in the robbery. And, what's more, this woman had been present when the teller created the demand note used by the robbers by cutting letters out of a magazine and pasting them on a piece of paper. She claimed to be in the same circle of friends with the teller and the men who robbed the bank, and named all of the robbers. Sure enough, when we got the phone records of the teller and the men whom the woman had named as the robbers, we learned that the teller had called several of the men in succession on the morning of the robbery. We then arrested the men, and each of them told us the same story. They admitted their involvement, and said that it had been an "inside job" led by the teller, who had promised them that she would get a large amount of cash out of the vault before the robbery went down. She even told them the best time of day to rob the bank and where the guards would be standing. Eventually, the teller pled guilty to being an accomplice in the bank robbery and admitted her complete involvement.

I was stunned that I had been so convinced of her innocence. Her performance was Oscar-worthy.

My work as an innocence lawyer has taught me the same lesson, again and again. I have had inmates apply for help from the Ohio Innocence Project (OIP) who came across very convincingly in our prison interviews with them, only to be confirmed guilty later by DNA testing. In some cases, I have had inmates who were later confirmed guilty talk about their feelings of being wrongfully convicted, and the stages they have had to go through psychologically to cope with being in prison for crimes they didn't commit. Their stories sometimes mirrored the psychological reactions of the truly innocent I have represented, and were exceptionally convincing. But the DNA testing confirmed their guilt.

It goes the other way as well. I have had clients who appeared nervous and shifty during the interviews, and who had trouble making eye contact with me when telling me their stories of innocence. They acted guilty, or sometimes even "creepy" to the students accompanying me on the prison visits. They seemed like they were lying. Their voices cracked and wavered. But DNA testing proved them innocent.

I now tell my students working in the OIP that while their instincts about whether a witness is lying or telling the truth should not be totally disregarded, their gut reactions should never be viewed as very important factors in the overall investigation. Judge on the hard evidence, I tell them, not on demeanor. But this is a hard lesson for the students to learn. Our societal belief in our lie-detection abilities is so ingrained that I still sometimes find students slacking on a case when they have not been moved by the demeanor of the inmate claiming innocence, or telling me that they are going to keep working hard on a case that appears dead in the water because they met the inmate and "know" from his "vibe" that he is innocent. I remind them that you can't take your instincts to the bank. Humans are just not good lie detectors.

I routinely see stubborn arrogance from police and prosecutors about their lie-detection abilities. It is not uncommon for prosecutors or police to react with great indignation when they learn that the Ohio Innocence Project is investigating one of their old convictions. I can't count the number of times I have called prosecutors or police officers to ask for files or evidence in an old case, only to be told something like, "You've got to be kidding me. I was the one who met with the witnesses. I'm the one that looked into their eyes and heard their stories. They were telling the truth and were not mistaken. There is no doubt about it. You're barking up the wrong tree with *this* case, sir."

I recall attending a conference on innocence work in New Orleans and meeting a board member from an innocence organization in another state. She had been a prosecutor her entire career, and decided to volunteer for this organization after her recent retirement. We struck up a conversation over lunch, as I was interested in why she decided to "switch sides." I asked her if someone she convicted as a prosecutor had turned out to be innocent and whether that is what caused her to take up innocence work. She said no, quite the opposite. She reported that she believes in innocence work because she has come to accept that some people are wrongfully convicted in this country, but the one inmate from her prosecutor's office who had been exonerated and released by the innocence organization she now volunteered for was most definitely guilty despite being exonerated and released!

Curious, I asked her why she felt so strongly that this exoneree was actually guilty. She replied, "Because my friends who prosecuted the case—and even the judge—later told me after this woman was exonerated that they *knew* she was lying when she testified in her defense back in her original trial." She went on to express absolute confidence in the lie-detection abilities of her friends and the judge in the case, and made clear that this confidence outweighed all other evidence of innocence that surfaced later. I just listened, of course, and didn't bring up the research and facts demonstrating her faulty reasoning. Nor did I mention how confirmation bias—stemming from a belief from the beginning of the trial that the woman was guilty—likely clouded the perceptions of her prosecutor friends and the judge as they watched the woman's testimony that day in court many years earlier.

OIP client David Ayers was exonerated in 2011 and released after spending twelve years in prison for a murder he didn't commit. Later, in his civil suit for monetary damages against the Cleveland detectives who had arrested him, a detective took the stand and explained why she initially focused on Ayers as a suspect and eventually brought charges against him. Her testimony, which took place in 2013, was as startling as it was illuminating. Throughout her testimony, she made clear that the primary justification for her decision to pursue and charge Ayers was her unwavering belief, from her years of experience, that she can tell which suspects are lying and which ones are telling the truth. And she was certain that Ayers was lying and being evasive about nearly everything he said in her interviews with him. Her instincts told her this and apparently spoke to her loudly and clearly. And based on these infallible instincts, honed through years on the street as a detective, she claimed that she had never arrested an innocent person. She can tell from her intuition right away if a person is innocent, she claimed, and wouldn't waste her time on an innocent person. She believed she was a human lie detector with no rate of error.[5] It was that simple to her. Indeed, at one point in her testimony, when asked why she thought Ayers was guilty, she stated: "I'd bet my life on it. And take my word for it, my partner would bet his life on it. We've been doing homicides for thirteen years, thirteen years. I can pick out a killer in five minutes. I can tell talking to a person within two minutes whether they're lying to me. After thirteen years of doing hundreds and hundreds of homicides, I think I know what I'm doing."

Armed with strong evidence of Ayers's innocence, including DNA test results and extensive evidence of police misconduct, Ayers's lawyers obtained a jury verdict in excess of $13 million against this detective and her partner. She promptly filed for bankruptcy and her partner died, and to date (as of 2017) Ayers hasn't collected a dime from either one.

· · ·

In the cases of the first 330 DNA exonerations in this country, approximately half the defendants had testified in their own defense at trial, proclaimed their innocence, and were flatly disbelieved by the jury. Instead, the jurors believed witnesses such as jailhouse snitches who were later proven to be liars, forensic scientists who provided exaggerated or false testimony, or witnesses who were lying to protect their own involvement in the crime. My clients Clarence Ekins, Robert McClendon, Raymond Towler, and Ricky Jackson all testified in their defense at their original trials and told the jury they had nothing to do with the crimes. The jury thought they were lying. Yet all four were later proven innocent. Elkins had served seven and a half years in prison, McClendon eighteen years, Towler twenty-nine years, and Jackson a whopping thirty-nine years, making him the longest-serving person in U.S. history to later be declared innocent and exonerated.

In Steven Avery's trial for the rape of Penny Beernsten, twenty different alibi witnesses testified for Avery that he was nowhere near the scene of the attack. But the police and the jury disbelieved every single one of them. Avery was later proven innocent by DNA testing and exonerated and released.[6]

In some cases, cops and juries are double-duped: they not only fail to believe the innocent party, but believe the false statements of the true perpetrator who is trying to pin the crime on an innocent person. In the Kansas case of Floyd Bledsoe, the police believed Floyd's brother Tom, who told them that Floyd had murdered the victim and dumped the body on their parents' property. Based on Tom's testimony, Floyd—who adamantly protested his innocence but was disbelieved by both the police and the jury—was convicted and sent to prison. Years later, DNA testing proved that Tom was the true perpetrator and that Floyd was entirely innocent, as he had claimed all along.[7]

My Ohio Innocence Project case of Walter Zimmer and Thomas Siller described earlier had a similar outcome. After an elderly woman was murdered in her Cleveland home, the police arrested Jason Smith. But Smith soon convinced the police that Zimmer and Siller were the true culprits, and that he had been waiting outside in a car when Zimmer and Siller began beating the victim, then gone inside the house and witnessed the attack from a distance for a few seconds, then left. DNA testing later proved that Smith was the real culprit, and Zimmer and Siller were exonerated after each spending more than a decade in prison. Eventually, they each won a sizeable settlement against the city of Cleveland for their wrongful convictions. The police and the jury believed Smith—a career criminal who was lying to save his own skin—and disbelieved Zimmer and Siller, who were innocent.[8]

THE RESEARCH ON HUMAN LIE DETECTION

Psychologist Paul Ekman has performed groundbreaking research over a period of decades demonstrating that, contrary to popular opinion, human beings are not very good at detecting truthfulness in others. In fact, Ekman's studies show that we are accurate at detecting lies at a rate that is only slightly better than a coin toss. In one study recounted in his influential book *Telling Lies*, Ekman divided a group of nursing students into two groups.[9] One group watched a video depicting a pleasant ocean scene and were then asked to accurately and honestly describe what they had just watched while being videotaped by Ekman. A second group of nursing students were shown a video of gory medical scenes but were asked to tell a fabricated story afterward that they had watched a pleasant video about flowers. The lies of this second group were also videotaped. Dr. Ekman set the stakes high. The nursing students were told that lying was a necessary part of being a nurse, because sometimes a nurse must hide bad facts from patients while appearing happy and relaxed until the doctor determines it is the appropriate time to tell the patients the bad news. The nursing students were told that they were being judged on how well they lied and how well they controlled and hid their emotions when lying. Thus, the nursing students in the "lying group" had a personal incentive to lie as effectively as possible to show that they could perform well on the job.

Dr. Ekman then had a group of subjects watch both tapes and render verdicts on which nursing students were lying and which were telling the truth. He divided the subjects into two groups. Ekman intentionally made the first group suspicious—he told them to be on the lookout for liars in the videotapes, as half of them would be lying. The second group was told nothing. But both groups performed barely above chance at detecting which group of nursing students were lying and which were telling the truth. The "suspicious group" did no better than the other group.

This study has been replicated in a number of settings with similar results. Psychologists Kraut and Vrij conducted independent studies that placed the accuracy rate of lie detection at about 57 percent—a strikingly low figure given that guessing or a coin toss should result in a correct answer 50 percent of the time.[10] A meta-analysis of more than two hundred studies on this topic involving more than twenty-four thousand different subjects shows an accuracy rate in the general public of lie detection at about 54 percent.[11] Many of these studies have also revealed what is called a "truth bias." That is, subjects correctly identify truthful statements about 67 percent of the time, while accurately identifying lies only 44 percent of the time—below chance. This result reflects the societal bias that we generally *want* to believe others; our default position, absent proof to the contrary, is to believe.

Furthermore, several studies have demonstrated that police officers are no better than lay subjects at ferreting out the truth. In various studies, police officers achieve between 50 percent and 57 percent accuracy. Secret-service agents, however, performed slightly better (67 percent accuracy rates), as did CIA agents (73 percent accuracy rates). Not surprisingly, those in law enforcement, while not particularly good at detecting lies, did not suffer from the same "truth bias" as the general public. Police officers are of course looking for lies and expect lies, and thus are presumably less likely to give others the benefit of the doubt than are members of the general public.

In 2004, a group of leading psychologists evaluated the ability of police officers to detect lies in a setting particularly true to life.[12] They took videotaped interrogations from fourteen real cases where the suspects at first lied (told a story that was later proven to be false) and then later gave a truthful version after more evidence of guilt surfaced. Cases were carefully selected to include only those where the eventual evidence of guilt was clear, such as DNA test results or an eventual confession by the suspect that included facts that corroborated the confession (such as where the murder weapon had been hidden).

The psychologists played both video segments from the cases to ninety-nine police officers of varying age and experience. When watching the videos, the officers could hear the suspects' voices well, and could pick up facial movements such as eye blinks. The group correctly identified the truthful statements 64 percent of the time and the false statements 66 percent of the time. Not surprisingly, more experienced police officers fared slightly better than those who were newer to the police force. While these success rates are higher than those of the studies discussed above, they are still a far cry from demonstrating that police officers are accurate lie detectors whose intuitions are rock solid. Notably, the police officers were incorrect approximately one-third of the time in this real-life setting.

This study had another important result. Objective factors that the public commonly believes indicate dishonesty, such as fidgety body movements or gaze aversion, had little to do with whether or not the suspect was telling the truth or lying. This supports the findings of numerous other studies undermining the commonly held belief that a person who acts fidgety or avoids eye contact is likely lying, or that a person who is calm and makes confident eye contact is telling the truth. It is simply not supported by the research. Indeed, police officers in the study who cited amounts of eye contact or nervous bodily movements as the reasons for their decisions were less accurate than officers who avoided such temptations and instead based their decisions on more objective factors, like whether the stories made sense internally or contradicted other evidence.

Given that police training manuals typically claim that police officers are excellent lie detectors, and instruct officers to strongly consider factors such as eye contact and fidgetiness, those officers who followed the lessons of well-known training techniques such as the Reid technique were far less accurate than those who ignored such training.[13] A supreme irony indeed. Yet this training seems to give police officers a false sense of infallibility about their lie-detection abilities.

But it is not only police officers and jurors who fall prey to inflated confidence in their lie-detection abilities. The federal government's Transportation Security Administration has spent nearly $1 billion in recent years training its agents at airports to detect passengers who are allegedly lying during screening interviews, and thus are potential terrorism threats, using the same indicators of dishonesty—fidgety behavior, minimal eye contact, and so on—that we now know are not accurate indicators.[14] The United States Government Accountability Office issued a scathing report to Congress on this practice in 2013 stating:

> Available evidence does not support whether behavioral indicators, which are used in the Transportation Security Administration's (TSA) Screening of Passengers by Observation Techniques (SPOT) program, can be used to identify persons who may pose a risk to aviation security. GAO reviewed four meta-analyses (reviews that analyze other studies and synthesize their findings) that included over 400 studies from the past 60 years and *found that the human ability to accurately identify deceptive behavior based on behavioral indicators is the same as or slightly better than chance.*[15]

Rep. Mike McCaul, R-Texas, the chairman of the House Homeland Security Committee, said that the GAO report is "concerning, particularly in light of the fact that TSA has spent almost $1 billion on the program."

He added, "While I believe that there is value in utilizing behavioral detection and analysis in the aviation environment, we can only support programs that are proven effective. The terrorist threats to our aviation system require us to constantly re-evaluate and evolve our security procedure, and if this program isn't working, we need to find something that will."[16]

In other words, when it came to wasting nearly $1 billion training agents to use these supposed deception-detecting techniques, the TSA was publicly criticized, and Congress began evaluating alternatives. Yet, when it comes to determining the guilt or innocence of our own citizens—and possibly sending them to prison for life, or worse, to death row—based on the same type of faulty reasoning, nothing changes.

DEMEANOR EVIDENCE

Any attorney who has engaged in innocence work for any length of time can cite numerous cases where the police claimed that when they arrived on the crime scene, the defendant appeared too "calm and collected" for someone who, for example, had allegedly just arrived home and found his wife dead with a stab wound to the chest. Or, conversely, "too upset and over-the-top." In both situations, the police's perception was that the defendant's demeanor was being staged. Police who arrive on a possible crime scene are, naturally, often somewhat suspicious of the person on the scene, and confirmation bias can kick in. If the person is calm, they may see this as suspicious. If the person is out of control with emotion, they may perceive it as a predesigned act. It's hard to win with something so subjective. Or, given the malleability of human memory, once some alleged evidence of guilt is later uncovered, the police officers may reflect, "Now that I think of it, he was a little too calm under the circumstances." This thought later becomes trial testimony that the defendant acted unnaturally calm, and this can be powerful evidence of guilt in the eyes of the jury. The following cases are just a few of the many that illustrate this point.

Cameron Todd Willingham (Texas)

In 1991, Cameron Todd Willingham's house caught fire and burned down, killing his three daughters.[17] At first it was believed that the fire originated from a nonhuman source, but later it was ruled an arson and Willingham was charged with murder. Before it was ruled an arson, Willingham's grief was perceived by his friends and neighbors to be genuine. But once he was accused of setting the fire, Willingham's devastation was perceived as a sign of a guilty conscience.

Indeed, the arson ruling caused a dramatic shift in the public's perception of the grieving father. Willingham's priest, who had initially described him as devastated, suddenly became suspicious of him, saying that "things were not as they seemed. I had the feeling that [Willingham] was in complete control." According to one neighbor, although Willingham was dramatically crying out for his children as the fire progressed, he "did not appear to be excited or concerned," implying that his emotion was an act. Another neighbor told the police that Willingham seemed more concerned about the fate of his car than the fate of his children, reporting that while he had moved the car out of the fire's path, he had made no attempt to enter the house and rescue his daughters until the firefighters arrived.

With no motive to explain why Willingham would murder his daughters, the prosecution pieced together the theory that Willingham was a sociopath—that his daughters interfered with his desired fast and loose lifestyle. But while Willingham was being painted as a sociopath in the media, the majority of those who knew him well did not believe he was capable of setting the fire.

After a two-day trial, Willingham was convicted of capital murder and sentenced to death. His demeanor during and after the fire and the interpretations of his demeanor by various witnesses were used heavily by the prosecution to suggest guilt. After several unsuccessful attempts to prove his innocence, Willingham was executed by lethal injection on February 17, 2004.[18]

After Willingham's death, the "science" used in the investigation of the fire that killed his daughters was deemed to be invalid by a panel of the nation's leading arson experts.[19] New understandings in fire science confirmed that the fire could *not* have been an act of arson, but rather supported the initial beliefs that the fire was of nonhuman origin. It is now widely believed that Willingham was innocent; several independent investigations have come to that conclusion.[20] Indeed, Willingham's conviction was the impetus for Texas passing a new law allowing those who were convicted on bad science to apply for a new trial and seek exoneration. And the prosecutor who convicted Willingham has recently faced disciplinary charges for hiding evidence that pointed to Willingham's innocence. At the time of this writing, those charges are still pending.

This case, like many others, shows how confirmation bias works in tandem with demeanor evidence. Willingham's demeanor was not considered suspicious until a fire investigator, using a method later determined to be bogus, ruled the fire an arson. Then, and only then, did witnesses come forward with "memories" of Willingham acting in feigned ways that they claimed were suggestive of guilt. Former homicide detective and now innocence reformer Jim Trainum said on the famous podcast *Serial,* when asked how much weight should be given to people's interpretations of the demeanor of the defendant in that case, Adnan Syed, "Toss it out all out because it's subjective, it's hindsight, and also, people tend to bend their memories to what they think the police want to hear."[21] I couldn't agree more.

Michael Morton (Texas)

Michael Morton spent twenty-five years in prison for the murder of his wife, Christine, before being exonerated in 2011 with DNA evidence. Morton's demeanor and actions before and after his wife's death were heavily scrutinized at trial and played a huge role in his conviction.[22] The police developed a motive based on a note that Michael had left his wife the morning of her death in which he complained about her refusal to have sex with him the night before. The prosecution fleshed out the motive at trial by claiming, falsely and without evidentiary support, that Michael was a sexual deviant who had masturbated over his wife's corpse after violently murdering her (sometimes the truth really is stranger than fiction).

The prosecution argued that Michael's stoicism in the aftermath of the murder demonstrated indifference toward his wife, and convinced the jury that he was a disturbed human being capable of murdering her. The most damning testimony against Michael came from the Mortons' neighbor and friend, Elizabeth Gee. She described the Mortons' marriage as unhappy, and recalled instances in which Michael had said unkind things to Christine. Gee also testified that Michael's stoic demeanor following the murder had bothered her. Moreover, the fact that Michael had cut down his wife's marigolds two days before her funeral seemed callous and suspicious to Gee, given the timing.

While it was true that Michael had showed little emotion when told of his wife's death and had made some odd decisions in the aftermath of the murder—like choosing to return home where the murder took place instead of staying in a hotel, and cutting down the marigolds—the perception that these behaviors somehow revealed his guilt was dead wrong. The DNA testing that proved Michael innocent also identified the individual actually responsible for the crime. Two years after Michael's release from prison, Mark Norwood was convicted of Christine Morton's murder and sentenced to life in prison.[23]

Russ Faria (Missouri)

On December 27, 2011, Russ Faria placed a hysterical call to 911 after discovering his wife's body covered in blood.[24] He told the operator that he believed his terminally ill wife had committed suicide. Although he had an alibi and there was little evidence implicating him, Faria was arrested and charged with his wife's murder a week later.

At trial, the prosecution argued that Faria's hysteria during the 911 call was staged. The prosecution played the 911 tape to the jury and called the supervisor of the 911 operator who took the call to testify as to his interpretation of Faria's demeanor. Amid his hysteria, Faria had lucid moments of relative composure. The supervisor testified that in his experience Faria's fluctuation between these extremes was unusual and suspicious. Faria was convicted.

Afterward, however, the 911 operator who actually took Faria's call told reporters that she found his demeanor during the call to be genuine. The operator explained that the fluctuation in his mood reflected the effectiveness of the common techniques used by all 911 operators to calm down hysterical callers. On the basis of this and other new evidence of innocence, Faria was granted a new trial. He was acquitted of all charges in November 2015 and exonerated.

Here again the reliance on demeanor evidence, and the belief that someone can be deemed guilty or innocent based on how they reacted in an unusual, unprecedented moment, is troubling. The fact that the operator who took the 911 call and the supervisor of the operator had such widely divergent views about Faria's reaction reflects the highly subjective and unreliable nature of this evidence. And while Willingham and Morton were accused of reacting too calmly to shocking news, Faria was criticized for allegedly overreacting.

It's damned if you do, damned if you don't.

Han Tak Lee (Pennsylvania)

Like Willingham, Han Tak Lee was convicted of intentionally setting a fire that resulted in the death of his daughter.[25] After spending twenty-four years incarcerated, Lee was exonerated through the invalidation of the arson science used to determine the origins of the fire.

At his original trial, Lee's demeanor in the wake of the tragedy was heavily scrutinized. The first officer who arrived at the scene described Lee as "nonchalant," impassively observing the fire. Other witnesses described him as "calm" and "cold."[26] A firefighter noted that Lee seemed "very depressed," as if he were "mad at himself."[27] In contrast, Lee's wife nearly collapsed when she learned of her daughter's death. Witnesses reported that Lee made no attempt to console his grieving wife; instead, he "walked right by [her] like nothing happened."[28] Lee's surviving daughter responded to the fire like Lee's wife, becoming so distraught that she had to be removed from the area.

The defense argued that Lee's demeanor was conventional by Korean cultural standards and not out of the ordinary within that context. However, the jury rejected this argument.

By the time of his exoneration and release, Lee was nearly eighty years old. The state appealed Lee's exoneration, turning to the same arguments about Lee's demeanor that were raised at the original trial:

> The accounts of Appellee's demeanor are significant in light of what a great majority of people would consider the apparent and immediate tragedy of losing a child in such a horrific way. Though there was some question raised in testimony that Appellee's demeanor was consistent with a cultural norm, it is significant that neither his wife nor his daughter shared his stoicism. . . . The jury could have interpreted this evidence as Appellee's callous disregard for the fatality in light of his hand in Ji Yun Lee's death.[29]

The prosecution's appeal was rejected and Lee's exoneration remains intact.

The Debelbots (Georgia)

Ashley and Albert Debelbot were jointly tried and convicted of murdering their newborn daughter just hours after bringing her home from the hospital.[30] The child's cause of death was alleged to be intentional blunt-force trauma. With no alternative explanation for the child's death, police believed the couple must have done it.

The prosecution relied heavily on circumstantial evidence of demeanor to advance the theory that Ashley was responsible for the child's death, while Albert played a minor role. Ashley was described as appearing calm and reserved, while Albert was visibly distraught.[31] The prosecution tactically exploited the contrast in the couple's demeanors to portray Ashley as especially callous:

PROSECUTOR DAILY: Did you have an opportunity to observe both Albert Debelbot and Ashley Debelbot's demeanor?

OFFICER TYNER: Yes.

PROSECUTOR DAILY: Can you describe Albert Debelbot's demeanor?

OFFICER TYNER: . . . Albert appeared to be very distraught . . . And he was very shaken by, appeared to be very shaken by what had happened.

PROSECUTOR DAILY: Okay. Can you describe Ashley Debelbot's demeanor?

OFFICER TYNER: Ashley was a little bit more alert, at least she appeared to be. She appeared to be a little bit more rational in her thinking and just appeared to be all around more alert.

PROSECUTOR DAILY: Alright. Did she appear distraught?

OFFICER TYNER: She was not near as distraught as her husband.

PROSECUTOR DAILY: Was she crying?

OFFICER TYNER: I don't recall her crying, no.

PROSECUTOR DAILY: Was Albert Debelbot crying?

OFFICER TYNER: Yes. Mr. Debelbot cried several times.[32]

Calling Ashley "emotionless," the prosecution argued that Ashley's failure to cry while writing her witness statement and the fact that she did not refer to the baby by name were additional proof of her indifference toward the child. But, as other testimony revealed, Ashley was anything but indifferent to her daughter's death.

OFFICER GARDNER: [Ashley] went through a few different changes in emotion as would be expected. At the hospital she was quite stressed . . . which is quite natural having just lost a baby. By the time we got back to the house she was more talkative and seemed a lot nicer. . . . We were investigating her child's death as a suspicious death. . . .

PROSECUTOR DAILY: . . . When you saw her at the hospital and at the residence, was she crying?

OFFICER GARDNER: She was a little teary at the residence. She wasn't flat-out crying, but she was teary. . . . I believe it was a mother or grandmother had called her while she was at the residence and she cried a little bit there when she spoke to her. But after she got off the phone with the person, she regained her composure.[33]

Both Ashley and Albert Debelbot were convicted of murder and sentenced to life in prison. In 2015, the Wisconsin Innocence Project and the Georgia Public Defender filed a motion on Albert Debelbot's behalf requesting a new trial based on newly discovered evidence showing that the death of his daughter was the result of brain and skull abnormalities formed while the child was in utero.[34] The litigation is currently ongoing with Ashley expected to proceed with similar filings soon.[35]

Jeffrey Deskovic (New York)

At the age of sixteen, Jeffrey Deskovic was found guilty of raping and murdering a fifteen-year-old classmate.[36] Deskovic's curiosity and fascination with the investigation of his classmate's death was mistaken by the police as a sign of his guilt. Eager to help with the investigation, Deskovic voluntarily met with the police on several occasions to put forward his own theories about the case. He was misled to believe that he would be allowed to participate in the investigation if he could just prove his worth to the investigators. Taking advantage of Deskovic's eagerness to please, the detectives manipulated the teenager into falsely confessing after a six-hour interrogation.[37]

Deskovic was exonerated with DNA evidence sixteen years later. After performing an internal review of the investigation that led to Deskovic's wrongful conviction, the local district attorney issued a report that made the following observation: "As the police theorized, Deskovic's actions could have been those of a killer inserting himself in the investigation and working up the gumption to confess. By the same token, Deskovic's actions could have been—and, indeed, apparently were—those of a troubled sixteen year old, who having experienced the death of a peer from the first time, became obsessed with it and naively believed that the detectives, who fed him pizza and spent time with him discussing the case, would invite him into their investigation if he could prove himself worthy."[38]

· · ·

A few years ago, I heard a loud noise in the bathroom and found my wife in the midst of a seizure on the floor of the bathtub while the water from the shower ran over her. Her eyes were unnaturally frozen open, foamy vomit dribbled from the side of her mouth, and her body was stiff like a board and twitching. She could not respond to anything I said. She just stared blankly and twitched from the seizure. I called 911 and reported what I was seeing, and answered questions about her age, health, the fact that she had no history of seizures, and so on. I had never seen anything like this before, and I was understandably shocked and quite worried. For all I knew, she could be dying.

But for some reason, my natural reaction was to be very calm. I spoke very slowly and deliberately to the 911 dispatcher and pronounced my words very carefully. There was no emotion in my voice.

Fortunately, my wife turned out to be fine, and there was no investigation, as it was clearly a medical condition rather than a crime. But I couldn't help thinking afterward that, for some unexplainable reason, I had become very calm and focused. And because of my line of work, it occurred to me that if for some reason my demeanor were later analyzed by suspicious police or prosecutors because they believed a crime had occurred, I would have been accused of being far too collected and calm. I was unnaturally emotionless, they would say. And that would mean I was guilty.

My client Ryan Widmer was not so lucky. When he found his wife dead in the bathtub and called 911, the sound of his voice during the call and his reactions at the scene once the paramedics and police arrived were aggressively used against him at trial. The police believed he'd drowned his wife, while the defense put on evidence that she suffered from a medical condition that caused her to lose consciousness and drown. When I listened to the 911 call, I heard nothing either way that told me if Widmer was innocent or guilty. It just seemed like a typical 911 call, devoid of clues. But law enforcement somehow *knew* that his voice was that of a murderer staging the scene as an accident, and they argued this over and over again to the jury. The jury found this convincing and they convicted with other fairly weak evidence.

Later, when I got involved in the case after Widmer was convicted, I met with the elected district attorney to try to get him to agree to release the deceased's bodily tissue samples so I could perform genetic testing to see if she suffered from a disorder like Long QT syndrome that could have caused her drowning. During her life, she demonstrated many of the symptoms of Long QT syndrome, such as a cleft palate, short stature, a heart murmur, and narcolepsy-like symptoms throughout her lifetime. In fact, her nickname was "Sleepy" because of her strange tendency to fall asleep in the sitting position at bizarre times, such as when the family was gathered together opening Christmas presents.

In rejecting my request for access to her tissue, the prosecutor cited the sound of Widmer's voice on the 911 tapes and the way he behaved on the scene once the police arrived: too calm. Also, the case had recently been on *Dateline NBC* shortly before my meeting with the prosecutor, and Widmer had decided to be interviewed on camera from prison for the show. The prosecutor said, "After that *Dateline* interview, no one around here believes he is innocent anymore. You could tell from the way he came across that he did it." I sure wish I possessed such amazing wizardry at divining the truth from one's demeanor.

To date, the prosecutor has still not released the tissue for biological testing, and the courts have said that he doesn't have to because there is no law in Ohio that expressly requires him to release it. Widmer remains in prison despite the fact that genetic testing could be done that could shed great light on what happened in his case.

While I don't know whether or not Widmer is innocent, as I was not there when his wife died, I find the supreme confidence of others in his guilt—based in large part on Widmer's demeanor—to be quite troubling, though it reflects our system's overreliance on demeanor evidence and our disturbing overconfidence in our lie-detection abilities.

7. Blind Tunnel Vision

I've talked about the Clarence Elkins case quite a bit already, and his case is a perfect illustration of tunnel vision. You'll recall that Elkins was wrongfully convicted of raping and murdering his mother-in-law and raping his six-year-old niece during the same attack. Immediately after the attack, the niece said that the perpetrator "looked like" her Uncle Clarence. When authority figures, including the police, talked to her, however, her story morphed into "it *was* my Uncle Clarence." But it was dark in the house where she and her grandmother had been attacked in the middle of the night, and the little girl had been knocked unconscious at the beginning of the assault. So she, of course, could not have gotten a very good look at the perpetrator. But despite this weak evidence, the police arrested Clarence at his home within hours of the crime and then assured the public that they had the dangerous criminal in custody. They patted themselves on the back for acting swiftly to protect the public.

From that point on, nearly every piece of evidence that was discovered during the investigation decisively pointed to Elkins's innocence. But the police routinely ignored all of it. Indeed, after the police had arrested Elkins and announced they had solved the crime, there was no going back. Their minds were made up. Tunnel vision had set in.

That evidence of innocence included the fact that Elkins's then-wife, Melinda, told the police that Clarence had been asleep in their bed at the time of the crime. One of their children had been awake all night sick, and Melinda had to stay up to take care of him. There is no way, she told police, that Clarence could have gotten out of bed, driven thirty minutes to his mother-in-law's house, committed a murder and two rapes, and driven thirty minutes back and gone back to bed without her knowing it. And he had no motive. There was some friction at times between Clarence and his mother-in-law but nothing out of the ordinary for a relationship of that nature.

Melinda said there was no way she would lie—after all, it was her *own mother* who had been murdered and *her own* sister's daughter who had been beaten and raped. But because of the police's tunnel vision, they *knew* that she was lying. She was labeled as a "stand by your man" countrywoman who would rather protect a murderous husband than her own mother and niece. The prosecutors eventually pressed that same theory to the jury when Melinda testified in Clarence's defense; in essence, they suggested to the jury that she should not be believed.

Yet every piece of forensic analysis failed to connect Elkins to the crime scene. The scene was a bloodbath, with bloody palm prints, hairs, and all sorts of evidence on the floors and walls. None of it matched Elkins. Not a shred. No matter, the police and prosecutors said. The mother-in-law's home was very dirty, they claimed, and she must not have cleaned it in ages. So the fingerprints and hairs and other such things must have been left by prior visitors. Somehow, they claimed, Elkins was able to commit this crime without leaving so much as a trace behind. And though the perpetrator would have no doubt been drenched in blood, they could find no blood connecting Clarence to the crime in his car, on any of his clothes, or anywhere in his house. The police even had the drains of Clarence's house scoured for blood, assuming Clarence showered the blood from his body. But their search turned up nothing.

At this point, an objective observer might think that the testimony of a six-year-old girl who witnessed her attacker for a few seconds in the dark, under great stress, was undermined by Elkins's solid alibi and the lack of forensic evidence connecting him to the scene. Indeed, it would seem unimaginable to any objective observer that Elkins could have committed such a bloody crime and left no evidence at the scene, while removing all traces of blood from his car, clothing, and house in just a few hours. Yet, because the police and prosecutors suffered from tunnel vision, they continued to push forward. And they did so with ferocity—seeking the death penalty against Clarence.

Based on the testimony of the child, Elkins was convicted. Thankfully, the jury rejected the death penalty but he was sentenced to life in prison.

After Elkins had served seven and half years, DNA testing exonerated him, as I've said already, and proved that Earl Mann was the true perpetrator. Earl Mann is now serving life in prison for the crimes for which Clarence Elkins had been originally convicted.

So, in addition to ignoring all the evidence that pointed to Elkins's innocence, police and prosecutors also ignored the fact that a violent child rapist had just been released from prison and was living two doors down from the crime scene. That should have been rather glaring. Earl Mann even looked quite a bit like Clarence Elkins. But it gets even worse. It was later discovered in Elkins's civil suit against the police department that *before* Elkins's trial, Earl Mann had been picked up by the same police department for a violent robbery and had said something to the effect of, "Why aren't you arresting me for the murder of Judy Johnson?" Judy Johnson was Elkins's mother-in-law. That comment was obviously a thunderbolt, and the arresting officer informed the detective bureau investigating the murder about it. But the detectives were so beholden to their theory of the case, and to Elkins's guilt, that this incriminating comment was never followed up on. It was just ignored. Despite the fact that Mann happened to live two doors down from the crime scene, happened to resemble Clarence Elkins, and was known to the police as a violent, serial offender. And the police report documenting Mann's statement wasn't even disclosed to Elkins's defense team prior to trial!

Thanks to appalling tunnel vision, Elkins spent seven and a half years in hell, and Earl Mann went on to rape and physically abuse several other children before he was eventually caught and imprisoned for life.

The Elkins story might seem bizarre, or almost unbelievable, to a person not familiar with the criminal justice system. But it is not atypical at all. Tunnel vision is rampant in our system.

· · ·

Tunnel vision occurs when we develop an initial belief or suspicion, become wedded to that belief, and then interpret or even twist all subsequent information we encounter in order to confirm it. It's a common human tendency that arises in a variety of situations in our lives, because it is "partly innate" and "part of our psychological makeup," as Keith Findley has observed.[1]

Tunnel vision at first glance appears to be similar to confirmation bias. But it's more than that. All of the psychological problems discussed in this book work together to create tunnel vision. Because of confirmation bias, we see new information through the warped lens of our initial belief, which we are loath to let go of. "People tend to see information that confirms their hypothesis and to avoid information that would disconfirm their hypothesis," Findley writes.[2]

And given our malleable memories, we recall past events with memories that we have reshaped to support our new belief. This sometimes results in the "knew-it-all-along effect" or "hindsight bias," or the tendency to see events as more predictable than they actually were. Cognitive research of memory has clearly demonstrated our tendency to reconstruct our memories of past events to be consistent with our later beliefs.[3]

Moreover, because humans are not good lie detectors, but rather not much better than a coin flip at determining who is telling the truth and who is lying, tunnel vision causes us to selectively make these determinations based on which witness accounts fit our hypothesis of the crime.

When external political pressure is applied to reach a certain conclusion consistent with an initial hypothesis, such as the pressure on police and prosecutors to solve a horrific crime, all of these problems are greatly exacerbated, and tunnel vision can wreak havoc.[4]

Tunnel vision served an important purpose in bygone eras. A tribal leader in charge of a hungry tribe needed to be decisive, and act quickly in interpreting various clues, to determine which direction the game herd likely moved in overnight so that his tribe could mobilize in time to keep pace with the herd. A deep thinker, on the other hand, who might take all day to reach a conclusion after evaluating all the available clues, might pick the right direction a higher percentage of the time than the decisive leader, but his or her tribe might starve, because such a deliberate, careful process would allow the game herd to advance beyond reach.

Evolution thus favored quick decisions and the ability to ignore distractions while remaining wedded to the most obvious option. As a result, our brains innately engage in what are called "heuristics"—hardwired mental shortcuts that help us to make decisions quickly—jumping to conclusions, one could even say, without getting bogged down in too many distracting details.[5] But psychologists have realized that while heuristics were necessary in past eras, and can be helpful in many aspects of life today, they can sometimes lead to disastrous results in our complex world. And in the criminal justice system, our innate psychological instincts can cause serious problems if we're not aware of them and don't try to keep them in check.

Tunnel vision is a powerful force. Political leaders, for example, frequently fall prey to it in matters of foreign policy. George W. Bush and his administration developed suspicions, if not paranoia, after 9/11 that Iraq and its leader, Saddam Hussein, were hiding weapons of mass destruction. Leading up to the U.S. invasion of Iraq in 2003, they repeatedly chose to believe unreliable sources, such as informants who had been "spoon-fed" to tell the administration what it wanted to hear, and forged and other unreliable documents on this matter. Meanwhile they discounted hard data and information from more reliable sources that indicated that Iraq had already destroyed its WMDs after the earlier Gulf War.[6] After the invasion commenced and it was discovered that Iraq no longer possessed WMDs, a governmental commission assigned to investigate the fiasco reported to the president:

In the case of Iraq, collectors of intelligence absorbed the prevailing analytic consensus and tended to reject or ignore contrary information. The result was "tunnel vision" focusing on the intelligence community's existing assumptions. . . . For example, several human sources asserted before the war that Iraq did not retain any WMDs. . . . But the pervasive influence of the conventional wisdom—that Iraq had WMDs and was actively hiding it from inspectors—created a kind of intellectual "tunnel vision" that caused officers to believe that information contradicting the conventional wisdom was disinformation. Potential sources for alternative views were denigrated or not pursued by collectors.[7]

In a nutshell, the Bush administration had become "too wedded" to its initial assumptions and then failed to analyze all new evidence objectively, resulting in an expensive and deadly war that disproved the very assumptions that the administration had so stubbornly refused to question.[8]

But George W. Bush is certainly not the only U.S. president to suffer from tunnel vision. Lyndon B. Johnson repeatedly ignored data and advice from his advisors that the war in Vietnam was unwinnable.[9] George Reedy, an advisor to Johnson, said that President Johnson "had a remarkable capacity to convince himself that he held the principles he *should* hold at any time, and there was something charming about the air of injured innocence with which he would treat anyone who brought forth evidence that he had held other views in the past. It was not an act. . . . He had a fantastic capacity to persuade himself that the 'truth' which was convenient for the present was *the truth* and anything that conflicted with it was the prevarication of the enemies. He literally willed what was in his mind to become reality."[10] Most if not all of us are guilty of similar self-delusions in our lives.

In 1962, John F. Kennedy and his administration clung to the belief that the Soviet Union would not place missiles in Cuba, and were very slow and reluctant to accept any contrary information, although it was mounting. In 1968, Johnson's administration discounted clear and reliable evidence that the Soviet Union was preparing to invade Czechoslovakia, because the evidence conflicted with officials' preconceived beliefs, until the invasion happened. Five years later, the Nixon administration could not be shaken from its belief that Egypt and Syria would not attack Israel, despite a "mountain of evidence" to the contrary.[11] A survey of nearly any past presidential administration would find similar examples of tunnel vision, often with disastrous results. But it's not just presidents who suffer from tunnel vision. Everyday people experience it in their daily lives, at work and at home.

Even love, for example, can be a strong facilitator of tunnel vision. Those who have been in troubled relationships may relate to this. Indeed, I know this from personal experience. In 2004, when my wife at the time first told me she wanted a divorce, I was devastated. We had had a near-perfect relationship for more than fifteen years, I believed. I pushed back against the divorce for more than two years, confused as to why it was happening and in anguish. After we were divorced in 2006, I was depressed for months, convinced my world was rocked forever. Things would never be the same. What a waste, I thought, to throw away such a wonderful relationship that had produced two beautiful, young children. And to put them through a painful divorce for no good reason seemed callous and incredibly unnecessary.

I had grown up in a household where divorce was greatly frowned upon. My parents enjoyed a storybook marriage filled with daily expressions of love, joy, and support, with no visible tension between them. Growing up, I knew I would have that too. I *knew* it because I didn't know anything else. My parents' relationship was my only example, and I naïvely thought that was just how it was with any couple that made a daily effort to love and support each other. It was easy. So a marriage like my parents' became an ingrained part of the vision I had for my life.

I was in love at the beginning of my relationship with my ex-wife, and saw growing old with her in happiness and joy, like my parents did with each other, as my only path in life. But as time passed after our divorce, I could feel the layers of tunnel vision that I had created during our marriage begin to peel off one by one. I began seeing our relationship in a different light, very gradually, step by step. I began to comprehend problems in our relationship, which I had simply been unable to see. I eventually realized that my ex-wife and I were quite incompatible and just weren't right together. She had been right all along.

I had not been happy in the marriage either, or at least wouldn't have been if I had been honest with myself, but had convinced myself that I was happy through self-rationalization about the problems and copious amounts of revisionist history. What had actually devolved into an unhappy and unsatisfying relationship remained a near-perfect union to me, given the way I had limited my field of vision. By the end of 2007, however, after enough time had passed, I was able to see more clearly, to shake myself loose from my self-delusions, and to feel thankful toward my ex-wife for having the courage to break things off despite my naïve and stubborn inability to see what she had realized long before I did—that it wasn't anyone's fault, but we just weren't right together.

I am, of course, not the only person who has suffered from tunnel vision in matters of troubled relationships. Although I didn't mention the role of tunnel vision in relationships in my short proposal for this book, a friend who read the proposal said, "You know, you should talk about how love can cause tunnel vision in bad relationships. I was in a terrible relationship for years. He was mean. He didn't have a job. Nothing about him was good, but I was somehow blinded. I was a wreck when he broke up with me. Everyone could see the problems but me. I could only see it much later. I had tunnel vision." And so it is with many in love, I believe, particularly those in unhealthy relationships. As Benjamin Franklin once quipped, couples in troubled relationships tend to keep their eyes "wide open" before marriage, and then "half-shut afterward."

But it's not just one's field of vision that becomes narrowed. Couples in rocky relationships constantly revise their memories to comport with their current perception of their relationships. As one psychologist has written, "distortions of past events—or complete amnesia—kick in to confirm" each partner's beliefs.[12] If a partner is like I was in my first marriage, and desperately wants to believe that they are in a good marriage, they will revise their memory of past events in a glowingly positive light to maintain that belief. But if a partner has decided that the marriage is over, and wants a divorce, they will tend to recast past events in an unfairly negative light. One marriage psychologist reports that when she asked a couple she was counseling how they met, the wife responded, "At school, where I mistakenly thought he was smart." The wife went on to say that she didn't make a mistake in choosing her husband; rather, he made a mistake by tricking her to make her think he was intelligent.[13] Alas, marriage counselors must be great repositories for twisted and revised memories.

· · ·

In like fashion, police and prosecutors, because they are human, are prone to fall in love with their initial suspicions and beliefs. Criminal investigation is a highly competitive and stressful enterprise, and police and prosecutors feel both internal and external pressures to solve cases on their docket. The inability to solve a horrendous crime is emotionally stressful and nerve-wracking, and can lead to low self-esteem and negative repercussions in the workplace. Indeed, police and prosecutors are often evaluated on their "clearance rates"—the percentage of cases assigned to them that they are able to solve and that result in convictions.[14]

They are not emotionless robots. They have to visit bloody crime scenes, and hold the hands of victims' families. They become personally sickened by violent crimes, because they are immersed in the horror, and become deeply emotionally invested in obtaining justice for the victims. As a result, nothing feels better than that initial "Ah-hah! This is very interesting. . . .

Here we go!" feeling when a suspicious fact surfaces that finally brings a suspect into focus. Police and prosecutors, particularly with heinous or high-profile crimes, are desperate for those initial suspicions to be correct, because otherwise they must start over from ground zero and deliver more bad news to the heartbroken victims or victims' families.

I know this from my own experience as a prosecutor. After that initial *Eureka!* moment when a solid suspect jumps to the forefront, your mind runs through all the old evidence in the case over and over again with great excitement. Facts that were meaningless before suddenly take on a sinister light now that you have a suspect. "That explains why he called the victim thirty minutes before she was murdered," you think. "He must have been making sure she was home by herself!" "Now it makes sense," you realize. The pieces of the puzzle start fitting together. The momentum builds. Your mental adrenaline kicks in. You get more and more excited with each new "realization" as you replay the case in your head. You try to make each piece of evidence fit your new theory.

A witness you interviewed who provided the suspect with an alibi was obviously lying, you now believe. You look for reasons not to believe him. "He's the suspect's friend, so of course he's lying to protect him. It makes sense now." Or: "Did you see how much he fidgeted and avoided eye contact with me? He seemed nervous like he was hiding something." You suddenly convince yourself that you never believed this witness, even if, in fact, you had—you knew something was fishy with him from the beginning. You knew it all along.

But the witness who provided damning evidence against the suspect was telling the truth, you now believe. And you convince yourself that you knew that all along, too. With each new rationalization, you become more and more entrenched in your belief.

I did this as a prosecutor. I did it every single day. And I did it honestly. I was completely unaware of confirmation bias. I didn't think my memory was malleable. I thought I could truly tell when witnesses were telling the truth or not, because I was a good lie detector. But I now know, as clear as day, that this isn't true. And I wouldn't have been able to admit to myself at the time that institutional political pressures had any bearing whatsoever on my decision making.

But tunnel vision was part of the culture of my prosecutor's office. We shared our theories with those around us. Everyone took part in bouncing their ideas off their colleagues, and coming up with ways to make the pieces fit together. The excitement of "cracking the case" and coming up with ways to make all the pieces fit was part of the fun of the office. And as each new piece was made to fit, we became more beholden to our hypothesis. We fed off each other. To the extent that we tried to see arguments on the other side, it was just so that we could be prepared to shoot them down at trial.

. . .

One of my first cases as a prosecutor illustrates how tunnel vision works. In the story that follows, I have changed the names of the participants and some less significant details for the sake of anonymity. The defendant, whom I'll call Diego Miranda, had been a low-level equipment manager for a professional sports team in the New York City area. The victim, whom I'll call Jackie, was a famous, all-star professional athlete for the same team. Although Jackie was a millionaire, he was young and disorganized and had a tendency to overspend. Jackie's accountant tried to rein in in his spending, so each month he sat down with Jackie and went over Jackie's returned checks to see what he had purchased and to lecture him about living within his means. At one such meeting, Jackie denied having written some of the larger checks, most of which had been written to pay off credit cards. Jackie noted that the checks in question had credit card account numbers written in the memo section, and those numbers didn't match any of Jackie's credit cards.

When the accountant asked him who had access to his checkbook and could have written them, Jackie named Diego Miranda. Jackie explained that Diego had been hanging around his house along with other "wannabes"— people who try to ingratiate themselves into the social circles of professional athletes. Jackie said Diego could have gotten his hands on one of his checkbooks, which Jackie just left sitting around, and that he recognized Diego's handwriting on some of the checks. Diego had obviously forged his signature, Jackie claimed, and used the checks to pay off his credit cards. So the accountant brought the checks to us and the investigation started.

When he brought the checks to us, the accountant told us that he had already confronted Diego about the checks, and Diego broke down and cried, apologizing for taking Jackie's money. So my office had Diego arrested.

Diego's attorney insisted, however, that Diego was innocent, and he asked to meet with me. At the meeting, he told me that Diego had worked for Jackie. Jackie had started using Diego as a personal assistant, having Diego run errands, purchase things Jackie needed like clothes and electronics, pick up his dry cleaning, get his car washed, make sure there was always food and beer in Jackie's refrigerator after games, and other things of that nature. The relationship escalated to the point where Diego was spending most of his time when not working for the team performing personal concierge services for Jackie.

Jackie had given Diego a checkbook to pay for some of the things Diego purchased for Jackie. But Jackie was disorganized, the attorney said. He rarely had cash on him, and he kept forgetting to pay Diego for all his work. When Diego asked Jackie to formally hire him so that he could receive a regular paycheck, Jackie told him that his accountant would never agree to such an arrangement, so it had to stay "off the books" and remain a secret.

Jackie told Diego, the attorney claimed, "Go ahead and buy some stuff to make up for what I owe you, and then buy yourself some stuff each month going forward as your salary. Put the things you buy for yourself on a credit card, and then use my checks to pay off your credit cards. That way my accountant will never know—he'll just think I wrote those checks to pay off my *own* credit cards." Diego's attorney said that even though such an arrangement would sound strange to a normal person, Jackie was a young millionaire who was disorganized and immature, and flew by the seat of his pants. Diego's attorney also told me that shortly before Jackie made the theft allegations against Diego, Jackie and Diego had had a falling out over Diego's interactions with a woman Jackie was dating, and that Diego had been fired from his under-the-table gofer job. He also claimed that there was a misunderstanding about Diego's alleged "confession" to Jackie's accountant. Jackie had told Diego that their business relationship had to remain a secret because the accountant would never approve of it. So when the accountant confronted him about the checks, Diego panicked, not knowing whether, if he revealed the secret, it would get Jackie in serious trouble, undermining a relationship important to Jackie that could hurt his chances for endorsements or God knows what else. So, with little time to think, Diego confessed, figuring that once he told Jackie what had happened, Jackie would best know how to fix the situation. But afterward, because of their falling out or because of Jackie's fear of the accountant knowing the truth, Jackie stabbed Diego in the back. Diego was Jackie's fall guy, he claimed.

After hearing this story, I interviewed Jackie. Jackie stated that he had never hired Diego as a personal assistant. Diego, Jackie claimed, was a groupie or "hanger-on" who tried to suck up to celebrity athletes. Diego was always showing up at his house and hanging around at parties, so all the professional athletes just used him to make beer runs or drive their girlfriends home from clubs—things of that nature. But they didn't pay Diego, other than picking up his tab for food and drinks when they were out on the town together. Rather, they just took advantage of him because he was one of the many eager fans who would do anything to hang around the professional athletes after hours.

I went forward with the case. My office had already brought charges against Diego. Jackie's story made sense, and Diego's story seemed far-fetched. After interviewing Jackie and watching his demeanor, I believed him. I discounted Diego's story as told to me by his lawyer. And the amount that appeared to have been stolen, around $100,000, seemed too high to constitute a salary for a mere gofer position, even for a multimillionaire like Jackie.

A day or two before the jury trial started, I finally received all of Jackie's bank records for the months around the time the alleged thefts had occurred. To my shock, there were checks in what I recognized as Diego's handwriting in small amounts written to businesses like dry cleaners, car washes, and grocery stores. Various checks of this nature, all in what I recognized as Diego's handwriting, with Jackie's signature as it looked when forged by Diego. When Diego's attorney received his copies of the checks, he called and said, "See, this is what I was talking about. Diego was picking up Jackie's dry cleaning, getting his groceries, and making a lot of Jackie's day-to-day purchases. He was Jackie's personal assistant. The remaining checks you're bringing charges on *were* written by Diego to pay off Diego's own credit card expenditures, but they were authorized by Jackie as Diego's payment for all his work. They had a bizarre setup, but that's Jackie for you."

My trial was starting in the next day or two, and I felt like I had been kicked in the stomach. These new checks seemed to support Diego's story, and contradicted what Jackie had told me, but I just somehow knew it couldn't be true. I was positive that I was right. By this time, I was deeply wedded to the notion that Diego was guilty. So I thought and thought. And then it finally dawned on me: Diego was smarter than I had given him credit for. He stole Jackie's checkbook, but rather than start immediately writing big checks to pay off his credit card debt, he devised a scheme whereby he would first use the checks to pay for dry cleaning or buy groceries—small, inexpensive purchases like that. These were "test checks" to see if the forged signatures would make it past the bank employees. And since some were for businesses near Jackie's house, everything would seem copacetic to Jackie's accountant. These "test checks" were designed to get the bank employees and Jackie's accountant used to seeing checks written in Diego's handwriting—to condition them to breeze past checks with Diego's handwriting. And if they *did* notice the handwriting and Diego got caught, it would only be for very small amounts—no big deal for a millionaire like Jackie. Nothing would come of it. But if time went by and no alarm bells sounded, then Diego would know it was smooth sailing, and he could start writing bigger checks to pay off his own credit cards.

As soon as this light bulb went on in my head, I knew I was right. I ran my theory past my colleagues, and they agreed with me. "That's awesome. That makes sense," they told me. And I was proud of myself for rescuing the case from the brink of disaster.

At trial, I presented to the jury my theory of Diego's brilliant scheme of writing test checks in smaller amounts, and then when they went undetected by the bank and Jackie's accountant, writing bigger checks to pay off his credit cards. Diego testified to his story that he worked for Jackie, and that the big checks written to Diego's credit cards were his salary, authorized by Jackie. Diego suggested that Jackie was lying because his accountant had busted him again for overspending, and because Jackie had a vendetta against Diego due to their falling out. Jackie denied all of this and said it was theft. I told the jury something like, "Why would a professional athlete like Jackie lie about this? He has so much to lose. He would have to be evil to frame a low-level employee that worked for his team. There's no evidence that he's evil." The jury convicted and Diego was sent to federal prison.

Although I believed Diego was guilty at the time, today I can no longer be completely sure. I look back on that case now, like most other cases I prosecuted, and I see that I approached the case with the same sort of tunnel vision that I now see from prosecutors and police in my innocence cases. Although I didn't know what really happened, I was convinced that I did. I came up with the theory about "test checks" out of the blue the day or two before trial, even though at first glance the checks seemed to support Diego's story. I did it because I was prone to twist and turn any new evidence I received to make it fit my preconceived theory, to which I had been wedded for weeks. I had worked so hard on the case, having for weeks believed that Diego was a liar, that the only option I could consider when the new checks arrived the day before trial was that they had to be part of some devious scheme by Diego. So I made up a theory that fit my preconceived beliefs and pushed forward as if my theory amounted to proof beyond a reasonable doubt.

Although I believed Diego was guilty at the time, today I have no idea whether Diego devised a brilliant "test check" scheme, or whether he worked as a personal concierge for Jackie as he claimed. My theory might have been correct, but I don't know. I have no idea whether Jackie framed Diego because he was mad at him, or because he didn't want to get in trouble with his accountant again for overspending, or both. But looking back on it, I do know that I was supposed to present proof beyond a reasonable doubt of Diego's guilt, and instead I presented a theory that I made up out of the blue right before trial. I presented it with passion because at the time

I *knew* that I was right, and firmly believed that Diego Miranda deserved to go to prison.

The criminal justice system believes this sort of ambiguity is perfectly fine, because the jury can look into the eyes of the witnesses and tell who is telling the truth and who is lying. If Diego were telling the truth and Jackie were lying, the jury would certainly know it. I believed that back then too. I believed Jackie was telling the truth and Diego was lying, and that the jury would be able to see the truth as I did. But I now know that none of us are accurate human lie detectors, and that our lie-detecting abilities are even worse when we are deeply committed to a theory. I was more apt to believe Jackie and disbelieve Diego simply because I was deeply invested in Diego's guilt. And so was the jury. As we saw earlier, despite our lofty "presumption of innocence," jurors tend to believe that the police and prosecutors wouldn't waste their time unless the defendant were actually guilty. Rather than presuming innocence, they tend to start off with a predisposition against the criminal defendant and in favor of the police and prosecution.

My tunnel vision was amplified in the case because it was high-profile, given Jackie's involvement along with that of several other famous professional athletes and coaches who testified. There was even a famous rapper slated to testify, who had been present at some of Jackie's parties when Diego was there. I knew the case was going to be covered by ESPN and the *New York Times*, among other media outlets. A week before trial, I had already arranged with a courtroom sketch artist, who had been contracted by the media for the case, to buy his original sketches after the trial to frame for my office wall. I still have two of those sketches today. One, which depicts me asking Jackie questions on the witness stand, hangs in my parents' home. With all the work I had invested in the case, and how my reputation was at stake, and all the attention the case was getting, I probably would have taken any new evidence of innocence and come up with any theory necessary to keep the case on track. Of course, with any serious case—like murder or rape—the stakes are naturally very high and the pressure intense, regardless of media attention.

Prosecutors obtain convictions like I did in Diego Miranda's case every single day. It's the norm in hotly contested, close cases. Prosecutors develop theories, or ways to spin the evidence, that are nothing more than speculation churned in a tub of biased, one-sided tunnel vision. They then confidently present these theories to the jury as fact—as "proof beyond a reasonable doubt." The system then relies on the jurors as human lie detectors to sort out the mess and determine which side's theory is right, with many jurors tending to start with a preexisting bias in favor of the prosecution.

And with the defense operating at a serious disadvantage in terms of resources, often without investigators or experts to back up its competing theories. That's just how our adversarial system works.

But it's important to recognize that this is far from an error-free process. It's actually quite flimsy and subjective, to be honest. It may be that we have no other option in hotly contested, close cases like Diego Miranda's than to just throw the evidence to the jury and let them decide. We can't just stop prosecuting crime because we haven't figured out a foolproof way to divine truth. But we need to at least call a horse a horse and recognize our system's unstable foundations, built on human beings and all the flaws they bring with them. Because of human limitations, we don't have a foolproof way of finding the truth—of reconstructing past events with a high level of accuracy. Instead of prosecutors presenting their made-up theories to the jury as unassailable facts, and then trying to convince the jury that the prosecutors *actually know* what happened, perhaps they should be honest and call their theories what they are—theories. Then let the jury decide between the various possibilities in a setting more conducive to objective evaluation. After all, it's a prosecutor's job to seek justice, not to win cases.

And as things currently operate in our world of unbridled tunnel vision, we treat each conviction as the "gospel," as if there's no chance juries ever get it wrong. So when new evidence comes to light years later suggesting that the person convicted and sent to prison might have been innocent all along, we pretend that the original conviction was the word of God, which can never be challenged. "How dare you argue that this guy could be innocent?" prosecutors often ask. "He was convicted by a jury of his peers. He's obviously guilty."

· · ·

Michael Morton of Williamson County, Texas, a case discussed earlier, was also a victim of tunnel vision. On the morning of August 13, 1986, Michael woke up a little miffed at his wife, Christine. The couple had gone out to dinner the evening before for Michael's birthday. When they got home, Michael was hoping for birthday sex and put on an adult film to watch with his wife. But Christine promptly fell asleep, leaving Michael upset and frustrated. Before leaving for work the next morning, Michael wrote Christine the following note: "Chris, I know you didn't mean to, but you made me feel really unwanted last night. After a good meal, we came home, you binged on the rest of the cookies. . . . I'm not mad or expecting a big production. I just wanted you to know how I feel without us getting into another fight about sex. Just think how you might have felt if you were left hanging on your birthday. I L Y—M [I love you—Michael]." Michael left the note on his wife's vanity and left for work. By the time he returned home later that day, he was a murder suspect.

The Mortons' friend and neighbor Elizabeth Gee discovered Christine's body. She'd entered the Morton household after finding the couple's two-year-old son wandering around outside wearing only a diaper. Upon entering the couple's bedroom, Gee found Christine bludgeoned to death on sheets stained in semen.[15]

Police arrived at the home before Michael was aware of what had happened. They immediately found Michael's note on his wife's vanity. The note fueled the police's inherent suspicion of Michael as the victim's spouse, leading them to jump to the conclusion that he was the murderer.

When Michael returned to find his home surrounded by police cars, his immediate concern was his son, not his wife, and when informed of her death, he showed little emotion. As is often the case, this only reaffirmed the detectives' suspicion. Michael then decided to stay in the house that night with his son, which many perceived as somewhat callous given what had taken place there earlier in the day. Michael also eventually resumed sleeping in the very room and on the very bed where his wife had been murdered—another indication to the police and prosecutors of the mindset of a remorseless killer.

Michael adamantly denied killing his wife and fully cooperated with the investigation. He willingly submitted samples of his hair, saliva, and blood, and agreed to take two lie-detectors tests, both of which he passed. Aside from the note and whatever conclusions could be drawn from his behavior and demeanor, not a shred of evidence tied Michael to his wife's death, despite a hoard of physical evidence recovered from the scene. None of it pointed to Michael. Fingerprints lifted from the doorframe of the family's sliding glass door failed to match anyone in the Morton family. The source of another fifteen fingerprints found inside the house and near the victim's body also could not be matched to anyone in the family. A fresh footprint was found inside the Mortons' fenced-in backyard. And nearby, next to a wooded vacant lot, a blue bandana stained in blood was discovered. None of this evidence could be connected to Michael.

The police not only ignored the striking fact that the forensic evidence pointed away from Michael; they helped bolster the prosecution's case by turning Elizabeth Gee against him. Leading up to the trial, sheriff's deputies frequently visited Gee, feeding her information and theories all predicated on Michael's guilt. At trial, Gee then provided insights into the Mortons' unhappy marriage, recalling specific fights and instances in which

Michael had said unkind things to Christine. Gee also testified that Michael's stoic demeanor following the murder and the fact that he had cut down his wife's marigolds two days before her funeral seemed insensitive and suspicious to her.

Michael's perceived insensitivity helped bolster the prosecution's case by supporting its contention that he was a depraved, porn-obsessed, sexual deviant who did not care about his wife. According to the state's theory, after being denied birthday sex, Michael continued watching the adult video, eventually becoming so turned on that he became absolutely incensed by his wife's refusal to sleep with him. Michael's sexual frustration and fury came to a head, the prosecution charged, leading him to bludgeon his wife to death. But here's the real kicker. The prosecution claimed that immediately after murdering his wife, Michael performed one last depraved act: he masturbated on top of her corpse.

Over the objections of the defense, the prosecution showed the sexually explicit video that Michael had rented that night to the jurors. After a six-day trial, the jury deliberated for only two hours before returning a guilty verdict.

Years later, during postconviction proceedings, Michael's attorneys obtained police reports detailing the investigation of Christine's murder. The reports revealed the existence of exculpatory evidence that had been withheld from the defense, uninvestigated and ignored leads that should have looked promising, and numerous witness accounts clearly pointing to a different perpetrator.

For example, the morning after the murder, a couple that lived down the street from the Mortons flagged down a sheriff's deputy to report seeing a man park a green van next to the wooded vacant lot that abutted the Mortons' backward. This was near the area where the bloody bandana had been found. Another family in the neighborhood contacted the police reporting a similar sighting, but no one ever returned the call. Another witness reported seeing the mysterious man walking through the woods near the van toward the Mortons' backyard. The police paid very little attention to these reports. In recalling a conversation that had taken place just a couple days after the murder, one witness recalled how the police seemed certain that they had already caught their man, "He didn't overtly say, 'We know who did it,' but he implied that this was not a random event. I can't remember his exact words, but the suggestion was that the husband did it."

In the days following the murder, the police also received several telephone calls indicating that Christine's purse had been stolen. A relative reported that a check he'd written to Christine had been cashed after her death with a signature that appeared forged. Another report indicated that Christine's credit card had been used in San Antonio two days after her murder. However, because the police were confident that Michael had staged the burglary, neither lead was investigated. Their reasoning is made clear in a note that accompanied the reports: "They seem to think that Chris' purse was stolen; of course, we know better than that."

The reports further revealed that at the time of the investigation, the Mortons' two-year-old son, who by then was in the care of his maternal grandmother, was questioned by the police. Due to the child's knowledge of the circumstances surrounding his mother's death, it became abundantly clear that he had witnessed the crime. When asked who was present, the two-year-old accounted only for himself, his mother and a "monster." When asked whether his father was present, the child very clearly stated no. This was not turned over to the defense. Rather, it was buried.

Twenty-five years after being convicted, Morton was exonerated, in part due to DNA testing. DNA testing on the blue bandana found near the scene of the murder revealed the DNA profiles of Christine Morton and Mark Norwood, a known offender whose DNA profile was available in the FBI's CODIS database. Norwood was tried and convicted of Christine Morton's murder in 2013. He was sentenced to life in prison.[16]

On October 4, 2011, Michael Morton was released from prison. He was officially exonerated two months later and has since been awarded over $1 million in compensation from the state of Texas. Michael later wrote the book *Getting Life: An Innocent Man's 25-Year Journey from Prison to Peace*, which detailed how he had been yet another victim of police tunnel vision.

• • •

In 1982, Marvin Anderson of Virginia was another such victim.[17] He was identified from a photo lineup as the perpetrator of a rape and robbery by the victim of the crime. Anderson's photo stuck out like a sore thumb in the array. It was the only photo in color, and the only one with the suspect's social security number printed across it. Twenty minutes later, with Anderson's face now firmly imprinted into her memory, the victim selected Anderson from a live, in-person lineup. The identification was the crux of the state's case at trial, the most powerful evidence against him. Anderson was convicted and sentenced to 210 years in prison.

Anderson had become a suspect through pure happenstance. Among the things the victim recalled about her attacker was that he had mentioned having a white girlfriend. She described the perpetrator as black, and a mixed-race relationship was apparently not that common in Hanover, Virginia, in 1982. The police happened to know one black man who resided with a white woman, Marvin Anderson. Thus, Anderson became the primary suspect.

From that point on, and based on nothing more, the police went after Anderson confidently and aggressively, as if they already had their man. But aside from being a person of color, Anderson did not fit the victim's description of the perpetrator. Anderson was taller, had a darker complexion, lacked a mustache, and did not have any scratches on his face as described by the victim. Plus, Anderson had four alibi witnesses accounting for his whereabouts during the time of the attack. And he had no criminal record or history of run-ins with the police. But he was nevertheless convicted based on the eyewitness identification by the victim.

The full extent of the tunnel vision that led to Anderson's conviction was only made clear after DNA testing identified the true perpetrator of the crime twenty years later. The DNA test results not only proved Anderson innocent, but revealed the identity of that perpetrator: John Otis Lincoln. His involvement in the rape had been rumored throughout the community since the time of Anderson's trial. During the initial investigation, several witnesses reportedly saw Lincoln riding a bicycle near where the crime had occurred. The witnesses also stated that Lincoln had been making lewd and threatening comments toward them that day. The bicycle that Lincoln was reportedly seen riding was later identified by its owner, who verified that it had been stolen by Lincoln on the day of the rape. The only people totally oblivious to Lincoln's possible involvement were the police, who quickly dismissed him as a suspect early on in their investigation, even though he matched the victim's description of the perpetrator, was present in the area that day with a stolen bike, and was awaiting trial for another sexual assault at the time. Consequently, Marvin Anderson spent twenty years in prison for a crime he did not commit.

. . .

The Norfolk Four case from Virginia highlights police tunnel vision in the extreme.[18] In this case, the police ended up charging no less than seven innocent men with the murder and rape of Michelle Moore-Bosko, before finally charging and convicting the actual culprit. Four of those innocent men served significant prison time, while three had their charges dismissed. In a series of events reminiscent of a *Three Stooges* episode, the lead detective focused first on Danial Williams and his roommate, Joe Dick, who lived near the victim, because a neighbor said that Williams had been "obsessed" with the victim. The detective, who was known for his aggressive interrogation techniques and was later imprisoned for misconduct in a different matter, coerced both Williams and Dick into falsely confessing, although their confessions did not match one another and flatly contradicted the evidence from the crime scene, including the way the victim was killed.

When the DNA testing from the crime scene excluded both Williams and Dick, instead of questioning his theory of the case, the lead detective went back to them and told them he knew they must have committed the crime with someone else. Which would explain why the DNA did not match them. Under coercion that included threats of the death penalty, Dick ended up offering a new name, Eric Wilson. The detective then arrested Wilson and coerced him into a false confession as well. But when the DNA from the crime scene didn't match him either, the detective went back to the well again and told the men they had to name who else was with them. Under great pressure, Dick eventually named Derek Tice, and Tice was also promptly arrested, and he too falsely confessed. When Tice's DNA did not match the crime scene evidence either, he was pressured to name more men, and so he provided the names of the three individuals whose charges were later dismissed. (They had not falsely confessed.)

Although the evidence from the crime scene strongly suggested that only one man committed the murder and rape, the lead detective's theory of the case changed as each suspect was excluded by DNA testing and a new man was offered up as an accomplice under coercion. Eventually, the detective's theory expanded to include eight different men participating in a gang rape and murder—a theory that was wholly contradicted by any unbiased analysis of the crime scene, including the inconvenient fact that only one man's DNA was present. Yet the state went forward and obtained convictions against Williams, Dick, Wilson, and Tice, based primarily on their confessions. That DNA from the crime scene came back to match Omar Ballard, who had no connection to the other men and who confessed to having committed the crime alone. The Norfolk Four were eventually released and fully pardoned after great public pressure was brought to bear on their case.[19]

. . .

In April 1989, a female jogger was brutally raped and nearly beaten to death in New York City's Central Park. An hour later, before the unconscious jogger was discovered, the police chased down a group of thirty teenage boys who were reportedly harassing people in the park in a moblike fashion. Five of them were apprehended and charged not only with participation in the mob, but also the jogger's rape. The boys, Antron McCray, Kevin Richardson, Yusef Salaam, Raymond Santana, and Korey Wise, ranged in age from fourteen to sixteen. Four of them subsequently confessed, which led to the convictions of all five. However, several years later, DNA testing would prove that all five of them were innocent and that a man named Matias Reyes, a serial rapist acting alone, was actually responsible for the crime.[20]

The jogger's attack received a great deal of media attention due to the nature of the case. It involved a sexual assault on a white female victim who was a wealthy, Ivy League–educated investment banker, and a gang of black and Latino teenage perpetrators. The case even caught the attention of none other than Donald Trump—who famously called for the immediate execution of all five boys. The case was as high-profile as they come, and the higher a case's profile, the more pressing the need to solve it. Under intense external and internal pressure to obtain convictions, those handling the jogger case became hell-bent on securing confessions from the boys.[21]

No one witnessed the attack on the jogger, and because she had sustained a head injury during the attack that caused her to black out, the jogger could not provide a description of the assailant. Aside from the boys' presence in the park and their alleged participation in the mob, the police had no reason to suspect them of the jogger's rape. Indeed, there was nothing indicating that the jogger had been attacked by more than one assailant. However, the police subjected the boys to intense and lengthy interrogations, ranging from fourteen to thirty hours.[22]

Their four confessions were inconsistent not only with one another, but with demonstrable facts of how the attack occurred, which should have led the Manhattan district attorney to question their reliability. But instead they were the primary evidence used to convict the boys. The confessions were admitted despite defense arguments that the use of overly manipulative and coercive interrogation tactics, including threats, physical abuse, and promises of release, effectively rendered them involuntary. Conveniently, only the confessions were recorded and not the actual interrogations preceding them, meaning there was no way to prove the extent of the coercion.

Aside from the confessions, there was no evidence linking the five boys to the jogger's rape.[23] In fact, the physical evidence suggested the contrary—that the boys were innocent. At the time of their trials, an early form of DNA testing was performed on several samples from the crime scene. The Manhattan DA's office reported to the press and the public that the results of the testing were inconclusive, but, in truth, the testing had failed to find a match between the defendants and the DNA samples: all five defendants were excluded. Furthermore, the testing showed that semen obtained from the victim's cervix matched semen found on her sock, which tended to suggest that there was only one perpetrator. Yet, rather than cease prosecution of the boys, the DA, in effect, suppressed the results by construing them as inconclusive.[24]

At trial, each of the five boys was convicted; they received five to fifteen years apiece. In 2002, Matias Reyes, who was serving a life sentence in a New York State prison, confessed to the rape and assault of the Central Park Jogger. Reyes had been regarded as one of New York's most notorious serial rapists. New DNA testing with advanced technology confirmed that the semen on the jogger's sock belonged to Reyes.[25] On December 19, 2002, the convictions of Antron McCray, Kevin Richardson, Yusef Salaam, Raymond Santana, and Korey Wise were overturned. Wise, the only one of the five boys to be charged as an adult, served eleven and a half years in prison. The Central Park Five received more than $40 million in compensation from New York City.

· · ·

In the prosecutor's office where I worked, there was no general awareness of the dangers of tunnel vision. Building a case and making each piece of new evidence fit our preexisting theory was often a group activity. We had fun picking each other's brains and brainstorming on how to spin evidence to fit our original hypothesis. It was a game. There was no sense of objectivity about the process whatsoever. There was never an attempt to disprove our original hypothesis. Rather, the point of the game was to see how clever you could be in making all new evidence fit your original hypothesis, thus making the case stronger. To the extent we played devil's advocate and put forth contrary arguments, it was only so we would be prepared to shoot down such arguments in court.

Not only are there no systematic policies in place at most police departments and prosecutor's offices to combat tunnel vision, but police are actually trained to *engage* in tunnel vision. The famous Reid interrogation technique, for example, which most police officers in this country are trained in, encourages police officers to assume the guilt of those under interrogation and to confidently inform the suspect that the officers *know* they are guilty. When suspects under interrogation try to offer up innocent explanations or alternative theories suggesting their innocence, officers are instructed not to listen and to gruffly cut off all such attempts. As one scholar has noted: "The very notion of the Reid 'interrogation,' therefore, expressly embraces the foundation problem with tunnel vision—a premature conclusion of guilt, and an unwillingness to consider alternatives. In this context, however, the tunnel vision is not inadvertent, but deliberate; police are taught that this is the way to advance their investigation. Cognitive biases are openly encouraged."[26]

. . .

Those like myself who work on postconviction innocence cases see another type of tunnel vision in our criminal justice system—defense attorney tunnel vision. In case after case, we see that the defense attorney at our client's original trial did very little work and often performed no independent investigation into the facts. They often simply just accepted the foundation of the state's case and worked within it, merely cross-examining the state's witnesses as their primary form of defense, without performing any of the independent investigation necessary to offer evidence supporting an alternative hypothesis. Part of the reason for this is that defense attorneys typically don't have the resources at their disposal to challenge the prosecution's theory of the case. But it often goes beyond that. As one postconviction innocence lawyer has noted:

> We've all read about tunnel vision and how it affects police
> investigations and prosecutors' decisions. Defense lawyers also fall prey
> to cognitive biases. They often see their clients as the jurors and judges
> saw them—guilty. And they often see their clients' cases as unwinnable.
> Because of these cognitive biases we often fail to raise the claims that
> could eventually lead to exoneration. Lawyers are wise to investigate all
> the facts and test all the theories, withholding judgment until the
> investigation is complete. Only when every theory has been debunked
> and every favorable relevant fact turns out to be false, can a post-
> conviction lawyer throw in the towel.[27]

Another scholar has noted, "After a year toiling as public defenders, most stop believing that any of the people they represent are actually innocent. In fact, in most criminal courtrooms, most people present believe that the police got it right and that the trial will simply confirm the defendant's guilt."[28]

This phenomenon was seen starkly in the Netflix docu-series *Making a Murderer*. After Brendan Dassey gave police what appears to be a demonstrably unreliable confession that he was Steven Avery's accomplice in the murder of Teresa Halbach, he was arrested. As the film progresses, the viewer sees that Dassey may very well have been entirely innocent, even though he was eventually convicted, and that he had many avenues available to make a strong defense. But his first court-appointed attorney, who represented Brendan at his initial appearance before bowing out due to a conflict of interest, stated in open court that Brendan had participated in the crime before even speaking at length to his client or doing any investigation. He just blindly accepted the prosecution's theory of the case. Dassey's next attorney, Len Kachinsky, did the same thing. During Kachinsky's representation of Dassey, Kachinsky never investigated the case nor made any effort to listen to what Dassey was telling him—that he was innocent and had falsely confessed. In fact, when Dassey protested his innocence, Kachinsky sent his defense investigator into the jail to intensely pressure Dassey to give up his claims of innocence. The investigator eventually got Dassey to sign another confession that mirrored his first one.

Part of the problem is that public defenders and court-appointed defense attorneys are conditioned to simply accept the state's theory because they do not have the funds to hire investigators, or expert witnesses, to perform their own full-scale investigations. But another part of the problem is defense attorney tunnel vision.

In my work with the Ohio Innocence Project, I cannot count the number of times when, after we have opened a case and begun reinvestigating it, I have called the client's original trial attorney to seek information about the case, only to receive a condescending laugh and a comment like, "That guy? The Ohio Innocence Project is looking into *that* case? That guy is totally guilty." When I have then asked them how they had investigated the case, if at all, and whether they had looked into the promising angles that the OIP had recently uncovered, the answer is often, "No. I didn't do any of that because it just seemed clear that the guy was guilty. I'm not gonna ask the judge for funds for investigators and stuff like that in a case where he's so obviously guilty. I'd get laughed out of court."

In cases when we are eventually able to build powerful evidence of innocence, the reaction from defense attorneys is mixed. Some are concerned, or embarrassed, and offer to help in any way possible. But many continue to believe that their former client is guilty. They cannot accept the fact that they might not have done enough, that their lapses may have caused an innocent person to be convicted. Tunnel vision, it seems, can be hard to shake, even for a lawyer charged with protecting the rights of the victims of tunnel vision.

NOBLE-CAUSE CORRUPTION

In any field there are, of course, bad apples. In the criminal justice system, no category of actor is immune to this problem. The public has been shocked in recent years when videos have surfaced of cops shooting and killing unarmed suspects who weren't fighting back.[29] There have been publicized cases of police officers framing innocent people, planting evidence, or even torturing suspects with electric shocks to obtain confessions.[30]

There has been no shortage of stories about forensic lab technicians who have been caught routinely fabricating results—rendering conclusions favorable to the prosecution without even running the tests. Massachusetts forensic lab technician Annie Dookin, for example, was sent to prison in 2013 after it was discovered that she routinely faked test results in thousands of cases.[31]

Defense lawyers have gone to prison for bribing witnesses or encouraging them to leave town so they couldn't testify against the lawyer's client at trial. Other defense lawyers have become immersed in the criminal activity of their clients, apparently unable to resist the monetary temptations.[32]

Even judges are sometimes bad apples. One judge in Pennsylvania, in what's known as the "Kids for Cash" scandal, was recently convicted for taking payoffs from a private prison company for each juvenile he sentenced to a juvenile detention center, thereby enriching the company by giving them yet another juvenile inmate it could charge the state for incarcerating.[33]

The public understands that sometimes bad people—people with personality disorders or criminal minds—infiltrate the criminal justice system as police officers, prosecutors, defense lawyers, judges, or in other roles. Just as disturbed people sometimes become doctors, accountants, or teachers. It can't be completely avoided, despite our best efforts to keep them out. We all know that.

But most of the injustice in the criminal justice system results from the actions of good people, not the rare bad apples. Indeed, good police and prosecutors can cause tragic injustices when they suffer from tunnel vision. A certainty that they have identified the guilty party can sometimes lead police or prosecutors to cut corners—or even engage in acts of outright dishonesty—to obtain the result that they *know* is the right result in the big picture. This phenomenon is called "noble-cause corruption."[34] Police and prosecutors who engage in noble-cause corruption are motivated by a sense of their important mission to protect the public. It is an "ends-based investigative culture that prompts investigators to blind themselves to their own inappropriate conduct, and to perceive that conduct as legitimate in the belief that they are pursuing an important public interest."[35]

Noble-cause corruption is different than outright corruption—such as accepting bribes to dismiss charges—because those who engage in it are not seeking a personal advantage, like money, but believe they are doing it for a laudable cause. A cop may think, "It would be a tragedy to the victims and society at large if this guilty murderer gets away with it. I need to bend a few rules to bring justice to the victims and to save the life of his next would-be victim."

Defense attorney Dean Strang, who in *Making a Murderer* raised the defense that the police had planted evidence against his client Steven Avery, captured this understandable human temptation: "I didn't see [the cops] plant evidence with my own two eyes. . . . But do I have any difficulty understanding what human emotions might have driven police officers to want to augment or confirm their beliefs that [Avery] must have killed Teresa Halbach? I don't have any difficulty understanding those human emotions at all." Strang also commented, "It is really unusual—and an abandoned act of evil—when a police officer sets out to frame someone who he knows to be innocent." Strang sees any police misconduct in Avery's case as arising not from bad intentions, but from a determination to convict the right person.[36]

Most everyone has been asked at one time or another, "What is the first thing you would do if you had a time machine?" I have heard people answer, "I would go back and stop Hitler before his rise to power, even if it meant killing him." I can understand the temptation and human desire to want to do this. Indeed, in a recent poll, when asked whether they would kill a baby Hitler if they had a time machine, 42 percent said yes, 30 percent said no, and 28 percent said unsure.[37]

And so it is with police officers and prosecutors who engage in noble-cause corruption. If one is convinced that a suspect under investigation is a heinous murderer who may get off scot-free unless a few rules are broken, the temptation to break those rules can be overpowering. It's human. In Robin Hood–type fashion ("steal from the rich and give to the poor"), law enforcement officers can convince themselves that their minor acts of dishonesty are necessary to promote an important public good, and that if they don't engage in such acts the public will suffer greatly.

But while police and prosecutors tend to always believe they are pursuing a heinous criminal, and that their suspect is dangerous and evil, history has proven that they are often wrong.

There have been many stark examples of noble-cause corruption, such as planting evidence or hiding evidence that is favorable to the defendant. Suppressing favorable evidence—what we legally called *Brady* violations— is so common that a judge on the U.S. Court of Appeals for the Ninth Circuit recently wrote in a judicial opinion that it has become an epidemic:

"I wish I could say that the prosecutor's unprofessionalism here is the exception, that his propensity for shortcuts and indifference to his ethical and legal responsibilities is a rare blemish and source of embarrassment to an otherwise diligent and scrupulous corps of attorneys staffing prosecutors' offices around the country. But it wouldn't be true. *Brady* violations have reached epidemic proportions in recent years, and the federal and state reporters bear testament to this unsettling trend."[38] Several of my innocence cases have involved egregious *Brady* violations, including the Gillispie case discussed earlier. My Ohio Innocence Project clients Wheatt, Glover, and Johnson were also victimized by atrocious *Brady* violations.

Wheatt, Glover, and Johnson were all convicted of murder based on the identification of a single eyewitness and alleged gunshot residue found in a couple small areas on their clothing shortly after a shooting occurred on a street in East Cleveland. Gunshot residue is what is often deposited on a person's hands or clothing from the "blowback effect" after he or she fires a gun. The prosecution had offered no motive for why the three men would have shot and killed the victim, and no other evidence. Calling themselves the "East Cleveland 3," the defendants adamantly protested their innocence both before and after their convictions.

Several years into their prison sentences, the eyewitness recanted, saying that she had been pressured by the police into making the identification. The judge who tried the case originally, and who later admitted that she had been concerned about the case since the jury handed down the three men's convictions years earlier, heard this witness's recantation, found it credible, and overturned the trio's convictions. The prosecution appealed, however, and the appellate court reinstated their convictions, finding that the gunshot residue evidence was still sufficient to implicate the East Cleveland 3 in the murder.

At that point, the OIP got involved. We got involved because we knew that the gunshot residue evidence—the sole evidence maintaining their convictions—was highly problematic. In the years since the trio's convictions, it had been discovered that the test used at the time of their trial was prone to produce "false positives"—meaning that the test would signal the presence of gunshot residue when that residue was in fact some other material found in the environment having nothing to do with firing a gun.

More important, the East Cleveland 3 had had their hands and clothing swabbed for gunshot residue *after* they had been handcuffed and taken to the police station in squad cars and interrogated. Recent studies revealed that police cars and police stations—even police uniforms—are awash in gunshot residue due to the amount of firearm training police officers must undertake on an ongoing basis.[39] This causes contamination, as suspects who are transported in a squad car can get gunshot residue on their clothing merely from being in the car. As one commentator has noted, if a suspect is arrested and taken to the police station in a squad car, and then swabbed for gunshot residue at the station, a subsequent test finding a particle of gunshot residue indicates guilt no more than a particle of sand on the bottom of a suspect's shoe indicates he had just been on a beach.[40] As a result of these findings, law enforcement across the nation have been advised to change the protocol for sampling such residue, and to take swabs from suspects when they are first apprehended and *before* being placed in a squad car, or only after bagging their hands to protect them from contamination until swabbing can be performed at the station.[41]

Based on the eyewitness's recantation, and these new scientific understandings undermining the probative value of the gunshot residue evidence, we moved to overturn the East Cleveland 3's convictions.

We lost. We also lost in the court of appeals. The case went cold from our perspective, and the East Cleveland 3 remained in prison.

A few years later, we filed a public records request for the original police file. The East Cleveland 3 had been trying from prison to get the file for years but the police had refused to turn it over. But this time, however, for reasons we don't know, we unexpectedly received the file in the mail. And what we found was alarming. In the file were police reports made during the initial investigation that revealed two things. First, a group of unknown males had been trying to kill the victim and his brother in the days leading up to the murder. In fact, the victim had been shot at just a few days before in drive-by fashion, similar to how he was ultimately killed. The car driven by the shooters in that incident was different from any car associated with the East Cleveland 3. And during the original investigation, the police showed photos of the East Cleveland 3 to the victim's brother, and he did not identify any of them as the drive-by shooters in the previous attempt. So it appeared that someone else had a motive to kill the victim at the time he was murdered. And he wasn't any of our clients.

Moreover, while the eyewitness in the original investigation (who later recanted, saying she had been pressured by police) had identified one of the East Cleveland 3 as the shooter, two other eyewitnesses had given statements that completely contradicted that witness, and, in fact, had identified the shooter as someone else entirely—a man those witnesses knew from the neighborhood.

All of this evidence pointed decisively to the East Cleveland 3's innocence. But it had been hidden by the police and, in violation of their constitutional rights, never turned over to the defense prior to trial. The defense attorneys at the original trial could not interview these witnesses or call them as witnesses, because they simply didn't know about them.

A few years after their convictions, and while they were in prison, the East Cleveland 3 sent a public records request to the police department asking for the full police file. Their request was ignored. But when we finally got the police file years later, it contained a letter from the prosecutor's office to the police department, sent after the East Cleveland 3 had asked for the file, telling the police department to ignore the request. In fact, the letter demanded that the police file be sent to the prosecutor's office for safekeeping. However, for reasons we don't know, the police department did not send the file to the prosecutor's office as the letter demanded. That is how we were able to obtain it years later when we filed our own public records request with the police department.

Thus, someone in the police department, before the original trial, had made the decision *not* to disclose the exculpatory police reports to the defense, though the *Brady* rule required them to do so. And then the prosecutors made the decision after trial to ensure that the police file would never see the light of day.

Talk about covering your ass.

It's perhaps easy in hindsight to cast these actions as attempts to manufacture and maintain a bogus conviction. Acts of evil, even. But I believe that the most likely reason for them is that those who committed these acts suffered from severe tunnel vision, were convinced that the East Cleveland 3 were guilty, and felt that they were doing a public service to bend some rules to guarantee that the East Cleveland 3 would be convicted and stay in prison for life. That's noble-cause corruption.

Armed with new evidence of these *Brady* violations by the prosecutors and police, we once again sought to exonerate the East Cleveland 3. In March 2015, the trial judge threw out their convictions and the trio were finally freed after they'd each spent twenty years in prison. The decision was upheld on appeal, and later the prosecution dropped all charges against them.

. . .

Noble-cause corruption occurs in more subtle forms as well. I have previously described the problem of "synthesized testimony." This occurs when police or prosecutors take witnesses who initially provided details helpful to the suspect and, convinced because of tunnel vision that the witness *must* be wrong, ask pointed questions of the witness suggesting that his or her memory is off. Some witnesses take the cue and begin to question their memory. Sometimes they will change their statements to correspond with what it is clear the police believe *must* have happened. Then they "remember" it this way.

But even worse is when these initial comments helpful to the defense are not written down by law enforcement. The *Brady* rule requires law enforcement to disclose to the defense all materially helpful evidence uncovered during an investigation. But if a witness gives an initial statement helpful to the defense, and then changes it to fit the police's theory after pointed questions are directed at him or her, the initial statements are often not written down. At trial, when the witness testifies, the defense lawyer will have no idea that the witness initially provided the client with an alibi, but then modified his or her statement only in response to police questioning.

As I said before, as a new prosecutor I was taught by mentors not to write down parts of a witnesses statements that I believed were incorrect (and harmed my case) until after the witness "came to Jesus" and told the "correct" story. I was told that if the initial "incorrect" statements were written down, I'd have to turn them over to the defense, and the defense attorney would then be able to tear the witness to shreds on the stand for changing her story. And that would be a shame, I was told. A guilty criminal shouldn't get off because of some careless witness who opened his mouth and blurted something out before thinking it through. The practice was described to me as a way of ensuring that the guilty got what they deserved, and that they didn't get off on some stupid mistake that a defense attorney could unfairly exploit at trial by blowing it out of proportion.

Noble-cause corruption also occurs in even subtler and more intangible forms. As depicted in *Making a Murderer*, the day after sixteen-year-old Brendan Dassey gave a confession implicating himself as the accomplice of Steven Avery in the gruesome murder of Teresa Halbach, prosecutor Ken Kratz held a press conference in which he gave dramatic, chilling details of the crime as allegedly revealed by Dassey's confession. Kratz told television viewers that the details he was about to provide were so gruesome that anyone under age fifteen should change the channel. He then took viewers through his theory of how the murder occurred, based on Dassey's confession, and seemed to revel in the drama of the gory and sordid tale.

But—wait—Dassey's "confession" was recorded, and the videotape suggested that Dassey knew nothing about the crime. Rather, it appeared that he had just given the interrogators what they wanted to hear in response to leading questions. Indeed, Dassey's confession appears on the videotape as the prototypical false confession. Dassey would give wrong answers to questions until the interrogators fed him the "right" answer, which he would then adopt. For example, the interrogators, wanting Dassey to reveal the crucial fact not yet known to the public—how Halbach was killed—asked Dassey, "What did you guys do to her head?" Apparently not knowing the right answer, Dassey could not provide one. After the officers repeated the question several times, Dassey finally guessed, "We cut her hair." But because that was not the answer the police wanted, they then asked him repeatedly, "What else did you do to her head? . . . Come on Brendan, what else do you do to her head?" Eventually, Dassey guessed again, "We punched it." Because this was still not the right answer, one of the officers ultimately lost his patience: "Okay, I'm just gonna come right out and say it. Which one of you *shot* her in the head?" At which point Dassey answered, "He did," meaning Steven Avery.

The videotape also makes clear that Dassey did not understand the importance of what he was doing or saying, as he asked the officers at the end of the interrogation whether he would be able to get back to school by 1:30 because he had a project due. Of course, he was not allowed to leave and he has remained in prison since that date. After the interrogation ended, and the police officers stepped out of the interrogation room, Dassey's mother entered the room and asked her son why he had confessed to something he didn't do. Dassey answered, "They got in my head." A subsequent search of the Avery property failed to corroborate the wild story that Dassey told, or more accurately, the "synthesized" story he adopted in response to the police questioning. Dassey later told his mother that he had merely "guessed" at what answers the police wanted during his interrogation.

But despite the obviously problematic nature of this confession, Ken Kratz went on television and told a gruesome tale to the public based on it. This had the effect of sealing Steven Avery's fate in the eyes of the public from which his jurors would eventually be taken. *Making a Murderer* cut from Kratz's press conference to news interviews with various members of the public. Some of these people said that while they had not been sure before the press conference whether or not Avery was guilty, after hearing about the "confession," they now firmly believed he did it. Though Dassey's confession wasn't even admitted into evidence at Avery's subsequent trial, Kratz had ensured that it was firmly entrenched in the public's consciousness, and thus in the minds of Avery's jurors, before even checking its reliability or knowing that it would be admitted into evidence.

Kratz's tunnel vision was so strong that he ignored the facial unreliability of the confession at his press conference. And I'm sure that, in his mind, there was no chance that the confession was untrue. Kratz seemed supremely confident in what he was saying, and by sharing the gory details he made the press conference that much more tantalizing and memorable to the public. Experts have called Kratz's conduct unethical because it contaminated the local jury pool. But no bar proceedings were instituted against him for violating the pretrial publicity rule.[42] Most prosecutors who engage in this conduct are not disciplined. Indeed, in the counties surrounding the city where I live, prosecutors routinely engage in this same type of pretrial publicity stunt when they bring charges in high-profile cases, which, of course, contaminates the jury pool in their favor.

When prosecutors do this sort of thing, however, they always think it's for the good. They believe they are fighting for a righteous cause to protect the public and to ensure that an evil person is punished. And holding a press conference of this nature is a good way to move one step closer to "justice."

· · ·

There are probably some cases in which, if the officer didn't bend the rules a little, the guilty person might end up getting off scot-free. And I understand that if a person's close family member was murdered, and he or she felt certain that a particular suspect was guilty, he or she might want the rules bent a little to ensure the perpetrator was brought to justice. That temptation is natural and understandable.

But our criminal justice system shouldn't be grounded in the basest and most retaliatory instincts of the victims at their time of deepest shock and grief. If we based our system of justice on such instincts, then we might as well shoot and kill those arrested for heinous crimes as soon as they are apprehended. Although my mind would tell me different, my basest instincts would want that done to anyone who I believed had just murdered one of my children. And I'm sure many parents would feel the same way. We cannot, of course, follow such retaliatory instincts, but must allow our deeper sensibilities and more rational understandings of fair process to prevail.

Turning a blind eye to noble-cause corruption would also mean that police officers and prosecutors, rather than the judicial system and the trial process, would be the ones who seal the fate of those charged with crimes. And when a police officer or prosecutor engages in an act of noble-cause corruption that seals the fate of a suspect—such as, for example, by manipulating a witness's memory to invalidate the suspect's alibi—it happens behind closed doors rather than in public view as when a person is convicted during a trial. As a result, the conduct cannot be reviewed or scrutinized. It never sees the light of day.

But most important, police officers and prosecutors are sometimes wrong, even when they're sure they're right. Because they are human, they are prone to suffering from tunnel vision, and this can cause them to focus on innocent suspects. If we truly believe the adage that "it's better that ten guilty persons escape than that one innocent suffer," upon which our criminal justice system is supposedly based,[43] then this type of behavior simply cannot be pardoned.

SYSTEMICALLY CORRUPTED CATEGORIES OF EVIDENCE

The intense pressure on law enforcement to solve crimes, which often brings with it tunnel vision and noble-cause corruption, has through time created entire categories of evidence that are systemically corrupted. Examples include eyewitness identification testimony, confession testimony, incentivized-witness testimony, and forensic testimony. When I say that each of these categories of evidence is corrupted, I do not, of course, mean that every single eyewitness identification introduced in a courtroom is inaccurate, that every confession introduced is false, or that every statement by a forensic "expert" or incentivized witness is misleading or fabricated. Far from it.

But these categories of evidence are: (1) sometimes unreliable or false; (2) *always* presented at trial by the prosecution as solid and entirely reliable in the case at hand; and (3) capable of being substantially improved and made more reliable. Yet we fail as a system to take steps to improve them. If certain categories of evidence were *sometimes* unreliable and we were *honest* about that fact to jurors, and there was nothing more we could do to improve them, that would be OK in my book. You can't just stop prosecuting people because some forms of evidence aren't perfect. And in such circumstances, we would be doing the best we could do and being honest about our limitations. But instead we overstate the reliability of these forms of evidence, which, in essence, amounts to hoodwinking the jurors, while simultaneously failing to take sufficient steps to improve their reliability.

Eyewitness Identification Testimony

Studies show that simple steps could be taken to improve the reliability of eyewitness identifications.[44] Eyewitness errors occur for a variety of reasons. Error can enter the process when an officer, convinced she knows who the perpetrator is and desperately wanting the eyewitness to select him, gives overt or slight hints to the witness as to which photo she should select. This can be very subtle, such as, "I see you are looking closely at #2. What about

#2 makes you think it could be him?" Or it could be unconscious, such as when each time the witness's eyes settle on photo #2, the officer suddenly tenses up, holds his breath, and leans over the suspect's shoulder to get a better look in anticipation of the "right" choice being selected, unaware that he is sending a strong signal to the witness that #2 is, indeed, the "right" answer. We speak more with our bodies than we do with our mouths. Professional poker players wear sunglasses and hats for this very reason—even those with practiced "poker faces" can't help but inadvertently tip their hand.[45]

Or the officer might tell the eyewitness after she makes a choice that she selected the suspect. As we've seen, after an eyewitness selects a photo, confirmatory feedback of this nature has the effect of increasing a witness's confidence level. This can easily turn what would have been "I picked #2 because he looks the most like the perpetrator, but I can't be sure," into "I'm 100 percent positive it is #2."

To curb such alterations of memory by police, the identification process must be double-blinded. This means that the officer administering the photo lineup shouldn't know which of the six photographs depicts the police's suspect. An officer not assigned to the case should thus be the one who performs the lineup process with the eyewitnesses. There are also easy methods that have been devised that allow the officer assigned to the investigation to administer the lineup but blind him to seeing the photographs, thereby reducing his ability to subtly sway the outcome.

The double-blind process is elemental to the scientific method, because it eliminates bias.[46] If a test is not performed blindly, we simply don't accept the results in other fields. To take a ridiculous example, if a Pepsi vs. Coke taste test is performed on customers strolling through a mall, and the person administering the taste test works for Coke and knows which cup contains Coke, we would call the results unscientific and flatly reject them. Even people doing taste tests at malls know that to be reliable a test has to be double-blinded. Yet we convict our own citizens of serious crimes, and sometimes even send them to death row, based on a multiple-choice test—which of the six photographs is the perpetrator?—that doesn't follow a core principle of the scientific method designed to remove subtle bias and maximize reliability.

In addition, there must be a process in place for immediately memorializing the eyewitness's confidence level as soon as she says, "I'm picking #2." Witnesses who are 60 percent confident at the time they make their pick, for example, are often 100 percent confident in their selection by the time they testify at trial, due to postselection confirmatory feedback. The most obvious confirmatory feedback occurs when the person the eyewitness selected is subsequently arrested and the eyewitness is asked to testify against him at trial. In the meantime, she's likely seen the suspect's face on the news, or learned that the prosecution has substantial other evidence against him. But if her actual confidence level is recorded by a double-blinded officer immediately after she selects a photograph, this problem is alleviated to a large extent. The defense attorney will be able to point out that the eyewitness was only 60 percent sure when she made the pick, and that the increase in her confidence after her selection was brought about by external factors.

Research shows that eyewitnesses should also be shown photographs one at a time rather than at the same time.[47] This is called the "sequential method." The theory behind this process is that when a witness sees all six photographs together, her mind makes comparative judgments, and she ultimately selects the person in the lineup who *most resembles* the perpetrator. But the process of selecting a perpetrator from six different faces alters her memory, so that, once she makes a selection and says, "It's #2," she then "remembers" the face of #2 as the perpetrator rather than the face of the person who actually committed the crime. And when the police are wrong about their suspect and the actual perpetrator's photo is *not* in the lineup, this can cause a witness to select an innocent person and then become convinced that this innocent person is the perpetrator. This problem has been documented not only in clinical studies but in case after case.

However, studies show that when an eyewitness is shown photographs sequentially, her mind is forced to compare only the photograph in front of her to her memory of the perpetrator's face, reducing the comparative-mixing effect of the traditional six-pack lineup format. This increases the chance that she will say, "The perpetrator is not in this lineup," in cases where the police have developed suspicions against an innocent person. While many psychologists and researchers have recommended the sequential method, in 2014 the National Academy of Sciences issued a report stating that more research is needed before it would recommend this process.[48]

The eyewitness identification process can also be made fairer and more reliable at trial by including jury instructions explaining to jurors the inherent problems with memory, and the fact that eyewitnesses are not always correct. And it can be improved by the liberal allowance of memory and psychology experts at trial to educate the jury about the process of identification and the proper weight to be given to the testimony of eyewitnesses. The identification process should be videotaped from beginning to end, to document the conditions associated with the initial identification.[49]

In its current form, however, eyewitness identification testimony is systemically corrupted because, by and large, these procedures are not followed except in limited jurisdictions. And the flaws inherent in eyewitness testimony are usually not presented to the jury. Rather, prosecutors always tell jurors they can take this type of evidence to the bank, and that the eyewitnesses who testified in this case are 100 percent reliable.

Confessions

The problem with false confessions can be significantly alleviated rather simply: interrogations must be videotaped from beginning to end. In this way, jurors can see the stages of the interrogation and whether the confession that resulted came about naturally and convincingly, or by the police pressuring the suspect and feeding him information about the crime for him to parrot back. Today, police typically do not videotape an entire interrogation; they turn on the camera only after hours of pressure, when the suspect is ready to recite from beginning to end his "synthesized" confession. The jury sees only the final product, often scripted, and not what went on before, which resulted in the manufactured product.

Branden Dassey's confession to participating in the murder of Teresa Halbach, and implicating Steven Avery as the mastermind of the killing, was videotaped from beginning to end only because Wisconsin had recently made this a requirement in the "Avery Bill." This bill came about because of Avery's wrongful conviction and DNA exoneration in the earlier Penny Beernsten rape case. Based on my experience, I know that if Dassey's interrogation had not been videotaped from beginning to end, the nuances that demonstrate its unreliability would have never come to public light. The police would have presented it at trial as a solid confession that Dassey gave without prompting and without being fed information about the crime. Because of tunnel vision and noble-cause corruption, police do not see themselves as feeding information to suspects during interrogations. They are always convinced the person they are interrogating is guilty, and when the confession finally materializes they are confident that it's reliable.

Dassey was convicted at trial even though the unreliability of his confession was, for the most part, depicted to his jury. But in some cases the existence of an interrogation videotape can facilitate an acquittal when that appears to be the proper outcome. And Dassey's conviction was overturned by a federal court because of the way the police interrogation went down, as depicted on the videotape.[50] Dassey wouldn't have had a snowball's chance in hell if his interrogation hadn't been recorded in full.

As with eyewitness identification, the reliability of confession evidence could also be improved through proper jury instructions and the liberal allowance of expert witnesses to discuss the psychological pressure points inherent in the interrogation process.

Departments should also explore alternatives to the Reid technique of interrogation, such as the HIG or the PEACE methods. The Reid technique is prone to false confessions because it creates a highly coercive environment where the interrogator assumes the guilt of the suspect and tries to force words into the suspect's mouth (whether true or not, with "truth" defined by the interrogator, who is often blinded by tunnel vision). Moreover, the Reid technique tends to cause the guilty—the savvy criminals—to clam up or demand a lawyer, leaving the innocent, who feel they should talk because they have nothing to hide, the more vulnerable to manipulation and false confessions. The HIG and PEACE methods, in contrast, focus on rapport building and getting the suspect to talk freely.[51] If done correctly, even savvy criminals, many of whom would "lawyer up" under the Reid technique, can be convinced to talk. The HIG technique (named after the High-Value Detainee Interrogation Group that created it) was developed in recent years by the FBI, CIA, and Pentagon as they searched for a new interrogation method to use in the war against terror that would be more effective than the Reid technique. The similar PEACE method of interrogation (which stands for Planning and preparation, Engage and explain, obtain an Account, Closure, and Evaluation) has been in use in the UK for over a decade. Under these techniques, interrogators go to great lengths to make the suspect feel comfortable and "prime" him to open up and let the information flow. His statements are then compared with readily identifiable objective facts. Many guilty suspects eventually dig their own graves. Research has found these techniques more effective than the Reid technique at obtaining valuable confessions. And more important, they are less prone to false confessions. The LAPD has experimented with the HIG interrogation method, but so far, they are the only domestic police department to have done so.[52]

But in its current form, confession evidence is systemically corrupted because it's presented by prosecutors as foolproof, when in reality it is often unreliable or misleading. Simple steps have not been taken in most jurisdictions to improve the accuracy of confession evidence.

Incentivized Witnesses

Our criminal justice system relies heavily on the use of incentivized witnesses, often called informants or "snitches" in legal slang, who testify for the prosecution in exchange for leniency in their own criminal cases. These witnesses are usually criminals who have a great incentive to lie—to tell the prosecution what it wants to hear—so that they can cut a deal for themselves. Although common sense suggests the testimony of such witnesses should be considered by jurors with a grain of salt, prosecutors always tell the jury that the snitch in *this particular case* is telling the truth and passionately urge the jury to believe him. With the deference that jurors typically give to prosecutors, who they figure know more about the case than they do, lying incentivized witnesses cause innocent people to be convicted. Indeed, in the cases of the first 325 DNA exonerations, 14 percent of the wrongfully convicted people had been convicted in part by the testimony of such witnesses.[53] According to the National Registry of Exonerations, more than 50 percent of wrongful conviction cases nationally have involved perjured testimony against the defendant, a good percentage of which involved incentivized witnesses.[54]

When I was a prosecutor, I never suffered for the lack of a snitch. In some cases, multiple criminals or co-defendants would compete for the right to testify against the defendant in my upcoming trial. I would interview them—in reality, audition them—to see who would be the best witness in my case. I would ascertain which one could give me the best details and who could come across the most convincingly. The prosecutors in my office had a little routine we went through to teach our snitches how to come across to the jury as truthful. We told them, "Admit all your past crimes. Don't minimize anything. Don't argue with the defense attorney—just admit the stuff she throws at you with your head down, ashamed. The point is to convince the jury that you have turned over a new leaf—you are starting a new life. And that you've realized that your first step toward an honest life—the way to get your life back on track—is to come clean and tell what you know about this case."

We had a specific image we shared with our snitches to describe how they were supposed to come across on the stand when telling their story—humble, remorseful for all their past deeds, with head down and "hat in hand." "Yes, yes," they were supposed to say, "I've done some bad things. But I realized that to start over, I had to start somewhere. And this is my way of joining the good side, of finally going against the bad guys and helping to put them in prison instead of being one myself. It took a lot of courage for me to do this. It isn't easy."

Of course, the whole thing was a rehearsed act. A dramatic production of some twelve-step, self-discovery, and self-improvement program that the jury would buy, thus believing the snitch. We prepared these witnesses like theatrical directors did with their actors down the street on Broadway. If pulled off properly, the jurors *wanted* to believe the snitches. The jurors understood their struggle and how hard it must be for someone who had lived a life of crime to decide to finally turn his life around and, for once, help the good guys get the bad guys. They felt sympathy for the snitch, or at least wanted to rally behind him and his efforts at self-improvement. And thus they believed him. Or so we hoped. Since we almost always got our convictions, it seemed to work.

But snitching is a business. It's cutting deals and negotiating to improve your lot. When I was a prosecutor, a defense attorney I frequently went up against was indicted for selling snitch information. For example, if he had a client who could help the feds on three cases, he knew that two cases would be enough to get the guy immunity, or at least get him some serious leniency come sentencing time. So he would, according to the charges, collect information from his client about the third case and sell it to another client who was empty-handed—who had no information to share. That way, both of his clients would have something to tell the feds about, and to testify about, to get leniency. He would allegedly split the profits with the client who sold him the information about the third case.

The annals of snitch lore are filled with similar stories. A chapter called "Snitch" in Jim Dwyer, Barry Scheck, and Peter Neufeld's book, *Actual Innocence*, is filled with colorful anecdotes of wrongful convictions caused by incentivized witnesses who, once a new inmate was brought into the jail awaiting trial, would read newspapers to learn details about that inmate's case so they could call the prosecutors and falsely claim that the new inmate had confessed to them. The confessions would appear reliable, because they would contain specific details about the crime that the snitch gleaned from the newspapers. One inmate was even called the "Snitch Professor," because not only did he do it himself time and time again, but he taught other inmates how to play the game to their benefit.

My client Dewey Jones was wrongfully convicted based on snitch testimony. After he was arrested for murder and put in jail to await trial, another inmate named Willie Caton came forward and claimed Jones confessed to him while they were in jail together. Jones was exonerated, after spending nineteen years in prison, when DNA test results showed not only that he was innocent but that Caton was a liar. After Caton had testified in Jones's trial, he became infamous in his region for his ability to repeatedly avoid prison sentences by cutting deals with police and prosecutors in exchange for testimony in criminal cases; he would dream up "confessions" by whomever the local law enforcement was hot to prosecute. This pattern of committing crimes and then testifying in exchange for leniency ultimately ended tragically in a car chase with police that culminated in a crash and shootout, the deaths of two young children, and the death of Caton himself. Caton was out on the streets in part because he had learned to work the system, and he wrongfully convicted at least one innocent person in the process.

Some cases can be solved only through the use of incentivized witnesses. That is understood. Thus, I don't agree with the suggestions of some scholars that the use of incentivized witnesses should be abolished. Rather, it must be more carefully controlled and regulated. Ninth Circuit Court of Appeals Judge Alex Kozinski, among others, has called for stricter controls.[55] In 1990, he noted, Los Angeles County instituted a new rule requiring a committee to screen such witnesses for objective signs of reliability before they could be used in court.[56] This resulted in a steep decline in the number of cases where such witnesses were used, which suggests that many unreliable snitches were weeded out.[57]

Our system's reliance on snitch testimony developed because of the intense pressure police and prosecutors feel to obtain convictions. And unreliable snitch testimony is often used in specific cases because of tunnel vision or even noble-cause corruption. Law enforcement believes that having a criminal testify against the suspect, and putting on a little show for the jury about why this criminal should be believed, helps get a bad guy off the street. It's a good thing, furthering a good cause.

But to anyone who knows the full story of how we currently use incentivized witnesses, and understands how this practice really works behind closed doors, it should seem quite unsavory and prone to fabricated testimony. But those in the system don't see it that way, not only because of tunnel vision but because it's been done that way so long that it's just accepted. It's like a stain on the furniture that's been there so long you no longer notice it. But there's no objectivity or reliability in the process as it currently operates.

Forensic Testimony

At present, forensic testimony is often unreliable because of confirmation bias and underlying methods that have not been properly validated. Prosecutors tell state-paid experts what result they need, and studies, as well as a plethora of wrongful conviction cases, repeatedly have shown that this confirmation bias leads to inaccurate results tilted toward the prosecution. But the problem is deeper than simple confirmation bias. Entire subdisciplines of forensics are systemically corrupt, even in cases where no such bias exists.

As with eyewitness identification evidence, confession evidence, and snitch testimony, the current problems with forensics are so deep and complicated that it would take an entire book to do them justice. And books *have* been devoted exclusively to the current problems with forensics and to these other forms of evidence.[58] There's a wealth of literature on forensics. In short, most types of forensic disciplines that we have used in the past and continue to use today in the criminal justice system are not based on scientific principles with a known error rate. For years we have been convicting people in this country based upon "expert" bite mark testimony (an expert claiming the suspect's teeth match the bite mark on the victim's body), shoe-pattern matching testimony (an expert claiming the shoe print left in the mud at the crime scene matches the defendant's shoe print), gunshot residue testimony (experts claiming gunshot reside was found on the suspect's clothing after a shooting), tire tread matching testimony, bullet fingerprinting testimony (experts claiming the bullet from the crime scene came from the suspect's gun), friction ridge analysis in fingerprint testimony, and many other so-called forensic "sciences."

With the exception of DNA testing, none of the disciplines used in forensics today was developed in an objective setting through a proper validation process with a known error rate. Experts often testify to such things as that the crowbar found in the defendant's house—and *only* the defendant's crowbar, *to the exclusion of all other crowbars in the world*—could have made the particular marks on the victim's doorframe. I have an Ohio Innocence Project case right now where that exact claim was made to convict my client. And that seems like very incriminating evidence indeed. But how can one testify with absolute certainty that the defendant's crowbar made the scratches on the doorframe in question when all other crowbars in the world look pretty much the same? No one can answer that question. There were never studies performed to show an accuracy or error rate, or to prove that such claims are even defensible. And we now know that such claims can't be justified, because many people who were later exonerated by DNA testing were originally convicted on such exaggerated, unscientific "expert" testimony. Also, the research of psychologists like Itiel Dror shows us that these "experts" will change their answers at alarming rates—for example, from a "match" to "no match"—depending on what they are led to believe the "right" answer is before they start.

It's not just me saying this. In 2009, as discussed earlier, the National Academy of Sciences came out with an alarming report on forensic science in the United States, one that called into question the basis for nearly every forensic discipline—the only one that passed muster was DNA testing—

and recommended that Congress create a National Institute of Forensic Science to help mitigate the problem. The NAS wanted the NIFS to create guidelines and rules to ensure that all forensic testimony in the courtroom is actually based on science with a known error rate, and that standards and accreditation are employed to ensure the accuracy and reliability of all such evidence. It recommended that all forensic crime labs be removed from the control of law enforcement agencies and prosecutors' offices and be made truly independent, and that methods be developed to eliminate the confirmation bias that currently pervades these fields. It proposed corrective measures that might include, for example, providing fingerprint samples from six different people, instead of just the suspect's fingerprint, to an expert who is trying to determine whether there is a match to the fingerprint from the crime scene, and removing the expert's bias by not revealing the "right" answer.

But, to date, the NAS's thirteen recommendations have been by and large ignored.[59] Most forensic disciplines are still systemically corrupt, and many are still being used in the courtroom. They are too often the products of tunnel vision and bias, masquerading to jurors as infallible, awe-inspiring wonders as depicted on television shows like *CSI*, on par with putting a man on the moon.

To use another example from the documentary *Making a Murderer:* part of Steven Avery's defense to the charge that he murdered Teresa Halbach was that Avery's blood found in Halbach's car had been planted by the police. It's conceivable that the police could have planted it, because they had Avery's blood samples in vials from his prior wrongful conviction case. To counter this defense, the prosecution sent the blood found in Halbach's car to the FBI to test for EDTA, which is a preservative that would have been present in Avery's blood contained in the vials. If no EDTA was detected in the blood found in the car, the prosecution surmised, that would prove the blood didn't come from the vials. Defense attorney Jerry Buting quipped when he learned of this plan, "I don't trust the FBI at all. And I think that they're going to come up with some dishonest test that somehow claims that the blood in the vial is different than what was found at the scene."[60]

I laughed out loud when I saw that scene, because I know how Buting feels. Like me, he's been engaged in this type of work so long that he knows how forensics are often used by prosecutors as a means to an end. And Buting's fears may have been founded. The FBI originally said it would take months to run such a test, because these tests had been abandoned years earlier due to concerns about their reliability, and thus a new testing mechanism would have to be created specifically for that case. But when the prosecution needed results immediately, the FBI was somehow miraculously able in a matter of a few weeks to run the test and get a result that favored the prosecution. And at trial, Buting pointed out that the FBI lab analyst was told by the prosecution what answer he was supposed to arrive at *before* he created the test. The evidence submission sheet stated the purpose of the test was to "eliminate the allegation" that the police had planted blood.

A defense expert at Avery's trial testified that the FBI's test was unreliable. (Indeed, the results of such a test had never before been admitted in court, when contested, out of unreliability concerns.) Furthermore, the defense expert noted that the FBI's results could not be subjected to scrutiny, because the FBI had refused to turn over the details and processes of the new test it had created just for that particular case. But juries usually don't get these nuances. They see an impressive FBI analyst who flew in from Washington DC to testify, and typically accept such testimony as the gospel. I have previously described this phenomenon as the "Reverse-CSI Effect."[61] And that's what may have happened in Avery's case, just as Buting feared.

And the FBI blood expert in Avery's case even gave an opinion on several samples of blood he hadn't tested! He stated that in his expert opinion those samples did not contain EDTA, meaning they could not have been planted. This statement caught Buting by surprise, causing him to ask the expert to repeat it. When the FBI expert repeated his statement, Buting commented, "OK, I wanted to know how far you were willing to go."

THE SNOWBALL EFFECT

Tunnel vision can produce a snowball effect in cases of wrongful conviction, where an initial, single piece of errant evidence gives rise to what appears to be an overwhelming case by the time of trial.[62] If an eyewitness mistakenly identifies an innocent person from a photo lineup, for example, the police may become even more convinced that they have the right suspect, leading them to put pressure on the forensic experts to find a fingerprint match with a smeared latent print left at the crime scene. After the expert then gives them the fingerprint match they were looking for, they may then—even more certain of the suspect's guilt than before—interview potential witnesses in the case and "suggest" additions or corrections to their statements to make the overall picture more compatible with the suspect's guilt. And with enough pointed questions, a witness or two might start "remembering" things the way the police want them to.

Now that the police have both an eyewitness and a fingerprint match, and other witnesses providing incriminating details that undermine the suspect's alibi, they may approach inmates in custody with that suspect and ask if any of them by chance overheard the suspect talk about committing the crime. With inmates eager to work time off their own sentences, it's often not hard for the police to find someone who is more than willing to concoct a story about overhearing the suspect talk about committing the crime. Or they may go right to the horse's mouth and elicit a false confession from the suspect himself, pressuring him with the facts that an eyewitness has already identified him and that his fingerprint has been found at the scene, making it appear that a quick confession and a plea for leniency is his only way to avoid the death penalty.

By the end, the case against the innocent suspect appears overwhelming. But each piece of evidence was created from the ones before it in a "feedback loop,"[63] and each can be traced back to the initial piece of errant evidence—the initial snowflake—that has become a giant snowball by the end.

8.   Seeing and Accepting Human Limitations

To improve our system of justice, two things need to change. First, we need to recognize that the criminal justice system is not a self-automated machine that has been calibrated through the decades to achieve perfect justice. Rather, it is comprised of human beings, and is deeply infused with the psychological flaws that humans bring to it. We need to embrace our humanity and not be afraid to acknowledge and mitigate human error. In other words, we need humility and the ability to accept our human limitations.

In episode 9 of *Making a Murderer*, Steven Avery's defense attorney Dean Strang says, "Most of what ails our criminal justice system lie[s] in an unwarranted certitude on the part of police officers and prosecutors and defense lawyers and judges and jurors that they are getting it right, that they are simply right. Just a tragic lack of humility of everyone who participates in our criminal justice system." Later, in an interview that was reported by the *New York Times*, Strang was asked, "How do we change that culture?" He answered, "I think it starts with humility, [with] recognizing that every one of these institutions that together compose the criminal justice system is itself made up of human beings, all of us flawed, all of us broken. . . . I think we need to have the humility to recognize that and correct serious mistakes."[1]

Those words could have come right out of my own mouth. In fact, I came to this realization myself—by accident. I left my prosecutor's office arrogant and with my eyes closed to the imperfections in the system. Only through a process of education brought about by being, in essence, forced to help supervise the Kentucky Innocence Project as a fledgling academic did I eventually recognize the need for change.

Second, we need to implement structural and procedural changes in the criminal justice system to compensate for our psychological flaws. From mistaken eyewitness identifications to false confessions to bad forensics, there are clear and obvious steps we can take to limit or remove the human influences that lead to unjust results.

These two types of change—attitudinal and procedural—go hand in hand. The more we understand that the system is infused with human flaws, the more likely we are to embrace procedural changes designed to minimize the human problems.

The procedural changes that must be implemented have been set forth throughout this book. Each could be the topic of a book in and of itself. Indeed, entire books have been written on the steps necessary to improve specific types of evidence, such as confession evidence, eyewitness identification evidence, and snitch and forensic testimony.[2]

In summary, the following procedural changes are needed:

- *Eyewitness identification.* A police officer administering a photo line-up should employ the double-blind, sequential method. Instructions to witnesses should be standardized, and witness confidence statement should be taken immediately after an identification is made. All identification procedures should be videotaped.

- *Interrogations.* Interrogations in cases of all serious crimes must be videotaped from beginning to end without interruption. Police departments should explore new interrogation techniques that are more productive and less likely to elicit false confessions than the Reid technique, such as the HIG or PEACE method.

- *Incentivized witnesses (snitches).* The use of such witnesses must be tightly controlled, with procedures implemented to improve reliability, such as those previously implemented in LA County and some parts of Canada.

- *Forensics.* "Blinding" procedures recommended by the 2009 NAS report and leading scholars must be implemented, which would remove confirmation bias from forensic analysis.[3] For example, forensic agencies should be removed from the control of law enforcement,[4] and experts should be given limited information about a case before performing their analysis so that they don't know the "right" answer before they start. A "blinded" supervisor should confirm the results of the first analysis. Procedures like this have been implemented already in Scotland.[5] In addition, accreditation and validation standards of forensic disciplines must be devised and enforced to ensure compliance with basic safeguards of reliability.

- *Defense attorneys.* We must work to level the playing field between the prosecution and defense, with adequate resources provided to defense counsel for investigative and forensic pursuits.[6]

- *Police and prosecutors.* Police officers and prosecutors should receive formalized training on the dangers of tunnel vision and how to combat it, and the dangers of the other psychological pitfalls outlined in this book.[7] Training of this nature has already been implemented in some jurisdictions in Canada.[8]

- *Elections of judges and prosecutors.* We must work to modify how judges and prosecutors are chosen, immunizing them from political pressure, and move from an election model to appointment by bipartisan commissions, similar to what already occurs in the federal system and some states, like Arizona.[9]

The structural changes that our system needs are easy to identify and articulate, and have been fully outlined in many different publications. The website of the Innocence Project, for example, delineates all of these procedural reforms on a single webpage, with links supplying detailed information on each topic.[10] Some of these reforms would be expensive to implement, like increased resources for defense investigations, and thus may take years to achieve. Others are relatively inexpensive and easy to implement, like eyewitness identification reforms and procedures in forensic labs to reduce human bias.

The problem, therefore, is not identifying which reforms are necessary, but rather getting system buy-in on their implementation. Implementation requires opening the eyes of those in the system so that we can shift from arrogance and resistance to openness and vigilance, always looking for ways we can improve and provide greater justice. But so far that's proven to be easier said than done, even for reforms that are inexpensive and would take little effort to carry out.

• • •

When an airplane disaster occurs, the National Traffic Safety Board and the Federal Aviation Administration swoop in and create a diversified task force to investigate the causes of the crash and propose reforms to reduce the chances of a similar crash happening in the future.[11] Where appropriate, changes are mandated, from modifications in air-traffic control procedures to improvements in airplane manufacturing.

In the private sector, if an executive working for a chain of restaurants on the East Coast decides that the company should expand into the

Southwest, the decision will usually be challenged internally. Supervisors in the company will typically play devil's advocate and demand that, before substantial company assets are earmarked, the idea must be thoroughly tested against any and all competing views. External focus groups will often be created to determine if the executive's hypothesis is accurate. Is there a taste for our brand of food in the Southwest? What competitors are already located in that region?

Anheuser-Busch, IBM, Royal Dutch Petroleum, and 3M, for example, are major corporations that have implemented formalized "devil's advocates" in their decision-making processes, but most companies inherently engage in this process regardless of whether or not it's formalized and labeled.[12] My next-door neighbor is an engineer at Proctor and Gamble. His job is to analyze the manufacture of Proctor and Gamble products, and to question whether existing processes for production are energy-efficient. His sole job is to play devil's advocate and challenge the status quo—to find a way to save energy at every step of the process. He is paid specifically *not* to accept the way it's always been done, but rather to aggressively challenge it.

The international bestseller *In Search of Excellence: Lessons from America's Best-Run Companies* champions the necessity of devil's advocacy in the private sector.[13] And business journals are full of articles extolling the necessity of fighting tunnel vision in business, replete with scary examples of companies that went bankrupt because they allowed tunnel vision and "groupthink" to go unchecked.[14]

The discovery of hundreds if not thousands of wrongful convictions in the past twenty-five years should be viewed by the criminal justice system as indicative of a disaster. A mass disaster. Innocent people walking out of prison on a weekly basis after spending twenty, thirty, or forty years in prison for crimes they didn't commit would be, in the aviation field, the equivalent of planes crashing left and right. In the restaurant business, it would be the equivalent of a company repeatedly opening up new branches that immediately go under, causing great financial loss and eventual bankruptcy. In the private sector, such results wouldn't be tolerated for long. Yet, the criminal justice system consistently resists introspection and change. When a police officer or prosecutor gets hot on a case and becomes singularly focused on a suspect, a race ensues to confirm the hypothesis. Unbridled tunnel vision sets in. The entire police department or prosecutor's office might join in to help turn the hypothesis into a conviction. And when an inmate who has been in prison for twenty years asserts that he was wrongfully convicted, and brings forth new evidence to support his claim, it's met with a knee-jerk denial from those in the criminal justice system. Rarely is there an objective inquiry. There is no built-in devil's advocacy here.

So why is the criminal justice system in a silo, seemingly immune from introspection and reform? Simply put, largely because actors in the system don't have to respond to market demands. In the private sector, if an airplane crashes, or a product is defective and causes injuries, or a hasty business decision costs the company millions of dollars, market pressures require the company to take steps to ensure that such risks are minimized in the future. To do so, they institutionalize checks and balances and require that all hypotheses or business intuitions be challenged and tested to some degree before they are put into practice.

But actors in the criminal justice system—police officers, prosecutors, judges, and so on—don't have to respond to a market in the same way. They operate in a stilted environment, where those injured by their actions—the wrongfully convicted—are not consumers of their product. They don't need to fix or tweak anything to induce those they've injured—the innocents—to come back and buy again. It simply doesn't work that way. And with the qualified immunity that the U.S. Supreme Court has generously supplied to prosecutors and police in recent decades, which protects these actors from civil liability for their misconduct, they're rarely held accountable through their pocketbooks or in any other way. If a wrongfully convicted person is somehow able to pierce the shield of qualified immunity and obtain a monetary verdict against a police department or prosecutor's office, insurance companies usually foot the bill. Actors in the criminal justice system are almost never held accountable for their actions as are players in other facets of the professional world.

And given the "tough on crime" political environment in which those in the criminal justice system operate, the public is happiest when their public officials flex their law enforcement muscles and convince them that the occasional wrongful conviction is a great aberration that could never happen to John Q. Public. That's what the public wants to hear, and they believe it. Until it happens to them. I can't count the number of times I have answered a call from a mother or wife who wants to tell me about her son's or husband's wrongful conviction, and the first thing she wants to tell me is how unfair the trial was, and how overzealous the prosecutors acted, and how she never thought a witch hunt like that could happen in America. She invariably tells me stories with great passion, as if she thinks I'm hearing something new and her stories will be a great revelation to me. I say, "Yeah, you were in the fog like everyone else—oblivious. Welcome to my world.

Now you know how our system really works, unfortunately. Sorry you have to be one of the enlightened ones."

· · ·

I said at the beginning of this book that this was not a doomsday book. And it's true. The good news is that, despite the silo in which the criminal justice system operates, change is beginning to happen. Change has taken place surely but slowly, because the innocence movement has continued to gain momentum and the public has gradually taken notice of the problem of wrongful convictions. So far, fourteen states have adopted eyewitness identification reforms,[15] and twenty-three states have policies requiring the recording of interrogations.[16] Twenty years ago, no jurisdictions were taking steps to curb wrongful convictions. The number of local jurisdictions adopting these "best practices"—either voluntarily or through legislative or court action—continues to grow each year. In 2017, one of the major national companies that trains police departments in interrogation methods announced that it was abandoning the Reid interrogation technique because of its tendency to produce to false confessions.[17] That was a major blow to the fortress of Reid, which was once thought impregnable.

In 2015, the FBI announced that more than two thousand convictions that involved microscopic hair comparisons required reexamination because of the flaws with this forensic discipline.[18] That review is under way, and exonerations have already begun to occur as a result.[19] In 2013, the Department of Justice created the National Commission on Forensic Science, whose mission is to "enhance the practice and improve the reliability of forensic science."[20] Sadly, the Trump administration killed this commission when it took the reins in 2017, but hopefully that action will merely be a temporary blip in a radar field that otherwise appears to be trending slowly but surely in the right direction.[21]

In 2003, when the Ohio Innocence Project was founded, I began talking to legislators in Ohio about the need for eyewitness identification and interrogation reform. I was met with blank stares and little patience. But I kept talking to them about these pressing needs. And each year the reception I received improved a little. By 2010, a reform bill my office drafted—which included eyewitness identification reform, interrogation recording policies, expanded access to postconviction DNA testing, and a DNA preservation law (so that law enforcement must save the DNA from a case until the inmate is released from prison)—was passed by both state houses and signed into law by the governor. It made Ohio a "national model" for innocence reform and was called by a sponsor "one of the most important pieces of criminal justice legislation in this state in a century."[22]

I learned a valuable lesson through this process: change happens very gradually. Activists must understand that if they at first encounter resistance, sometimes people must hear about a problem many times, over a course of many years, before the message sinks in and they start to take notice. The "effective frequency" theory in the field of marketing, for example, holds that when a person hears a new idea for the first time she often instinctively throws it to the wayside. But each time she hears it thereafter, the idea sounds less strange. Eventually, the idea sounds within the range of "normal" and can be openly considered and debated.[23]

I found this to be true with innocence reform. Activists sometimes get frustrated and give up when results are not immediate. But change—particularly change of this magnitude across a vast criminal justice system—will happen slowly but surely when we are resolute and keep "screamin' and hollerin'," as my friend and exoneree Dean Gillispie always says, until the truth wins out.

This is true with any civil rights movement. When I was in high school in the early 1980s, a fellow student in speech class gave a speech on the evils of homosexuality, and no one in the class batted an eye—not even the teacher. Thirty years later, such a speech would be received in an entirely different way. Indeed, I have seen tremendous shifts in societal views in my lifetime, on issues ranging from gay rights to marijuana legalization. And so it will be with innocence reform. I believe that if we keep pressing and educating, we will see massive transformation in our criminal justice that will make it more accurate, fair, and just.

With the forces that bring procedural changes comes humility—attitudinal change. For example, in recent years, more than twenty-five prosecutors' offices across the country have opened what are known as conviction integrity units (CIUs), which delve into postconviction claims of innocence in an attempt to free the wrongfully convicted. The Conviction Review Unit in Brooklyn District Attorney's office, for example, exonerated twenty inmates in the first two years of its operation. The DA who created it, Ken Thompson, who late in 2016 sadly passed away at age fifty, called it a "national model"—and he was right. His office freed more innocent people between 2014 and 2016 than my Ohio Innocence Project and probably any other innocence organization in the world.[24] Except, that is, for the CIU in the prosecutor's office in Houston, Texas. Prosecutors there freed forty-two inmates on grounds of innocence in 2015 alone.[25] No law school innocence organization, including my own, can come close to matching those numbers.

The CIUs in Brooklyn and Houston are, of course, a welcome and much-needed addition to the innocence movement. Combined with independent innocence organizations like my Ohio Innocence Project, they provide a blueprint for how we can eventually conquer the problem of wrongful convictions. But the failings of CIUs in other jurisdictions show that success in this area is hard to attain. Many of the other CIUs thus far appear to pay little more than lip service to the problem of wrongful convictions, because the prosecutors in charge seem understandably unable to move past their own psychological barriers to adequately reexamine old cases with a fresh eye. A 2016 report issued by the Quattrone Center for the Fair Administration of Justice at the University of Pennsylvania School of Law recognized this problem, issuing a series of recommendations to make CIUs more effective, like the ones in Brooklyn and Houston. Included in the report was a recommendation that CIUs employ criminal defense attorneys and others from outside the prosecutor's office to combat the inevitable confirmation bias and tunnel vision to which any human being may succumb when reviewing his or her own work, or the work of a close colleague.[26]

But in 2015, 58 of the 149 exonerations in this country came from prosecutors' offices—from CIUs. Those 58 exonerations came from the small group of CIUs that have proven to be effective, ones that have seemingly been able to get past the psychological roadblocks. This small group of effective CIUs exonerated nearly as many innocent people in 2015 as did all the law school and freestanding innocence organizations combined. One can only imagine that if every major city in the United States had a CIU as effective as the ones in Brooklyn and Houston, it would be a complete game changer. The number of annual exonerations nationally would be staggering. Such is the hope for the future.

·   ·   ·

Our Ohio Innocence Project client Ricky Jackson was exonerated in November of 2014 after serving thirty-nine years in prison. Ricky spent more than two years of that time on death row, coming within a few months of his execution date and escaping death only because of a lucky paperwork error that had occurred at his sentencing. Ricky's thirty-nine years gave him a dubious distinction at the time, making him the longest-serving exoneree in U.S. history. Ricky and his two best childhood friends had been convicted in 1975 based on the testimony of a twelve-year-old boy, Ed Vernon, who said he saw Ricky and his friends commit the murder. We were able to exonerate them nearly four decades later because Ed Vernon, by then a man in his fifties, recanted. He explained that he'd lied at trial because of intense police pressure and manipulation. That lie, he later said on the stand at our hearing in Cleveland, had ruined his life.

Going into our court hearing to exonerate Ricky, I felt the odds were stacked against us. It is very difficult to win a case like Ricky's without ironclad evidence of innocence, like DNA test results. I knew from my experience that prosecutors and judges will virtually never agree that a recantation like Vernon's is valid—they will claim in a knee-jerk manner that someone pressured or paid the witness to recant. Simply put, they are usually unable, because they are human, to reexamine such a case with an open mind, and thus they typically fight back with ferocity.

Prior to the court hearing, the prosecutors in Cleveland asked if they could meet with Ed Vernon alone, in advance of the hearing, to get a sense of whether or not he was telling the truth. Earlier in this book, I told the story of a similar request from a prosecutor's office in a different case. When our witness in that case arrived to meet with the prosecutors, they didn't bother to interview him, but rather had him arrested for a series of unpaid traffic tickets in an effort to intimidate him from testifying. The requested interview was nothing more than a sham.

But in Ricky's case, we agreed to let Vernon meet with the prosecutors in advance of the hearing. We agreed because we had sensed, from our frequent dealings with the prosecutors in Cleveland, that their attitude toward innocence had evolved in recent years. When we first started bringing cases to their attention, shortly after the OIP opened in 2003, we were often met with the same type of close-minded resistance described throughout this book. But that attitude seemed to have changed a bit over the years. Not in every case, and not with every prosecutor in that office, but there were several prosecutors in the Cleveland office who we felt had listened to the message of the innocence movement, and who were doing their best to achieve justice on a case-by-case basis in an open-minded manner. And one of those prosecutors, Mary McGrath, had been assigned to defend the Ricky Jackson conviction.

When Mary met with Ed Vernon, she didn't try to have him arrested or otherwise try to intimidate him. Rather, she listened to him. Carefully.

The hearing commenced in November 2014 with the testimony of Ed Vernon. Ed explained how he had lied as a child. He told how he had informed the police back in 1975 that he was lying, but how they screamed at him and threatened him to make him go forward with his testimony. And how he had lived with the burden of that lie for nearly forty years. Mary and her colleagues cross-examined Ed and questioned his story. But Ed held firm. Then Ricky Jackson testified. He said he was innocent and described his decades behind bars for a crime he didn't commit. I felt that Ed's and Ricky's testimonies were both extremely compelling. In fact, their stories were so moving that they brought several spectators in the courtroom to tears. But I had no idea how the prosecutors or the judge viewed them.

After the testimony of the witnesses ended, the judge said that he would hear closing arguments after a lunch break. During the break, OIP staff attorney Brian Howe, who was in charge of the case, prepared for his closing argument, and we were all sick with anxiety over Ricky's fate. We agonized over the judge's facial expressions during the hearing, trying to guess how he had received the evidence that would determine how Ricky would spend his remaining years on earth—in prison, or as a free man.

When we returned to the courtroom at the predetermined time, the prosecutors and judge were nowhere to be seen. After thirty more minutes passed, there was still no sign of the prosecutors or the judge. We sat in the courtroom and waited, confused and exceedingly nervous.

After about forty-five minutes of waiting, the courtroom doors swung open and Mary and her team of prosecutors entered the courtroom. With them was the elected prosecutor—the head of the office. They entered the courtroom at the same time that the judge entered through his private door behind the bench, as if their entrances had been orchestrated. The prosecutors walked straight up to the bench and said something to the effect of, "We agree that Ricky Jackson is innocent and that a terrible injustice has occurred in this case. We are dismissing all the charges and agreeing that he may be set free."

In all my years of doing postconviction innocence work, I have never been so shocked. Ricky looked up at the heavens and then began to cry, as did all of us on his team. The prosecutors and the judge continued to talk about mundane matters, such as the paperwork that would have to be done to complete the exoneration and how quickly Ricky could be released from custody. But none of us heard what they were saying. We just cried and hugged one another in stunned disbelief.

A few days later, Mary and her team agreed to financial compensation for Ricky, filing papers that once again declared that Ricky Jackson was innocent and that he deserved full compensation for the pain he had suffered at the hands of the State of Ohio.

I am still to this day in awe of what Mary and her team were able to do in Ricky Jackson's case. I know from years of experience in this type of case that because of confirmation bias, tunnel vision, cognitive dissonance, dehumanization, and the bureaucratic prosecutorial mindset, it is hard for any prosecutor to evaluate postconviction innocence evidence objectively. That is true even when the evidence of innocence is rock-solid, as with DNA test results. The fact that they were able to make themselves step out of that role, to step away from all of the psychological pressures to confirm their office's preconceived belief in Ricky's guilt, and to look at Ricky's case objectively and fairly without ironclad evidence of innocence, is a truly impressive human accomplishment. I don't know that I could have done it when I was a prosecutor. I doubt it.

Immediately after Ricky was released, he said he had a very important thing to do. He asked Brian Howe for the phone number of Ed Vernon's pastor, as the pastor was the person who had first notified us of Vernon's agony and his desire to correct the tragic injustice he had helped perpetuate as a young boy. Brian gave Ricky the pastor's phone number. Later, Ricky told us that he had called the pastor and asked him to arrange a meeting between Ricky and Ed Vernon at the pastor's church. The pastor set it up. On the day of the meeting, Ricky saw Vernon enter the chapel in the same way he had appeared during his courtroom testimony a few days earlier—a broken, bent-over, and dispirited man, worn and weary from living with a lie that had sent Ricky and two other innocent men to death row nearly forty years earlier. On the stand at Ricky's hearing, Vernon had called it "the lie from the pits of hell."

When Vernon entered the chapel that day, Ricky walked up to him, hugged him, and whispered in his ear, "I forgive you. I want you to live a good life." Ricky then continued to hold him while Vernon sobbed in his arms. Ricky later told me that as Vernon sobbed, he became lighter in Ricky's arms, and Vernon gradually began to stand more upright. A physical transformation occurred before Ricky's eyes, as Vernon's burden began to dissipate.

Ricky later explained to me that he had lived those thirty-nine years in prison hating Ed Vernon. He had put the "enemy image" on Vernon (though he didn't use that term), and imagined him living a life of freedom, blessed with a wife, children, a good job, and all the things that Ricky had been so painfully deprived of.

But Ricky had also studied the great philosophers and all the major religions in prison, and in the process he had internalized their lessons of open-mindedness and open-heartedness. He had come to understand that there are always two sides to every story, and to recognize that every human being, no matter what they have done, is worthy of being treated with decency and respect, and to be forgiven. With that attitude, Ricky challenged himself to overcome his greatest bias. A bias greater than most of us have ever faced in our lifetimes. Ricky challenged himself to see the world—to see Ed Vernon—in a way that questioned his decades of hardened hatred. His decades of close-minded certainty. Ricky wanted to do this not only for Ed Vernon, but for himself. He wanted to see if he could instantly impart true justice to Ed Vernon in a way that our criminal justice system had been unable to impart to Ricky Jackson for thirty-nine long years.

The criminal justice system is beginning to change for the better, to correct some of its flaws. Prosecutor Mary McGrath's act of freeing Ricky Jackson with an open mind and open heart is a testament to the power of this change. But we must continue to speak, write, share, educate, and inform. As exoneree Dean Gillispie would say, we must keep "screamin' and hollerin'." And we must encourage others to join the cause to create a groundswell—a critical mass that will cause a shift in societal thinking such as we have seen with other social justice movements in recent decades. It is starting now. The shift is still in its embryonic form. But if we are not vigilant and steadfast going forward, then change will die on the vine.

Notes

CHAPTER 1. EYE OPENER

1. Registry of Exonerations, www.law.umich.edu/special/exoneration/Pages/about.aspx (accessed April 29, 2017).

CHAPTER 2. BLIND DENIAL

1. Later, after the DNA from the crime scene matched Earl Mann, the judge exonerated Clarence Elkins. It may have occurred to her at that point that her initial decision in the case was erroneous and could have caused an innocent man to spend the rest of his life in prison, if not for new evidence connecting Earl Mann to the crime scene. To her great credit, in her next Ohio Innocence Project case, she issued a well-reasoned opinion exonerating our client Douglas Prade, over the objection of the prosecution. See, "Former Police Captain Freed after Murder Conviction Overturned," *Cleveland News 19*, www.cleveland19.com/story/20761689/judge-overturns-douglas-prades-murder-conviction (accessed Nov 19, 2016); *State v. Prade*, 2013 WL 658266 (Ohio Com.Pl.). This decision was overturned on appeal, and the Ohio Innocence Project is continuing to litigate the case to seek Prade's release.

2. Elizabeth Mendes, "Americans Down on Congress, OK with Own Representative," Gallup, May 9, 2013, www.gallup.com/poll/162362/americans-down-congress-own-representative.aspx.

3. Daniel S. Medwed, *Prosecution Complex: America's Race to Convict and Its Impact on the Innocent* (New York: New York University Press, 2012), 163; see also, Dahlia Lithwick, "When Prosecutors Believe the Unbelievable," *Slate*, Jul 16, 2015, www.slate.com/articles/news_and_politics/jurisprudence/2015/07/mark_weiner_conviction_vacated_chelsea_steiniger_text_case_finally_overturned.html.

4. Oren Yaniv, "Brooklyn Jury Acquits Man of Murder 24 Years after He Was Jailed for the Crime," *New York Daily News*, Nov 18, 2013, www

.nydailynews.com/new-york/nyc-crime/brooklyn-jury-acquits-man-murder-24-years-jail-article-1.1521151.

5. Ibid.

6. Medwed, *Prosecution Complex*, 119–21.

7. See "Innocence Lost: The Plea," *Frontline*, PBS and WGBH/Frontline, www
.pbs.org/wgbh/pages/frontline/shows/innocence/etc/other.html (accessed Apr 4,
2017); "Outcomes of High Profile Daycare Sexual Abuse Cases of the 1980s,"
Frontline, PBS and WGBH/Frontline, www.pbs.org/wgbh/pages/frontline
/shows/fuster/lessons/outcomes.html (accessed Apr 4, 2017). See also, Mark
Pendergrast, *Victims of Memory: Sex Abuse Accusations and Shattered Lives*
(Hinesburg, Vt.: Upper Access Books, 1996).

8. "Haunted Memories, Part 1," *Dateline*, NBC News, Apr 9, 2012, www
.nbcnews.com/video/dateline/46994994/#46994994.

9. See, for reference, Eddie Harmon-Jones and Judson Mills, "Introduction
to Cognitive Dissonance Theory and an Overview of Current Perspectives on
the Theory," in *Cognitive Dissonance: Progress on a Pivotal Theory in Social
Psychology*, ed. Eddie Harmon-Jones and Judson Mills (Washington D.C.:
American Psychological Association, 1999); see also Leon Festinger, *A Theory
of Cognitive Dissonance* (Evanston, Ill.: Row, Peterson, 1957).

10. Harmon-Jones and Mills, "Introduction to Cognitive Dissonance," 6–7.

11. Carol Tarvis and Elliot Aronson, *Mistakes Were Made but Not by Me*
(San Diego: Harcourt, 2007), 12–13.

12. Ibid., 22.

13. See Steve Orr and Gary Craig "Ruling Alters Legal Landscape in
NY Shaken-Baby Cases," *Democrat and Chronicle*, Nov 16, 2016, www
.democratandchronicle.com/story/news/2016/11/16/ruling-alters-legal-land
scape-ny-shaken-baby-cases/93952304.

14. "Doctor Who Denies Shaken Baby Syndrome Struck Off," *The
Guardian*, Mar 21, 2016, www.theguardian.com/uk-news/2016/mar/21
/doctor-waney-squier-denies-shaken-baby-syndrome-struck-off-misleading-
courts.

15. Michael Mansfield et al., "General Medical Council Behaving Like a
Modern Inquisition," *The Guardian*, March 21, 2016, www.theguardian.com
/society/2016/mar/21/gmc-behaving-like-a-modern-inquisition-by-striking-
off-dr-waney-squier.

16. Brandi Grissom, "Texas Science Commission Is First in the U.S. to
Recommend Moratorium on Bite Mark Evidence," Trail Blazer's Blog, *Dallas
Daily News*, Feb 12, 2016, http://trailblazersblog.dallasnews.com/2016/02
/texas-science-commission-is-first-in-the-u-s-to-recommend-moratorium-on-
bite-mark-evidence.html.

17. Radley Balko, "A Bite Mark Matching Advocacy Group Just Conducted
a Study That Discredits Bite Mark Evidence," The Watch, *Washington Post*,
Apr 8, 2015, www.washingtonpost.com/news/the-watch/wp/2015/04/08/a-
bite-mark-matching-advocacy-group-just-conducted-a-study-that-discredits-
bite-mark-evidence.

18. Radley Balko, "Attack of the Bite Mark Matchers," The Watch, *Washington Post,* Feb 18, 2015, www.washingtonpost.com/news/the-watch/wp/2015/02/18/attack-of-the-bite-mark-matchers-2/?tid=a_inl.

19. Balko, "Bite Mark Matching Advocacy Group."

20. Balko, "Attack of the Bite Mark Matchers."

21. Andrew Wolfson, "Louisville to Pay Whistleblower Cop $450,000," *The Courier-Journal,* Apr 16, 2014, www.courier-journal.com/story/news/crime/2014/04/16/louisville-pay-whistleblower-cop/7771933/; "Detective Demoted after He Helps Kentucky Innocence Project," Wrongful Convictions Blog, Oct 17, 2012, http://wrongfulconvictionsblog.org/2012/10/17/detective-demoted-after-he-helps-kentucky-innocence-project.

22. Paige Lavender, "Sharon Snyder, Court Clerk Fired for Helping Free Wrongly Convicted Man: 'I Would Do It Again,'" *Huffington Post,* Aug 15, 2013, www.huffingtonpost.com/2013/08/15/sharon-snyder-robert-nelson_n_3759185.html.

23. Guy B. Adams, "The Problem of Administrative Evil in a Culture of Technical Rationality" (abstract), *Public Integrity* 13 (Sum 2011): 275–85, doi: 10.2753/PIN1099–9922130307.

24. Guy B. Adams and Danny L. Balfour, *Unmasking Administrative Evil,* 4th ed. (New York: Routledge, 2014), 152.

25. Ibid., 277.

26. Michelle Maiese, "Dehumanization," Beyond Intractability, Jul 2003, www.beyondintractability.org/essay/dehumanization.

27. "'Less Than Human': The Psychology Of Cruelty," *Talk of the Nation,* National Public Radio, Mar 29, 2011, www.npr.org/2011/03/29/134956180/criminals-see-their-victims-as-less-than-human.

28. Ibid.

29. Medwed, *Prosecution Complex,* 79–80.

30. "Lead Prosecutor Apologizes for Role in Sending Man to Death Row," *Shreveport Times,* Mar 20, 2015, www.shreveporttimes.com/story/opinion/readers/2015/03/20/lead-prosecutor-offers-apology-in-the-case-of-exonerated-death-row-inmate-glenn-ford/25049063.

31. Raeford Davis, "Why I Hated Being a Cop," *Life Inside,* Marshall Project, Apr 21, 2016, www.themarshallproject.org/2016/04/21/why-i-hated-being-a-cop#.cN1tPIBto.

32. Upton Sinclair, *I, Candidate for Governor: And How I Got Licked* (Oakland: University of California Press, 1994), 109.

CHAPTER 3. BLIND AMBITION

1. Hilary Hylton, "The Tale of the Texting Judge," *Time,* Nov 1, 2013, http://nation.time.com/2013/11/01/the-tale-of-the-texting-judge.

2. "Fact Sheet on Judicial Selection Methods in the States," American Bar Association, www.americanbar.org/content/dam/aba/migrated/leadership/fact_sheet.authcheckdam.pdf (accessed Apr 27, 2016).

3. Madeline Meth, "New Report Finds Explosive Campaign Spending and 'Soft-on-Crime' Attack Ads Impact State Supreme Court Rulings in Criminal Cases," Center for American Progress, Oct 28, 2013, www.americanprogress .org/press/release/2013/10/28/78184/release-new-report-finds-explosive-campaign-spending-and-soft-on-crime-attack-ads-impact-state-supreme-court-rulings-in-criminal-cases.

4. *Woodward v. Alabama*, 134 S. Ct. 405 (Sotomayor, J., dissenting).

5. Ibid., 409.

6. Christie Thompson, "Trial by Cash," Marshall Project, Dec 11, 2014, www.themarshallproject.org/2014/12/11/trial-by-cash#.bzdp2LFiT. See also, "State Supreme Court Judges Are on the Ballots, and Outside Groups Have Broken the Record on TV Ad Spending," *USA Today*, Oct 26, 2016, www .usatoday.com/story/opinion/2016/10/26/judicial-elections-2016-editorials-debates/92788886.

7. Thompson, "Trial by Cash."

8. *Elected Judges*, YouTube video, 13:26, from *Last Week Tonight with John Oliver*, posted by "LastWeekTonight," Feb 23, 2015, www.youtube.com /watch?v=poL7l-Uk3I8 (accessed Apr 28, 2017).

9. Quoted in Thompson, "Trial by Cash."

10. Ibid.

11. Billy Corriher, "Criminals and Campaign Cash," Center for American Progress, Oct 2013, www.americanprogress.org/wp-content/uploads/2013/10 /CampaignCriminalCash-6.pdf.

12. Kate Berry, "How Judicial Elections Impact Criminal Cases," Brennan Center for Justice at New York University School of Law (2015), www .brennancenter.org/sites/default/files/publications/How_Judicial_Elections_ Impact_Criminal_Cases.pdf.

13. For an additional discussion of the role that corporations and super PACS play in judicial elections, particularly focusing on criminal issues, see Thompson, "Trial by Cash."

14. Adam Liptak and Janet Roberts, "Campaign Cash Mirrors a High Court's Rulings," *New York Times*, Oct 1, 2006, www.nytimes.com/2006/10/01 /us/01judges.html?pagewanted=all&_r=0.

15. Andrew Cohen, "'A Broken System': Texas's Former Chief Justice Condemns Judicial Elections," *The Atlantic*, Oct 18, 2013, www.theatlantic .com/national/archive/2013/10/a-broken-system-texass-former-chief-justice-condemns-judicial-elections/280654.

16. See also Joanna M. Shepherd, "Money, Politics, and Impartial Justice," *Duke Law Journal* 58 (Jan 2009): 623.

17. For state judge statistics, see David A. Harris, *Failed Evidence: Why Law Enforcement Resists Science* (New York: New York University Press, 2012), 110; for federal judge statistics, see "The Homogeneous Federal Bench," *New York Times*, Feb 6, 2014, www.nytimes.com/2014/02/07/opinion/the-homogeneous-federal-bench.html?_r=0.

18. See, Ronald F. Wright, "How Prosecutor Elections Fail Us," *Ohio State Journal of Criminal Law* 6 (2009): 581–610; Bryan C. McCannon, "Prosecutor Elections, Mistakes, and Appeals," *Journal of Empirical Legal Studies* 10 (Oct 2013): 696–714, doi: 10.1111/jels.12024; Siddartha Bandyopadhyay and Bryan C. McCannon, "The Effect of the Election of Prosecutors on Criminal Trials," working paper, forthcoming in *Public Choice*, http://ideas.repec.org/p/bir /birmec/11–08.html.

19. Daniel S. Medwed, *Prosecution Complex: America's Race to Convict and Its Impact on the Innocent* (New York: New York University Press, 2012), 78.

20. Ibid., 78–79.

21. Ibid., 77.

22. Ibid.

23. Saki Knafo, "How Aggressive Policing Affects Police Officers Themselves," *The Atlantic*, Jul 13, 2015, www.theatlantic.com/business /archive/2015/07/aggressive-policing-quotas/398165.

24. Jim Hoffer, "NYPD Officer Claims Pressure to Make Arrests," ABC, WABC-TV New York, Mar 2, 2010, http://abc7ny.com/archive/7305356.

25. Joel Rose, "Despite Laws and Lawsuits, Quota-Based Policing Lingers," *Weekend Edition Saturday*, National Public Radio, Apr 4, 2015, www.npr .org/2015/04/04/395061810/despite-laws-and-lawsuits-quota-based-policing- lingers.

26. Mensah M. Dean, "Retired Philly Cop Recalls the Blue Wall of Silence," *The Inquirer*, Oct 26, 2016, www.philly.com/philly/news/20161026_Retired_ Philly_cop_recalls_the_Blue_Wall_of_Silence.html. See also, Stephanie Clifford, "An Ex-Cop's Remorse," *New Yorker*, Oct 24, 2016, www.newyorker .com/magazine/2016/10/24/an-ex-cops-remorse.

27. See "ISU Team Calculates Societal Costs of Five Major Crimes; Finds Murder at $17.25 Million," Iowa State University News Service, Sept 27, 2010, www.news.iastate.edu/news/2010/sep/costofcrime#sthash.7Znl39yJ.dpuf. See also, "Trial Proceedings: Length and Cost," Washington Courts, www.courts .wa.gov/newsinfo/index.cfm?fa=newsinfo.displayContent&theFile=content /deathPenalty/trial.

28. Lincoln Caplan, "The Right to Counsel: Badly Battered at 50," *New York Times*, Mar 9, 2013, www.nytimes.com/2013/03/10/opinion/sunday/the-right- to-counsel-badly-battered-at-50.html?_r=1.

29. See, for example, Julia O'Donoghue, "Plaquemines Parish Public Defenders Office to Close after State Cuts," *Times-Picayune*, Feb 16, 2016, www.nola.com/politics/index.ssf/2016/02/louisiana_public_defenders.html; Oliver Laughland, "When the Money Runs Out for Public Defense, What Happens Next?" Marshall Project, Sept 7, 2016, www.themarshallproject .org/2016/09/07/when-the-money-runs-out-for-public-defense-what-happens- next#.nQIRnitGk.

30. Brentin Mock, "Why the ACLU Is Suing the New Orleans Public Defenders Office," *The Atlantic* City Lab, Jan 20, 2016, www.citylab.com

/crime/2016/01/why-the-aclu-is-suing-new-orleans-public-defenders-office
/424689; Ailsa Chang, "Not Enough Money or Time to Defend Detroit's Poor,"
All Things Considered, National Public Radio, Aug 17, 2009, www.npr.org
/templates/story/story.php?storyId=111811319.

31. Matt Ford, "A Governor Ordered to Serve as a Public Defender," *The Atlantic,* Aug 5, 2016, www.theatlantic.com/politics/archive/2016/08/when-the-governor-is-your-lawyer/494453.

32. Tina Peng, "I'm a Public Defender: It's Impossible for Me to Do a Good Job Representing My Clients," *Washington Post,* Sept 3, 2015, www.washingtonpost.com/opinions/our-public-defender-system-isnt-just-broken—its-unconstitutional/2015/09/03/aadf2b6c-519b-11e5-9812-92d5948a40f8_story.html.

33. "Minor Crimes, Massive Waste: The Terrible Toll of America's Broken Misdemeanor Courts," National Association of Criminal Defense Lawyers, Apr 2009, https://www.nacdl.org/reports/misdemeanor.

34. Ben Myers, "Orleans Public Defender's Office to Begin Refusing Serious Felony Cases Tuesday," *Times-Picayune,* Jan 11, 2016, www.nola.com/crime/index.ssf/2016/01/orleans_public_defenders_to_be.html. See also, James Fuller, "Kane County Public Defender: We Can't Always Provide Rigorous Defense," *Daily Herald,* May 13, 2016, www.dailyherald.com/article/20160513/news/160519415.

35. "Innocents Have Gone to Jail, Say Nola Public Defenders," CBS News, Apr 13, 2017, www.cbsnews.com/news/innocents-have-gone-to-jail-say-nola-public-defenders (accessed May 8, 2017).

36. Alexa Van Brunt, "Poor People Rely on Public Defenders Who Are Too Overworked to Defend Them," *The Guardian,* Jun 17, 2015, www.theguardian.com/commentisfree/2015/jun/17/poor-rely-public-defenders-too-overworked; Andrew Cohen, "How Much Does a Public Defender Need to Know about a Client?" *The Atlantic,* Oct 23, 2013, www.theatlantic.com/national/archive/2013/10/how-much-does-a-public-defender-need-to-know-about-a-client/280761. See also, Justin A. Hinkley and Matt Mencarini, "Court-Appointed Attorneys Paid Little, Do Little, Records Show," *Lansing State Journal,* Nov 4, 2016, www.lansingstatejournal.com/story/news/local/watchdog/2016/11/03/court-appointed-attorneys-paid-little-do-little-records-show/91846874.

37. Chang, "Not Enough Money or Time to Defend Detroit's Poor."

38. Ibid.

39. Daniel S. Medwed, "Anatomy of a Wrongful Conviction: Theoretical Implications and Practical Solutions," *Villanova Law Review* 51, no. 2 (2006): 370, http://digitalcommons.law.villanova.edu/vlr/vol51/iss2/3; Allen St. John, "The $40/Hr Defense Lawyer: 'Making a Murderer' Attorney Dean Strang Discusses the Economics of Innocence," *Forbes,* Jan 24, 2016, www.forbes.com/sites/allenstjohn/2016/01/24/the-40hr-defense-lawyer-making-a-murder-attorney-dean-strang-discusses-the-economics-of-innocence/#11064a0dca18.

40. https://www.washingtonpost.com/opinions/our-public-defender-system-isnt-just-broken—its-unconstitutional/2015/09/03/aadf2b6c-519b-11e5-9812-92d5948a40f8_story.html?utm_term=.e36a74de8ee9

41. Keith Findley, "The Presumption of Innocence Exists in Theory, Not Reality," *Washington Post,* Jan 19, 2016, www.washingtonpost.com/news/in-theory /wp/2016/01/19/the-presumption-of-innocence-exists-in-theory-not-reality.

42. Hon. Alex Kozinski, "Preface: Criminal Law 2.0," *Georgetown Law Journal Annual Review of Criminal Procedure* 44 (2015): iii–xliv, https:// georgetownlawjournal.org/assets/kozinski-arcp-preface-9a990f08f3f006558 eaa03ccc440d3078f5899b3426ec47aaedb89c606caeae7.pdf.

CHAPTER 4. BLIND BIAS

1. Raymond S. Nickerson, "Confirmation Bias: A Ubiquitous Phenomenon in Many Guises," *Review of General Psychology* 2, no. 2 (1998): 175–220.

2. J.M. Darley and P.H. Gross, "A Hypothesis Confirming Bias in Labelling Effects," *Journal of Personality and Social Psychology* 44 (1983): 20–33.

3. E.J. Langer and R.P. Abelson, "A Patient by Any Other Name—Clinician Group Difference in Labeling Bias," *Journal of Consulting and Clinical Psychology* 42 (Feb 1974): 4–9.

4. Brendan Nyhan and Jason Reifler "When Corrections Fail: The Persistence of Political Misperceptions," *Political Behavior* 32 (Jun 2010): 303–30, doi:10.1007/s11109-010-9112-2.

5. D. Kuhn, "Children and Adults as Intuitive Scientists," *Psychological Review* 96 (Oct 1989): 674–89.

6. N. Pennington and R. Hastie, "The Story Model for Juror Decision Making," in *Inside the Juror: The Psychology of Juror Decision Making,* ed. R. Hastie (New York: Cambridge University Press, 1993), 192–221.

7. P.C. Wason, "On the Failure to Eliminate Hypotheses in a Conceptual Task," *Quarterly Journal of Experimental Psychology* 12, no. 2 (1960): 129–40.

8. Nickerson, "Confirmation Bias," 175.

9. Ibid., 205.

10. "The Causes of Wrongful Conviction," Innocence Project, www .innocenceproject.org/causes-wrongful-conviction (accessed May 1, 2016).

11. Itiel E. Dror, David Charlton, and Ailsa E. Péron, "Contextual Information Renders Experts Vulnerable to Making Erroneous Identifications," *Forensic Science International* 156 (2006): 74–78, doi:10.1016/j.forsciint.2005.10.017.

12. Ibid.

13. Federal Bureau of Investigation and J. Edgar Hoover, *The Science of Finger-Prints: Classification and Uses* (Washington, D.C.: United States Government Printing Office, 2006), iv, www.gutenberg.org/files/19022/19022-h/19022-h.htm.

14. D.R. Ashbaugh, "The Premise of Friction Ridge Identification, Clarity, and the Identification Process," *Journal of Forensic Identification* 44 (1994): 499–516.

15. Sherry Nakhaeizadeha, Itiel E. Dror, and Ruth M. Morgana, "Cognitive Bias in Forensic Anthropology: Visual Assessments of Skeletal Remains Is Susceptible to Confirmation Bias," *Science and Justice* 54 (May 2014): 208–14, doi:10.1016/j.scijus.2013.11.003.

16. R.D. Stoel, I.E. Dror and L.S. Miller, "Bias among Forensic Document Examiners: Still a Need for Procedural Changes," *Australian Journal of Forensic Sciences* 46, no. 1 (2014): 91–97.

17. Itiel E. Dror and Greg Hampikian, "Subjectivity and Bias in Forensic DNA Mixture Interpretation," *Science and Justice* 51 (Dec 2011): 204–8, doi:10.1016/j.scijus.2011.08.004.

18. For a complete review of the Brandon Mayfield case, see "A Review of the FBI's Handling of the Brandon Mayfield Case," Office of the Inspector General, Jan 2006, https://oig.justice.gov/special/s0601/exec.pdf.

19. Itiel E. Dror and Simon A. Cole, "The Vision in 'Blind' Justice: Expert Perception, Judgment, and Visual Cognition in Forensic Pattern Recognition," *Psychonomic Bulletin and Review* 17, no. 2 (2010): 163, doi:10.3758/PBR.17.2.161.

20. Itiel E. Dror, "Practical Solutions to Cognitive and Human Factor Challenges in Forensic Science," *Forensic Science Policy and Management* 4 (2013): 1–9, doi: 10.1080/19409044.2014.901437.

21. Submission form received by author from Dr. Itiel E. Dror, which he obtained from a case file during his research.

22. Sandra Guerra Thompson, *Cops in Lab Coats: Curbing Wrongful Convictions through Independent Forensic Laboratories* (Durham, N.C.: Carolina Academic Press, 2015), 130–31.

23. Linda Geddes, "Forensic Failure: 'Miscarriages of Justice Will Occur,'" *New Scientist*, Feb 11, 2012, www.newscientist.com/article/mg21328514-600-forensic-failure-miscarriages-of-justice-will-occur.

24. For further discussion of this issue, see Radley Balko, "New Study Finds That State Crime Labs Are Paid per Conviction," *Huffington Post*, Aug 8, 2013, www.huffingtonpost.com/2013/08/29/in-some-states-crime-labs_n_3837471.html. See also, Roger Koppl and Meghan Sacks, "The Criminal Justice System Creates Incentives for False Convictions," *Criminal Justice Ethics* 32, no. 2 (2013): 126–62, doi:10.1080/0731129X.2013.817070.

25. Sandra Guerra Thompson, *Cops in Lab Coats: Curbing Wrongful Convictions through Independent Forensic Laboratories* (Durham, N.C.: Carolina Academic Press, 2015), 127.

26. Mike Wagner et al., "Scientist's Work Records Show Litany of Problems, but Praise from Cops," *Columbus Dispatch*, Dec 7, 2016, www.dispatch.com/content/stories/local/2016/10/30/records-show-litany-of-problems-but-praise-from-cops.html.

27. Jill Riepenhoff, Lucas Sullivan, and Mike Wagner, "State Crime Lab: Do Thank You Notes Hint at Impropriety?" *Columbus Dispatch*, Nov 19, 2016, www.dispatch.com/content/stories/local/2016/11/19/domissin-thank-you-notes-hint-at-impropriety.html.

28. Committee on Identifying the Needs of the Forensic Sciences Community, National Research Council, *Strengthening Forensic Science in the United States: A Path Forward*, available at the National Criminal Justice Reference Service, www.ncjrs.gov/pdffiles1/nij/grants/228091.pdf (accessed May 8, 2017).

29. Ibid., 22 and 24.

30. Jordan Smith, "FBI and DOJ Vow to Continue Using Junk Science Rejected by White House Report," *The Intercept*, Sept 23, 2016, https://theintercept .com/2016/09/23/fbi-and-doj-vow-to-continue-using-junk-science-rejected-by-white-house-report.

31. Jessica Gabel Cino, "Sessions's Assault on Forensic Science Will Lead to More Unsafe Convictions," *Newsweek*, Apr 20, 2017, www.newsweek.com /sessionss-assault-forensic-science-will-lead-more-unsafe-convictions-585762.

32. For more information about the Ray Krone case, see the National Registry of Exonerations, last updated Jan 4, 2015, www.law.umich.edu/special /exoneration/Pages/casedetail.aspx?caseid=3365.

33. Krone spent time on death row before being retried and once again convicted. Upon the second conviction, Krone was sentenced to life in prison.

34. For the complete facts, see the Larry Pat Souter case on the National Registry of Exonerations, www.law.umich.edu/special/exoneration/Pages /casedetail.aspx?caseid=3656 (accessed Apr 18, 2016).

35. For the complete facts, see the Robert Lee Stinson case on the National Registry of Exonerations, last updated Apr 9, 2014, www.law.umich.edu /special/exoneration/Pages/casedetail.aspx?caseid=3666.

36. "Two Innocent Men Cleared Today in Separate Murder Cases in Mississippi, 15 Years after Wrongful Convictions," Feb 15, 2008, www.innocence project.org/Content/Two_Innocent_Men_Cleared_Today_in_Separate_Murder_ Cases_in_Mississippi_15_Years_after_Wrongful_Convictions.php.

37. For the complete facts, see the George Allen case on the National Registry of Exonerations, last updated Jan 18, 2013, www.law.umich.edu/special /exoneration/Pages/casedetail.aspx?caseid=4091.

38. For the complete facts, see the Walter Zimmer case on the National Registry of Exonerations, last updated Apr 7, 2014, www.law.umich.edu/special /exoneration/Pages/casedetail.aspx?caseid=4283.

39. For the complete facts, see the Bob Gondor and Randy Resh case on the National Registry of Exonerations, last updated Jan 13, 2016, www.law.umich .edu/special/exoneration/Pages/casedetail.aspx?caseid=3245.

40. Documents relating to the James Parsons case on file with author.

41. Riepenhoff, Sullivan, and Wagner, "State Crime Lab: Do Thank You Notes Hint at Impropriety?"

42. Documents relating to the Ed Emerick case on file with author.

43. Documents relating to the Ryan Widmer case on file with author.

CHAPTER 5. BLIND MEMORY

1. Brandon Garrett, *Convicting the Innocent: Where Criminal Prosecutions Go Wrong* (Cambridge, Mass.: Harvard University Press, 2012), 66.

2. "John Jerome White," National Registry of Exonerations, www.law .umich.edu/special/exoneration/pages/casedetail.aspx?caseid=3735 (accessed Apr 18, 2017).

3. See Germain Lussier, "/Film Interview: Sarah Polley Explains Secrets of Her Brilliant Documentary 'Stories We Tell,'" */Film,* May 17, 2013, www .slashfilm.com/film-interview-sarah-polley-explains-secrets-of-her-brilliant-documentary-stories-we-tell.

4. D.L. Schacter, J.L. Harbluk, and D.R. McLachlan, "Retrieval without Recollection: An Experimental Analysis of Source Amnesia," *Journal of Verbal Learning and Verbal Behavior* 23 (Sept 1984): 593–96.

5. Dan Simon, *In Doubt: The Psychology of the Criminal Justice Process* (Cambridge, Mass.: Harvard University Press, 2012), 100.

6. Leon Festinger, *A Theory of Cognitive Dissonance* (Evanston, Ill.: Row, Peterson, 1957).

7. Elizabeth F. Loftus and John C. Palmer, "Reconstruction of Automobile Destruction: An Example of the Interaction between Language and Memory," *Journal of Verbal Learning and Verbal Behavior* 13 (Sept 1974): 585–89, doi: 10.1016/S0022-5371(74)80011-3.

8. Ibid., 585.

9. Ibid., 587.

10. Ibid., 588.

11. Elizabeth F. Loftus and Jacqueline E. Pickrell, "The Formation of False Memories," *Psychiatric Annals* 25 (Dec 1995): 720–25; 720. Italics added.

12. Ibid.

13. Ibid., 721.

14. Ibid., 723.

15. Ibid., 724.

16. Ibid., 724–25.

17. "Elizabeth Loftus: How Reliable Is Your Memory?" *TED Conferences, LLC,* filmed Jun 2013, www.ted.com/talks/elizabeth_loftus_the_fiction_of_ memory (accessed Apr 20, 2016).

18. See "The Causes of Wrongful Conviction," Innocence Project, www .innocenceproject.org/causes-wrongful-conviction (accessed May 1, 2016). Chart taken from website.

19. "% Exonerations by Contributing Factor," National Registry of Exonerations, www.law.umich.edu/special/exoneration/Pages/Exonerations ContribFactorsByCrime.aspx (accessed Dec 10, 2016).

20. Ibid. Perjury or false accusation is a contributing factor in 57 percent of the wrongful convictions reported, as of Apr 2016.

21. See, for example, Siegfried L. Sporer, *Psychological Issues in Eyewitness Identification* (New York: Taylor and Francis, 1996); Brian L. Cutler and Margaret Bull Kovera, *Evaluating Eyewitness Identification* (Oxford: Oxford University Press, 2010); Committee on Scientific Approaches to Understanding and Maximizing the Validity and Reliability of Eyewitness Identification et al., *Identifying the Culprit:: Assessing Eyewitness Identification* (Washington D.C.: National Academies Press, 2015).

22. Affidavit of Dr. Charles Goodsell from author's case of Douglas Prade, on file with the author.

23. See Morgan et al., "Misinformation Can Influence Memory for Recently Experienced, Highly Stressful Events," *International Journal of Law and Psychiatry* 36 (2013): 11–17; see also, Jon B. Gould and Richard A. Leo, "One Hundred Years Later: Wrongful Convictions after a Century of Research," *Journal of Criminal Law and Criminology* 100 (Summer 2010): 841.

24. N.M. Steblay, "A Meta-Analytic Review of the Weapon Focus Effect," *Law and Human Behavior* 16, no. 4 (1992): 413–24; K.L. Pickel, "Unusualness and Threat as Possible Causes of 'Weapon Focus,'" *Memory* 6, no. 3 (1998): 277–95.

25. Radley Balko, "NYPD Shooting Demonstrates Flaws in Eyewitness Identification," *Washington Post*, May 15, 2015, www.washingtonpost.com /news/the-watch/wp/2015/05/15/nypd-shooting-demonstrates-the-flaws-in-eyewitness-memory.

26. Affidavit of Charles A. Goodsell, Ph.D., at 4, *Ohio v. Prade*, Court of Common Pleas Summit County Ohio (Case No. CR 1998-02-0463); E.F. Loftus, "Creating false memories," *Scientific American* 277 (1997): 70–75; E.F. Loftus and K. Ketcham, *The Myth of Repressed Memory* (New York: St. Martin's Press, 1994); E.F. Loftus and J.C. Palmer, "Reconstruction of Automobile Destruction: An Example of the Interaction between Language and Memory," *Journal of Verbal Learning and Verbal Behavior*, 13 (1974): 585–89; J.T. Wixted and E.B. Ebbesen, "On the Form of Forgetting," *Psychological Science* 2 (1991): 409–15; J.T. Wixted and E.B. Ebbesen, "Genuine Power Curves in Forgetting: A Quantitative Analysis of Individual Subject Forgetting Functions," *Memory and Cognition* 25 (1997): 731–39; A.D. Yarmey, M.J. Yarmey, and A.L. Yarmey, "Accuracy of Eyewitness Identification in Showups and Lineups," *Law and Human Behavior* 20 (1996): 459–77.

27. J.W. Shepherd, H.D. Ellis, and G.M. Davies, *Identification Evidence: A Psychological Evaluation* (Aberdeen: Aberdeen University Press, 1982).

28. Affidavit of Dr. Charles Goodsell and other documents relating to the Douglas Prade case on file with the author.

29. Daniel L. Schacter, "The Seven Sins of Memory: Insights from Psychology and Cognitive Neuroscience," *American Psychologist* 54, no. 3 (1999): 182–203, http://scholar.harvard.edu/files/schacterlab/files/schacter_american_psychologist_1999.pdf.

30. For a discussion of similar studies, see Jeffrey S. Neuschatz et al., "The Effects of Post-Identification Feedback and Age on Retrospective Eyewitness Memory," *Applied Cognitive Psychology* 19 (Mar 2005): 435–53, doi: 10.1002/acp.1084. See also, Amy Bradfield, Gary Wells, and Elizabeth Olson, "The Damaging Effect of Confirming Feedback on the Relation between Eyewitness Certainty and Identification Accuracy," *Journal of Applied Psychology* 87 (Feb 2002): 112–20.

31. "The State of Wisconsin vs. Steven A. Avery," *Dateline*, NBC News, Jan 29, 2016, www.nbcnews.com/dateline/video/full-episode-the-state-of-wisconsin-vs-steven-a-avery-618615875727.

32. Laura Ricciardi and Moira Demos, "Eighteen Years Lost," *Making a Murderer*, Netflix Streaming, Dec 18, 2015. Documentary web series, episode 1, sixty minutes.

33. See the Justice Project, "John Willis' Story," in *Eyewitness Identification: A Policy Review*, 12–14, https://public.psych.iastate.edu/glwells/The_Justice%20Project_Eyewitness_Identification_%20A_Policy_Review.pdf (accessed May 8, 2017); "25 Years after Wrongful Conviction, Steven Phillips Set to Be Exonerated in Dallas Based on DNA and Other Evidence," Innocence Project, Aug 4, 2008, www.innocenceproject.org/25-years-after-wrongful-conviction-steven-phillips-set-to-be-exonerated-in-dallas-based-on-dna-and-other-evidence.

34. For examples of suggestive lineup procedures, Brandon Garrett, *Convicting the Innocent: Where Criminal Prosecutions Go Wrong* (Cambridge, Mass.: Harvard University Press, 2012), 61.

35. Laura A. Bischoff, "Sometimes I Wonder If Death Ain't Better," *Dayton Daily News*, Jun 3, 2007.

36. Elizabeth F. Loftus, "Juries Don't Understand Eyewitness Testimony," *New York Times*, Sept 1, 2011, www.nytimes.com/roomfordebate/2011/08/31/can-we-trust-eyewitness-identifications/juries-dont-understand-eyewitness-testimony.

37. Christie Thompson, "Penny Beerntsen, the Rape Victim in 'Making A Murderer,' Speaks Out," Marshall Project, Jan 5, 2016, www.themarshallproject.org/2016/01/05/penny-beernsten-the-rape-victim-in-making-a-murderer-speaks-out?ref=hp-3–121#.fJu9vltXt.

38. Jennifer Thompson-Cannino, Ronald Cotton, and Erin Torneo, *Picking Cotton: Our Memoir of Injustice and Redemption* (New York : St. Martin's Press, 2009); "Eyewitness, Part 1," *60 Minutes*, CBS News, Jul 12, 2009; "Eyewitness, Part 2," *60 Minutes*, CBS News, Jul 12, 2009.

39. Lesley Stahl, ""Eyewitness: How Accurate Is Visual Memory?" CBS News, Mar 6, 2009, www.cbsnews.com/news/eyewitness-how-accurate-is-visual-memory/2.

40. "Eyewitness, Part 2."

41. "The Words 'Guilty Your Honor' May Hold Far Less Authority Now That the 300th Person Has Been Exonerated by DNA Evidence," *Sky Valley Chronicle*, Oct 1, 2012, www.skyvalleychronicle.com/FEATURE-NEWS/THE-WORDS-GUILTY-YOUR-HONOR-FROM-A-JURY-MAY-HOLD-LESS-AUTHORITY-BR-Now-that-the-300th-person-has-been-exonerated-by-DNA-evidence-1132961.

42. Ibid.

43. Ibid.

44. Ibid.

45. Ibid.

46. Douglas A. Blackmon, "Louisiana Death-Row Inmate Damon Thibodeaux Exonerated with DNA Evidence," *Washington Post*, Sept 18, 2012, www.washingtonpost.com/national/louisiana-death-row-inmate-damon-thibode

aux-is-exonerated-with-dna-evidence/2012/09/28/26e30012-0997-11e2-afff-d6c7f20a83bf_print.html.

47. Ibid.

48. Ibid.

49. "Words 'Guilty Your Honor' May Hold Far Less Authority."

50. Blackmon, "Louisiana Death-Row Inmate Damon Thibodeaux Exonerated."

51. Ibid.

52. "Words 'Guilty Your Honor' May Hold Far Less Authority."

53. Ibid.

54. Ibid.

55. "The Causes of Wrongful Conviction," Innocence Project, 2016, www .innocenceproject.org/causes-wrongful-conviction (accessed May 1, 2016).

56. "% Exonerations by Contributing Factor," National Registry of Exonerations, last updated Dec 10, 2016, www.law.umich.edu/special/exoneration /Pages/ExonerationsContribFactorsByCrime.aspx.

57. *Colorado v. Connelly*, 479 U.S. 157.

58. See "John Mark Karr and the False Confession: Why?" WebMD, www .webmd.com/mental-health/features/john-mark-karr-false-confession-why (accessed Apr 20, 2016).

59. Richard A. Leo, *Police Interrogation and American Justice* (Cambridge, Mass.: Harvard University Press, 2009): 201–10; Tom Wells and Richard A. Leo, *The Wrong Guys: Murder, False Confessions, and the Norfolk Four* (New York: New Press, 2008); John Grisham, *The Innocent Man: Murder and Injustice in a Small Town* (New York: Doubleday, 2006).

60. Ken Burns, David Mcmahon, and Sarah Burns, *The Central Park Five* (PBS, Florentine Films, WETA-TV, 2012), 120 minutes. Documentary film.

61. See Leo, *Police Interrogation and American Justice*, 210–25; Saul M. Kassin, "Internalized False Confessions," *Handbook of Eyewitness Psychology* 1 (2007), http://web.williams.edu/Psychology/Faculty/Kassin/files/Kassin_07_ internalized%20confessions%20ch.pdf.

62. Kassin, "Internalized False Confessions," 171.

63. Julie Shaw and Stephen Porter, "Constructing Rich False Memories of Committing Crime," *Psychological Science* (Jan 2015).

64. Ibid., 298.

65. Kassin, "Internalized False Confessions," 176.

66. Ibid., 177.

67. For the complete facts of the Peter Reilly case, see Donald S. Connery, in *True Stories of False Confessions*, ed. Rob Warden and Steven A. Drizin (Evanston, Ill.: Northwestern University Press, 2006), 47–70; Kassin, "Internalized False Confessions," 175–94; D.S. Connery, *Guilty until Proven Innocent* (New York: Putnam, 1977), 173.

68. Douglas T. Kenrick, Steven L. Neuberg, and Robert B. Cialdini, *Social Psychology: Unraveling the Mystery*, 3rd ed. (Boston: Pearson, 2005), 173.

69. John Wilkens and Mark Sauer, "Haunting Questions: The Stephanie Crowe Murder Case," parts 1 and 2, SignOnSanDiego.com, Union-Tribune Publishing, May 11–12, 1999, http://legacy.utsandiego.com/news/reports /crowe/crowe2.html.

70. Frances E. Chapman, "Coerced Internalized False Confessions and Police Interrogations: The Power of Coercion," *Law and Psychology Review* 37 (2013): 159–92, http://heinonline.org/HOL/Page?handle=hein.journals /lpsyr37&div=8&g_sent=1&collection=journals.

71. Ibid., 185.

72. "Rock Hill Man Convicted of 2001 Rape, Murder of Daughter Seeks New Trial," *The Herald,* Jul 20, 2015, www.heraldonline.com/news/local/crime /article27957517.html.

73. Simon, *In Doubt,* 146.

74. Barry Berke and Eric Tirschwell, "New Rule Proposed on Note Taking in Criminal Cases," *New York Law Journal* 238, no. 47 (2007): 4.

75. Dan Simon, "The Limited Diagnosticity of Criminal Trials," *Vanderbilt Law Review* 64, no. 143 (2011): 150–51.

76. Danielle M. Loney and Brian L. Cutler, "Coercive Interrogation of Eyewitnesses Can Produce False Accusations," *Journal of Police and Criminal Psychology* 31, no. 1 (Mar 2016): 29–36, http://link.springer.com/article /10.1007/s11896-015-9165-6.

77. Wendy Gillis, "Aggressive Police Questioning May Boost False Accusations, Study Finds," *Toronto Star,* Feb 2, 2015, www.thestar.com/news /crime/2015/02/15/aggressive-police-questioning-may-boost-false-accusations-study-finds.html.

78. Stéphanie B. Marion et al., "Lost Proof of Innocence: The Impact of Confessions on Alibi Witnesses," *Law and Human Behavior* (Aug 24, 2015), http://dx.doi.org/10.1037/lhb0000156.

79. Simon, *In Doubt,* 95.

80. Ibid.

81. Marisol Bello, "Brian Williams Not Alone in Having False Memories," *USA Today,* Feb 6, 2015, www.usatoday.com/story/news/2015/02/05/brian-williams-helicopter-memory/22928349; see also, Brittny Mejia, "Scientists Explain How Brian Williams' Memory May Have Failed Him," *Los Angeles Times,* Feb 6, 2015, www.latimes.com/science/sciencenow/la-sci-sn-memory-blame-brian-williams-20150206-story.html.

82. Luke Johnson and Sam Stein, "Mitt Romney Recalls Parade That Occurred Before He Was Born," *Huffington Post,* Feb 27, 2012, www.huffingtonpost .com/2012/02/27/mitt-romney-remembers-golden-jubilee_n_1305110.html.

83. Nicholas Thompson, "Lie or Mistake, Paul Ryan's Marathoning Past," *New Yorker,* Sept 1, 2012, www.newyorker.com/news/news-desk/lie-or-mistake-paul-ryans-marathoning-past.

84. Daniel Greenberg, "President Bush's False Flashbulb Memory of 9/11/01," *Applied Cognitive Psychology* 18 (2004): 363–70, doi: 10.1002/acp .1016.

CHAPTER 6. BLIND INTUITION

1. *U.S. v. Scheffer*, 523 U.S. 303.

2. See, for example, *4-76 Modern Federal Jury Instructions—Civil P 76.01* ("How did the witness appear; what was his or her demeanor—that is, his or her carriage, behavior, bearing, manner, and appearance while testifying? Often it is not what a person says but how he or she says it that moves us"); *3-3-43 Instructions for Virginia and West Virginia § 114–115; 1-II Criminal Jury Instructions for DC Final Instructions Instruction 2.200.*

3. Steve Drizin, "Dancing Eyebrows, Amanda Knox, and Jerry Hobbs: Assessing Guilt Based on Body Language Is a Dangerous Game," Huffington Post Crime Blog, Jul 14, 2014, www.huffingtonpost.com/steve-drizin/dancing-eyebrows-amanda-k_b_5291451.html.

4. John Ferak, "Politician: Steven Avery's Eyes Prove He's Guilty," USA Today Network, Apr 6, 2016, www.postcrescent.com/story/news/local/steven-avery/2016/04/06/politician-averys-eyes-prove-hes-guilty/82586402.

5. Documents relating to the David Ayers case on file with the author.

6. Laura Ricciardi and Moira Demos, "Eighteen Years Lost," *Making a Murderer*, Netflix Streaming, Dec 18, 2015. Documentary web series, episode 1, sixty minutes.

7. Dave D'Marko, "Kansas Man Who Maintained His Innocence in Murder Case Released from Prison," WDAF-TV, Dec 8, 2015, http://fox4kc .com/2015/12/08/kansas-man-who-maintained-his-innocence-in-murder-case-released-from-prison. For more, see Maurice Possley, "Floyd Bledsoe," National Registry of Exonerations, last updated Dec 14, 2015, www.law.umich .edu/special/exoneration/pages/casedetail.aspx?caseid=4809.

8. For the complete facts, see the Walter Zimmer case on the National Registry of Exonerations, last updated Apr 7, 2014, www.law.umich.edu/special /exoneration/Pages/casedetail.aspx?caseid=4283.

9. Paul Ekman, *Telling Lies: Clues to Deceit in the Marketplace, Politics, and Marriage* (New York: W.W. Norton, 2001).

10. Samantha Mann, Aldert Vrij, and Ray Bull, "Detecting True Lies: Police Officers' Ability to Detect Suspects' Lies," *Journal of Applied Psychology* 89, no. 1 (2004): 137–49, University of Portsmouth, http://eprints.port.ac.uk/id /eprint/23; R.E Kraut, "Humans as Lie Detectors: Some Second Thoughts," *Journal of Communication* 30 (1980): 209–16.

11. Charles F. Bond, Jr., and Bella M. DePaulo, "Accuracy of Deception Judgments," *Personality and Social Psychology Review* 10, no. 3 (2006): 214–34, www.communicationcache.com/uploads/1/0/8/8/10887248/accuracy_of_ deception_judgments.pdf.

12. Mann, Vrij, and Bull, "Detecting True Lies," 137–49.

13. F.E. Inbau et al., *Criminal Interrogation and Confessions*, 4th ed. (Gaithersburg, Md.: Aspen, 2001).

14. Joel Seidman, "GAO: $1 Billion TSA Behavioral Screening Program 'Slightly Better than Chance,'" NBC News, Nov 13, 2013, www.nbcnews.com

/news/other/gao-1-billion-tsa-behavioral-screening-program-slightly-better-chance-f2D11588343.

15. "Aviation Security TSA Should Limit Future Funding for Behavior Detection Activities," *United States Government Accountability Office*, Nov 2013, http://msnbcmedia.msn.com/i/msnbc/sections/news/GAO-TSA_SPOT_Report.pdf. Italics added.

16. Seidman, "GAO: $1 Billion."

17. For the complete facts of the Willingham case see David Grann, "Trial by Fire: Did Texas Execute an Innocent Man?" *New Yorker*, Sept 7, 2009, www.newyorker.com/magazine/2009/09/07/trial-by-fire.

18. "Cameron Todd Willingham: Wrongfully Convicted and Executed in Texas," Innocence Project, Sept 13, 2010, www.innocenceproject.org/news-events-exonerations/cameron-todd-willingham-wrongfully-convicted-and-executed-in-texas.

19. Douglas J. Carpenter et al., "Report on the Peer Review of the Expert Testimony in the Cases of State of Texas v. Cameron Todd Willingham and State of Texas v. Ernest Ray Willis," *Arson Review Committee: A Peer Review Panel Commissioned by the Innocence Project*, www.innocenceproject.org/wp-content/uploads/2016/04/file.pdf (accessed May 1, 2016); Craig L. Beyler, "Analysis of the Fire Investigation Methods and Procedures Used in the Criminal Arson Cases against Ernest Ray Willis and Cameron Todd Willingham," Hughes Associates, Aug. 17, 2009, www.scribd.com/doc/20603037/Analysis-of-the-Methods-and-Procedures-Used-in-the-Cameron-Todd-Willingham-Arson-Case; see also Grann, "Trial by Fire."

20. Beyler, "Analysis of the Fire Investigation."

21. Sarah Koenig, *Serial*, episode 9, "To Be Suspected," podcast audio, Nov 20, 2014, https://serialpodcast.org/season-one/9/to-be-suspected.

22. Pamela Colloff, "The Innocent Man, Part One," *Texas Monthly* (Nov 2012), www.texasmonthly.com/politics/the-innocent-man-part-one/#sthash.2HNay7ea.dpuf.

23. "Michael Morton," National Registry of Exonerations, www.law.umich.edu/special/exoneration/pages/casedetail.aspx?caseid=3834 (accessed Apr 21, 2016).

24. Maurice Possley, "Russell Faria," National Registry of Exonerations, www.law.umich.edu/special/exoneration/Pages/casedetail.aspx?caseid=4792 (accessed Nov 16, 2015).

25. Unless otherwise indicated, facts derived from: *Lee v. Tennis*, 2014 U.S. Dist. LEXIS 110736, 2014 WL 3894306 (M.D. Pa. Jun 13, 2014); Transcript of Record, *Commonwealth v. Lee*, 433 Pa. Super. (No. CP-45-CR-0000577–1989).

26. Transcript of Record at 162, 621, *Commonwealth v. Lee*, 433 Pa. Super. (No. CP-45-CR-0000577-1989).

27. Ibid., 156.

28. Ibid., 257.

29. Appellant's Brief at 33, *Lee v. Cameron*, 2014 U.S. Dist. LEXIS 117115 (2015) (No. 14-3876) Doc. 003111853826.

30. Unless otherwise indicated, facts derived from: Transcript of Record, *Georgia v. Debelbot*, Superior Court of Muscogee County (Indictment No. SU-09-CR-1843).

31. Ibid., 251.

32. Ibid., 250–52.

33. Ibid., 288–89.

34. Defendant's Brief in Support of Amended Motion for New Trial, *Georgia v. Debelbot*, Superior Court of Muscogee County (Indictment No. SU-09-CR-1843).

35. Tim Chitwood, "Whether Parents Crushed Infant's Skull Subject of New Trial Hearing," *Ledger Enquirer*, Jan 12, 2015, www.ledger-enquirer.com /news/local/crime/article29383837.html#storylink=cpy.

36. Unless otherwise indicated, facts derived from: Judge (ret.) Leslie Crocker Synder et al., *Report on the Conviction of Jeffrey Deskovic: Prepared at the Request of Janet DiFiore, Westchester County District Attorney* (Jun 2007), www.westchesterda.net/Jeffrey%20Deskovic%20Comm%20Rpt .pdf.

37. "Jeff Deskovic," Innocence Project, www.innocenceproject.org/cases-false-imprisonment/jeff-deskovic#sthash.UnH4jzsp.dpuf (accessed Apr 22, 2016).

38. Synder et al., *Report on the Conviction*, 16.

CHAPTER 7. BLIND TUNNEL VISION

1. Keith Findley and Michael S. Scott, "The Multiple Dimensions of Tunnel Vision in Criminal Cases," *Wisconsin Law Review* 2 (Jun 2006): 307, http:// ssrn.com/abstract=911240.

2. Ibid., 309.

3. Ibid., 317.

4. Tunnel vision in this context is generally understood to mean that "compendium of common heuristics and logical fallacies," to which we are all susceptible, that lead actors in the criminal justice system to "focus on a suspect, select and filter the evidence that will 'build a case' for conviction, while ignoring or suppressing evidence that points away from guilt." This process leads investigators, prosecutors, judges, and defense lawyers alike to focus on a particular conclusion and then filter all evidence in a case through the lens provided by that conclusion. Through that filter, all information supporting the adopted conclusion is elevated in significance, viewed as consistent with the other evidence, and deemed relevant and probative. Evidence inconsistent with the chosen theory is easily overlooked or dismissed as irrelevant, incredible, or unreliable. Properly understood, tunnel vision is more often the product of the human condition as well as institutional and cultural pressures, than of maliciousness or indifference. See Keith Findley, "Tunnel Vision," in *Conviction of the Innocent: Lessons from Psychological Research*, ed. Brian Culter (Washington, D.C.: APA Press, 2010), http://ssrn.com/abstract=1604658.

5. For more on heuristics and decision making, see Amos Tversky and Daniel Kahneman, "Judgments under Uncertainty: Heuristics and Biases," *Science* 185 (Sept 1974): 1124–31, doi:10.1126/science.185.4157.1124; Amos Tversky and Daniel Kahneman, "Availability: A Heuristic for Judging Frequency and Probability," *Cognitive Psychology* 5 (Sept 1973): 207–33, doi:10.1016/0010-0285(73)90033-9; Daniel Kahneman and Gary Klein, "Conditions for Intuitive Expertise: A Failure to Disagree," *American Psychologist* 64 (Sept 2009): 515–26, doi:10.1037/a0016755.

6. MatthewAid.com, "Analyst Liabilities and the Iraqi WMD Intelligence Failure," blog entry by Matthew Aid, Sept 7, 2013, www.matthewaid.com /post/31058119160/analyst-liabilities-and-the-iraqi-wmd-intelligence.

7. The Commission on the Intelligence Capabilities of the United States Regarding Weapons of Mass Destruction, Rep. to the President (Mar 31, 2005), at 162, https://fas.org/irp/offdocs/wmd_report.pdf.

8. Ibid., 3.

9. Carol Tavris and Elliot Aronson, *Mistakes Were Made (But Not by Me): Why We Justify Foolish Beliefs, Bad Decisions, and Hurtful Acts* (New York: Houghton Mifflin Harcourt Publishing, 2015), 3–7.

10. Ibid., 7.

11. MatthewAid.com, "Analyst Liabilities and the Iraqi WMD Intelligence Failure."

12. Tavris and Aronson, *Mistakes Were Made*, 175.

13. Ibid.

14. Findley and Scott, "The Multiple Dimensions of Tunnel Vision," 325.

15. Unless otherwise indicated, facts derived from: Pamela Colloff, "The Innocent Man, Part One," *Texas Monthly* (Nov 2012), www.texasmonthly .com/politics/the-innocent-man-part-one/#sthash.2HNay7ea.dpuf; and, Colloff, "The Innocent Man, Part Two," *Texas Monthly* (Dec 2012), www.texasmonthly .com/articles/the-innocent-man-part-two.

16. "Michael Morton," National Registry of Exonerations, www.law.umich .edu/special/exoneration/pages/casedetail.aspx?caseid=3834 (accessed Apr 28, 2016).

17. Facts derived from Findley, "Tunnel Vision."

18. Facts derived from Tom Wells and Richard A. Leo, *The Wrong Guys: Murder, False Confessions, and the Norfolk Four* (New York: New Press, 2008).

19. "Convictions Vacated for Two Cases of the So-Called 'Norfolk Four,'" Associated Press/WAVY, Oct 31, 2016, http://wavy.com/2016/10/31/judge-to-hold-hearing-in-norfolk-four-cases; Priyanka Boghani, "Norfolk Four Pardoned 20 Years after False Confessions," *Frontline*, PBS/WGBH, Mar 22, 2017, www .pbs.org/wgbh/frontline/article/norfolk-four-pardoned-20-years-after-false-confessions.

20. Findley and Scott, "The Multiple Dimensions of Tunnel Vision," 305–7.

21. Syndney H. Schangberg, "A Journey through the Tangled Case of the Central Park Jogger," *Village Voice*, Nov 19, 2002, www.villagevoice.com/news /a-journey-through-the-tangled-case-of-the-central-park-jogger-6436053.

22. Findley and Scott, "The Multiple Dimensions of Tunnel Vision," 305–7.

23. Schangberg, "Journey through the Tangled Case of the Central Park Jogger."

24. Ibid.

25. Findley and Scott, "The Multiple Dimensions of Tunnel Vision," 305–7.

26. Ibid., 335. See also, Adam Benforado, *Unfair: The New Science of Criminal Injustice* (New York: Penguin Random House, 2015), 31.

27. Carrie Sperling, "Defense Lawyer Tunnel Vision: The Oft-Ignored Role Defense Counsel Plays in Wrongful Convictions," *The Defender* (Fall 2010): 19, http://ssrn.com/abstract=1802654.

28. Wendy J. Coen, "The Unparalleled Power of Expert Testimony," in *Forensic Science Testimony: Science, Law, and Expert Evidence,* ed. C. Michael Bowers (Oxford: Academic Press, 2014), 221.

29. Michael Martinez, "South Carolina Cop Shoots Unarmed Man: A Timeline," CNN, Apr 9, 2015, www.cnn.com/2015/04/08/us/south-carolina-cop-shoots-black-man-timeline.

30. Matt Gelb, "Former Philly Narcotics Cop Jeffrey Walker Sentenced to 3 1/2 Years in Prison," Philadelphia Media Network, Jul 31, 2015, www.philly .com/philly/news/20150730_Former_Philly_narcotics_cop_Jeffrey_Walker_ sentenced_to_31_2_years_in_prison.html; Michael E. Miller, "Cop Accused of Brutally Torturing Black Suspects Costs Chicago $5.5 Million," *Washington Post,* Apr 15, 2015, www.washingtonpost.com/news/morning-mix/wp/2015 /04/15/closing-the-book-on-jon-burge-chicago-cop-accused-of-brutally-torturing-african-american-suspects.

31. Dahlia Lithwick, "Crime Lab Scandals Just Keep Getting Worse," *Slate Magazine,* Oct 19, 2015, www.slate.com/articles/news_and_politics/crime /2015/10/massachusetts_crime_lab_scandal_worsens_dookhan_and_farak .html.

32. Katie Mulvaney, "R.I. Criminal Defense Lawyer Sentenced to 6 Years in Prison for Bribery Scheme," *Providence Journal,* Sept 11, 2013, www .providencejournal.com/article/20130911/News/309119971; Debra Cassens Weiss, "California Criminal Defense Lawyer Convicted of Laundering Money for Client," *ABA Journal,* Jul 21, 2010, www.abajournal.com/news/article /california_defense_lawyer_convicted_of_laundering_money_for_client; Martha Neil, "Attorney Is Convicted of Conspiring to Bilk Criminal Defense Clients Out of Big Bucks," *ABA Journal,* May 29, 2015, www.abajournal.com /news/article/defense_attorney_is_convicted_of_conspiring_to_dupe_criminal_ clients_into_p.

33. Eyder Peralta, "Pa. Judge Sentenced to 28 Years in Massive Juvenile Justice Bribery Scandal," *The Two-Way,* National Public Radio, Aug 11, 2011, www.npr.org/sections/thetwo-way/2011/08/11/139536686/pa-judge-sentenced-to-28-years-in-massive-juvenile-justice-bribery-scandal.

34. Bruce A. MacFarlane, "Wrongful Convictions: The Effect of Tunnel Vision and Predisposing Circumstances in the Criminal Justice System," *Prepared for the*

Inquiry into Pediatric Forensic Pathology in Ontario, the Honourable Stephen T. Goudge, Commissioner (2008), 20, www.attorneygeneral.jus.gov.on.ca/inquiries /goudge/policy_research/pdf/Macfarlane_Wrongful-Convictions.pdf.

35. Ibid.

36. Brigit Katz, "*Making a Murderer* Lawyer Says Humility Is Needed to Change a Flawed Legal System," *New York Times,* Jan 29, 2016, http://nytlive .nytimes.com/womenintheworld/2016/01/29/making-a-murderer-lawyer-says-humility-is-the-answer-to-flawed-legal-system.

37. Matt Ford, "The Ethics of Killing Baby Hitler," *The Atlantic,* Oct 24, 2015, www.theatlantic.com/international/archive/2015/10/killing-baby-hitler-ethics/412273.

38. Tim Lynch, "An 'Epidemic' of Prosecutorial Misconduct," Cato Institute, Dec 12, 2013, www.policemisconduct.net/epidemic-prosecutorial-misconduct.

39. Diana M. Wright and Michael A. Trimpe, "Summary of the FBI Laboratory's Gunshot Residue Symposium," *Forensic Science Communications* 8, no. 3 (2005), www.fbi.gov/about-us/lab/forensic-science-communications/fsc /july2006/research/2006_07_research01.htm. See also, R. E. Berk et al., "Gunshot Residue in Chicago Police Vehicles and Facilities: An Empirical Study," *Journal of Forensic Science* 52 (July 2004): 838–41; B. Cardinetti et al., "X-ray Mapping Technique: A Preliminary Study in Discriminating Gunshot Residue Particles from Aggregates of Environmental Occupational Origin," *Forensic Science International* 143 (Jun 2004): 1–14.

40. Dennis L. McGuire, "The Controversy Concerning Gunshot Residues Examinations," *Forensic Magazine,* Aug 1, 2008, www.forensicmag.com /articles/2008/08/controversy-concerning-gunshot-residues-examinations.

41. Wright and Trimpe, "Summary of the FBI Laboratory's Gunshot Residue Symposium."

42. John Ferak, "Legal Experts Blast Avery Prosecutor's Conduct," USA Today Network—Wisconsin, Jan 24, 2016, www.postcrescent.com/story/news /local/steven-avery/2016/01/15/kratzs-pretrial-behavior-called-unethical /78630248.

43. Vidar Halvorsen, "Is It Better That Ten Guilty Persons Go Free than That One Innocent Person Be Convicted?" *Criminal Justice Ethics* 23, no. 2 (2004): 3–13.

44. See, e.g., Amy Klobuchar, Nancy K. Steblay, and Hilary Lindell Caligiuri, "Improving Eyewitness Identifications: Hennepin County's Blind Sequential Lineup Pilot Project," *Cardozo Public Law, Policy, and Ethics Journal* 4 (2006): 381–413; Gary L. Wells et al., "Eyewitness Identification Procedures: Recommendations for Lineups and Photospreads," *Law and Human Behavior* 22 (Dec 1998): 603–47, www.psychology.iastate.edu/FACULTY/gwells/Wells_ articles_pdf/whitepaperpdf.pdf.

45. The poker analogy was taken from Justin Brooks, "The Role of the Innocence Project in the United States and the Current Situation," keynote speech, Ritsumeikan University, Osaka Japan, Mar 20, 2016.

46. *Farlex Partner Medical Dictionary*, s.v. "double-blind study," http://medical-dictionary.thefreedictionary.com/double-blind+study (retrieved May 9, 2016).

47. See for reference, R.C. Lindsay and Gary L. Wells, "Improving Eyewitness Identifications from Lineups: Simultaneous versus Sequential Lineup Presentation," *Journal of Applied Psychology* 70 (Aug 1985): 556–64, http://dx.doi.org/10.1037/0021–9010.70.3.556; R.C. Lindsay et al., "Biased Lineups: Sequential Presentation Reduces the Problem," *Journal of Applied Psychology* 76 (Dec 1991): 796–802, http://dx.doi.org/10.1037/0021-9010.76.6.796. However, according to a report published by the National Academy of Sciences, more research is needed before the superiority of this method over others can be resolved. Thomas D. Albright et al., *Identifying the Culprit: Assessing Eyewitness Identification*, National Academy of Sciences (Washington D.C.: National Academies Press, 2014), 3.

48. "Report Urges Caution in Handling and Relying upon Eyewitness Identifications in Criminal Cases, Recommends Best Practices for Law Enforcement and Courts," National Academies, Oct 2, 2014, www.8.nationalacademies.org/onpinews/newsitem.aspx?RecordID=18891.

49. Ibid.

50. As of early 2017, prosecution has appealed this ruling and the case is currently pending in the U.S. Court of Appeals for the Seventh Circuit. See Steve Almasy, "Making a Murderer: Brendan Dassey Conviction Overturned," CNN, Aug 12, 2016, www.cnn.com/2016/08/12/us/making-a-murderer-brendan-dassey-conviction-overturned.

51. For information on the HIG and PEACE interrogation techniques, see James L. Trainum, *How the Police Generate False Confessions: An Inside Look at the Interrogation Room* (Lanham, Md.: Rowman and Littlefield, 2016); Kelly McEvers, "In New Age of Interrogations, Police Focus on Building Rapport," *All Things Considered*, National Public Radio, May 23, 2016, www.npr.org/2016/05/23/479207853/in-new-age-of-interrogations-police-focus-on-building-rapport; "Symposium Facilitates Exchange of Research on Lawful Interrogations," FBI, Oct 27, 2015, www.fbi.gov/news/stories/symposium-facilitates-exchange-of-research-on-lawful-interrogations; Robert Kolker, "Nothing but the Truth," Marshall Project, May 24, 2016, www.themarshallproject.org/2016/05/24/nothing-but-the-truth#.IkBS3CvTk.

52. Robert Kolker, "A Severed Head, Two Cops, and the Radical Future of Interrogation," *Wired*, May 24, 2016, www.wired.com/2016/05/how-to-interrogate-suspects.

53. "Contributing Causes of Wrongful Convictions (First 325 DNA Exonerations)," Innocence Project, www.innocenceproject.org/causes-wrongful-conviction (accessed May 5, 2015).

54. "% Exonerations by Contributing Factor," National Registry of Exonerations, www.law.umich.edu/special/exoneration/Pages/Exonerations ContribFactorsByCrime.aspx (accessed Dec 10, 2016).

55. Hon. Alex Kozinski, "Preface: Criminal Law 2.0," *Georgetown Law Journal Annual Review of Criminal Procedure* 44 (2015): iii–xliv, http://georgetownlawjournal.org/files/2015/06/Kozinski_Preface.pdf.

56. Ibid. See also, Henry Weinstein, "Use of Jailhouse Testimony Is Uneven in State," *Los Angeles Times,* Sept 21, 2006, http://articles.latimes.com/2006/sep/21/local/me-jailhouse21.

57. Ibid. See also, Russell D. Covey, "Abolishing Jailhouse Snitch Testimony," *Wake Forest Law Review* 49 (Jan 2014): 1375.

58. See David A. Harris, *Failed Evidence: Why Law Enforcement Resists Science* (New York: New York University Press, 2012); Kevin J. Strom and Matthew J. Hickman, *Forensic Science and the Administration of Justice: Critical Issues and Directions* (New York: Sage Publications, 2014). See also, Sandra Guerra Thompson, *Cops in Lab Coats: Curbing Wrongful Convictions through Independent Forensic Laboratories* (Durham, N.C.: Carolina Academic Press, 2015).

59. Stephen A. Cooper, "D.C. Judge Rejects Junk Science but the Law Is Slow to Follow," *Huffington Post,* Jan 25, 2016, www.huffingtonpost.com/stephen-a-cooper/dc-judge-rejects-junk-sci_b_9063476.html.

60. Quoted in Laura Ricciardi and Moira Demos, "The Last Person to See Teresa Alive," *Making a Murderer,* Netflix Streaming, Dec 18, 2015. Documentary web series, episode 5, sixty minutes.

61. Mark A. Godsey and Marie Alou, "She Blinded Me with Science: Wrongful Convictions and the 'Reverse CSI-Effect,'" *Texas Wesleyan Law Review* 17 (2011): 481.

62. This "cascading effect" is most frequently found in cases involving false confession. Saul M. Kassin, Daniel Bogart, and Jacqueline Kerner, "Confessions That Corrupt: Evidence from the DNA Exoneration Case Files," *Psychological Science* 23 (Jan 2012): 41–45, doi: 10.1177/0956797611422918.

63. Findley, "Tunnel Vision."

CHAPTER 8. SEEING AND ACCEPTING HUMAN LIMITATIONS

1. Brigit Katz, "*Making a Murderer* Lawyer Says Humility Is Needed to Change a Flawed Legal System," *New York Times,* Jan 29, 2016, http://nytlive.nytimes.com/womenintheworld/2016/01/29/making-a-murderer-lawyer-says-humility-is-the-answer-to-flawed-legal-system.

2. See, for reference, Siegfried L. Sporer, *Psychological Issues in Eyewitness Identification* (New York: Taylor and Francis, 1996); Brian L. Cutler and Margaret Bull Kovera, *Evaluating Eyewitness Identification* (Oxford: Oxford University Press, 2010); Committee on Scientific Approaches to Understanding and Maximizing the Validity and Reliability of Eyewitness Identification et al., *Identifying the Culprit: Assessing Eyewitness Identification* (Washington D.C.: National Academies Press, 2015); Ethan Brown, *Snitch: Informants, Cooperators, and the Corruption of Justice* (New York: Public Affairs, 2007); David A. Harris, *Failed Evidence: Why Law Enforcement Resists Science* (New

York: New York University Press, 2012); Sandra Guerra Thompson, *Cops in Lab Coats: Curbing Wrongful Convictions through Independent Forensic Laboratories* (Durham, N.C.: Carolina Academic Press, 2015); Richard A. Leo, *Police Interrogation and American Justice* (Cambridge, Mass.: Harvard University Press, 2009); Tom Wells and Richard A. Leo, *The Wrong Guys: Murder, False Confessions, and the Norfolk Four* (New York: New Press, 2008).

3. Committee on Scientific Approaches to Understanding and Maximizing the Validity and Reliability of Eyewitness Identification et al., *Identifying the Culprit*; Itiel E. Dror and Simon A. Cole, "The Vision in 'Blind' Justice: Expert Perception, Judgment, and Visual Cognition in Forensic Pattern Recognition," *Psychonomic Bulletin and Review* 17 (2010): 163, doi:10.3758; Itiel E. Dror, "Practical Solutions to Cognitive and Human Factor Challenges in Forensic Science," *Forensic Science Policy and Management* 4 (2013), doi: 10.1080/19409044.2014.901437; Itiel E. Dror, "Cognitive Neuroscience in Forensic Science: Understanding and Utilizing the Human Element," *Philosophical Transactions of the Royal Society B* (Mar 2015), http://dx.doi.org/10.1098/rstb.2014.0255; Kevin J. Strom and Matthew J. Hickman, *Forensic Science and the Administration of Justice: Critical Issues and Directions* (New York: Sage Publications, 2014); Harris, *Failed Evidence*; Thompson, *Cops in Lab Coats*.

4. Ibid., 198–99, 211.

5. See Sophie Stammers and Sarah Bunn, "Unintentional Bias in Forensic Investigation," *Postbrief*, Parliamentary Office of Science and Technology (Oct 2015), researchbriefings.files.parliament.uk/documents/POST-PB-0015/POST-PB-0015.pdf; see also, Dror and Cole, "The Vision in 'Blind' Justice."

6. Inadequate defense lawyering is a major contributing factor to wrongful conviction: "The failure of overworked lawyers to investigate, call witnesses or prepare for trial has led to the conviction of innocent people. When a defense lawyer doesn't do his or her job, the defendant suffers. Shrinking funding and access to resources for public defenders and court-appointed attorneys is only making the problem worse." "Inadequate Defense," Innocence Project, www.innocenceproject.org/causes/inadequate-defense (accessed May 20, 2016). See also the Innocence Project's report by Dr. Emily M. West, "Court Findings of Ineffective Assistance of Counsel Claims in Post-Conviction Appeals among the First 255 DNA Exoneration Cases," Innocence Project, Sept 2016, www.innocenceproject.org/wp-content/uploads/2016/05/Innocence_Project_IAC_Report.pdf; "Inadequately Funded Public Defender Services Threaten Criminal Justice System, ACLU Testifies," American Civil Liberties Union, Mar 26, 2009, www.aclu.org/news/inadequately-funded-public-defender-services-threaten-criminal-justice-system-aclu-testifies.

7. This kind of training is already implemented in the business world, where executives often engage in high-stakes decision making. For reference, see Max H. Bazerman and Dolly Chugh, "Decisions without Blinders," *Harvard Business Review*, Jan 2006 (discussing the benefits of training individuals to recognize tunnel vision when engaging in the decision-making process),

https://hbr.org/2006/01/decisions-without-blinders; Judith Winters Spain et al., "Tunnel Vision: A Multi-Perspective Model and Case Application of Organizational Social Responsibility," paper distributed by the Department of Management, Marketing, and Administrative Communication at Eastern Kentucky University, (suggesting that executives train employees to recognize their own biases to engage in better decision making), http://people.eku.edu /englea/TunnelVisionconfproceed.htm. See also, Daniel S. Medwed, *Prosecution Complex: America's Race to Convict and Its impact on the Innocent* (New York: New York University Press, 2012); Keith Findley, "Tunnel Vision," in *Conviction of the Innocent: Lessons from Psychological Research,* ed. Brian Culter (Washington, D.C.: APA Press, 2010), http://ssrn.com/abstract=1604658; Keith Findley and Michael S. Scott, "The Multiple Dimensions of Tunnel Vision in Criminal Cases," *Wisconsin Law Review* 2 (Jun 2006), http://ssrn.com /abstract=911240; Laurie L. Levenson, "The Cure for the Cynical Prosecutors' Syndrome: Rethinking a Prosecutor's Role in Post-Conviction Cases," *Berkeley Journal of Criminal Law* 20 (Aug 2015); Loyola Law School, Los Diegoes Legal Studies Research Paper No. 2015-27, available at SSRN, https://papers.ssrn .com/sol3/papers.cfm?abstract_id=264829 (accessed May 1, 2017).

8. See "Tunnel Vision," in *FPT Heads of Prosecutions Committee Report of the Working Group on the Prevention of Miscarriages of Justice,* Government of Canada Department of Justice, Jan 7, 2015, www.justice.gc.ca/eng/rp-pr /cj-jp/ccr-rc/pmj-pej/p4.html#s44.

9. "A Messy Supreme Court Case Shows Why Judges Should Be Appointed, Not Elected," *Washington Post,* Jan 21, 2015, www.washingtonpost.com /opinions/a-messy-supreme-court-case-shows-why-judges-should-be- appointed-not-elected/2015/01/21/dab54610-a0f6-11e4-9f89-561284a573f8_ story.html; John L. Dodd et al., "The Case for Judicial Appointments," Federalist Society, Jan 1, 2003, www.fed-soc.org/publications/detail/the-case-for-judicial- appointments. For a general discussion of how the current system to elect pros- ecutor's came about in the United States, see Michael J. Ellis, "The Origins of the Elected Prosecutor," *Yale Law Journal* 121, no. 6 (Apr 2012): 1528–69.

10. "The Causes of Wrongful Conviction," Innocence Project, www .innocenceproject.org/causes-wrongful-conviction (accessed May 19, 2016).

11. See Phil Locke, "Why a Wrongful Conviction Is Like a Plane Crash—or Should Be," Wrongful Convictions Blog, Feb 16, 2015, https://wrongfulconvic tionsblog.org/2015/02/16/why-a-wrongful-conviction-is-like-a-plane-crash- or-should-be; Sarina Houston, "Inside the Aircraft Accident Investigation Process," *About Money,* Dec 19, 2014, http://aviation.about.com/od/Accidents /a/Inside-The-Aircraft-Accident-Investigation-Process.htm.

12. Fred C. Lunenburg, "Devil's Advocacy and Dialectical Inquiry: Antidotes to Groupthink," *International Journal of Scholarly Academic Intellectual Diversity* 14 (Nov 2012): 5–6.

13. Thomas J. Peters and Robert H. Waterman, Jr., *In Search of Excellence: Lessons from America's Best-Run Companies* (New York: Harper Business, 2006).

14. See, e.g., Max H. Bazerman and Dolly Chugh, "Decisions without Blinders," *Harvard Business Review,* Jan 2006, https://hbr.org/2006/01/decisions-without-blinders.

15. "Eyewitness Misidentification," Innocence Project, www.innocence project.org/causes/eyewitness-misidentification (accessed May 19, 2016).

16. Thomas P. Sullivan, "Compendium: Electronic Recording of Custodial Interrogations," National Association of Criminal Defense Lawyers, Jan 8, 2016, www.nacdl.org/criminaldefense.aspx?id=31573&libID=31542 (pdf available for download).

17. Wicklander-Zulawski and Associates, press release, "WZ Discontinues Reid Method," Mar 6, 2017, www.w-z.com/portfolio/press-release.

18. See Spencer S. Hsu, "FBI Admits Flaws in Hair Analysis over Decades," *Washington Post,* Apr 18, 2015, www.washingtonpost.com/local/crime/fbi-overstated-forensic-hair-matches-in-nearly-all-criminal-trials-for-decades/2015/04/18/39c8d8c6-e515-11e4-b510-962fcfabc310_story.html.

19. See Spencer S. Hsu, "Santae Tribble Cleared in 1978 Murder Based on DNA Hair Test," *Washington Post,* Dec 14, 2012, www.washingtonpost.com/local/crime/dc-judge-exonerates-santae-tribble-of-1978-murder-based-on-dna-hair-test/2012/12/14/da71ce00-d02c-11e1-b630-190a983a2e0d_story.html; "North Carolina Man Convicted Based on Erroneous Microscopic Hair Evidence Exonerated after Wrongly Serving 25 Years," Innocence Project, Mar 2, 2016, www.innocenceproject.org/north-carolina-man-convicted-based-on-erroneous-microscopic-hair-evidence-exonerated-after-wrongly-serving-25-years; George Graham, "After 30 Years in Jail, George Perrot of Springfield Freed after Rape Conviction Overturned," Mass Live, Feb 11, 2016, www.masslive.com/news/index.ssf/2016/02/george_perrot_springfield_man.html.

20. "General Information," National Commission on Forensic Science, www.justice.gov/ncfs (accessed May 19, 2016).

21. Spencer S. Hsu, "Sessions Orders Justice Dept. to End Forensic Science Commission, Suspend Review Policy," *Washington Post,* Apr 10, 2017, www.washingtonpost.com/local/public-safety/sessions-orders-justice-dept-to-end-forensic-science-commission-suspend-review-policy/2017/04/10/2dada0ca-1c96-11e7-9887-1a5314b56a08_story.html?utm_term=.346af0d125aa.

22. "Ohio Enacts Historic Reforms," Innocence Project, Apr 5, 2010, www.innocenceproject.org/ohio-enacts-historic-reforms. See also, Alana Salzberg, "Ohio Passes Major Package of Reforms on Wrongful Convictions; Governor Is Expected to Sign Bill, Making Ohio a National Model," Innocence Project, Mar 16, 2010, www.innocenceproject.org/ohio-passes-major-package-of-reforms-on-wrongful-convictions-governor-is-expected-to-sign-bill-making-ohio-a-national-model.

23. See, for reference, Michael J. Naples, *Effective Frequency: The Relationship between Frequency and Advertising Effectiveness* (New York: Association of National Advertisers, 1979).

24. Conviction Review Unit, *Brooklyn District Attorney's Office,* http://brooklynda.org/conviction-review-unit (accessed May 19, 2016).

25. Noah Fromson, "Conviction Integrity Units Expand beyond Texas Roots," *Texas Tribune*, Mar 12, 2016, www.texastribune.org/2016/03/12 /conviction-integrity-units-expand-beyond-texas-roo.

26. "Quattrone Center Issues National Report on Best Practices for Conviction Review Units," press release, Penn Law, University of Pennsylvania Law School, Apr 28, 2016, www.law.upenn.edu/live/news/6125-quattrone-center-issues-national-report-on-best#.VzEdGGDtye4.

Index